PUT MONEY IN YOUR POCKET
THE ART OF SELECTING NO-LOAD MUTUAL FUNDS FOR MAXIMUM GAIN
by Sheldon Jacobs

74-5849

SIMON AND SCHUSTER : NEW YORK

To my parents, Bert and Ruth,
who through hard work and consummate ability
both lead full lives at an age when many are retired.
Community leaders and successful business persons,
they are unforgettable to all who know them.

CONTENTS

PREFACE How I Came to Mutual Funds 7

SECTION I NO-LOAD MUTUAL FUNDS: THE NEW
WAY TO MAKE MONEY GROW 15

CHAPTER 1 You Can Get Trampled by the Institutions 17
CHAPTER 2 Buy Mutual Funds to Join the Pros 31
CHAPTER 3 Defining No-Load Mutual Funds 49
CHAPTER 4 No-Loads and Loads Perform Equally Well 53
CHAPTER 5 Evaluating the Load 60
CHAPTER 6 You *Can* Select a No-Load Fund Yourself 67

SECTION II HOW TO INVEST IN NO-LOAD
MUTUAL FUNDS 73

CHAPTER 7 Match Funds to Investment Objectives 75
CHAPTER 8 How to Select Top Maximum Capital Gains Funds 108
CHAPTER 9 Guidelines for Future Performance 120
CHAPTER 10 How to Select Quality Growth and Growth-Income
Funds 140
CHAPTER 11 The Dangers of Buying Newly Organized Funds 148
CHAPTER 12 When to Sell Mutual Funds 155
CHAPTER 13 Making the Most of Market Cycles 165
CHAPTER 14 "Trading" Mutual Funds 187
CHAPTER 15 Withdrawal Plans 192
CHAPTER 16 Mutual Fund Advisory Services 198
CHAPTER 17 The Mutual Fund Prospectus 216

APPENDIX I Alphas and Betas: The Newest Investing Tool 237
APPENDIX II No-Load Fund Directory 245

5

PREFACE HOW I CAME TO MUTUAL FUNDS

I am an investor with twenty years' experience buying stocks, bonds, and mutual funds. For the first thirteen of these years, I bought only stocks; I wouldn't touch mutual funds. Funds' sales commissions seemed far too high, their growth potential appeared unsatisfactory, and the thought of letting someone else make my investment decisions was beneath me. Like many other "sophisticated" investors, I thought mutual funds were for "know-nothings," not for me.

I preferred to buy stocks which my own research had uncovered, although on occasion I would accept the advice of a broker or a friend. At first I made frequent mistakes, but as I gained experience, my investing performance improved. I know from my income tax returns that over the long run I made money. However, like most investors, I don't know exactly how much. Perhaps it averaged out to 5% per year, maybe even 10% or 15%. It is laborious to make the needed calculations, so I never did.

Although I made money from stocks, I seldom got a great deal of satisfaction out of that type of investment. I usually felt that whether I had profited or lost on a transaction was due more to luck than to skill. Take my first two investments as illustrations.

I went into the Army in 1952, shortly after graduation from college. The following summer, I received orders to go to Korea. Since I had about $600 saved at that time, I walked into a nearby brokerage firm, asked for a broker, and bought equal amounts of United Aircraft at $30 and Texaco at about $50. (You may wonder how someone in the service had a brokerage firm nearby. Well, fortune had smiled on me. My first duty station was Governors

7

Island, New York, a military installation lying about 2,000 yards directly south of Wall Street.)

I never considered keeping my $600 in a savings account. You may perhaps recall the early 1950's was a period of considerable inflation. In 1951, the cost of living had increased 7.9%, and in 1952, 2.1%. The typical savings bank paid only 2.4% interest at the time. These figures don't say very much for savings accounts. To me, the moral was clear. If I wanted to make money grow, I had to invest it elsewhere. This was true then; it is true today.

I distinctly remember my reason for buying United Aircraft. I thought helicopters had a big future, and United owns Sikorsky. I bought Texaco because someone recommended it. I no longer remember who or for what reason.

I went to Korea and never saw a stock quotation for a year. Upon returning to the States, I found that United Aircraft had doubled to $60 and Texaco had risen to about $62. I was elated until I investigated and found that my double in United had very little to do with helicopters.

I sold United and held Texaco. Texaco rewarded my faith (but not my knowledge) by adding about 40 more points; and United continued on to $90. I realized there was a lesson in all this. I had simply been lucky—and this bothered me. I would have been much happier if my gain had resulted from solid analysis of these stocks' potentials. I knew it took more than luck to maximize profits over the long run.

Upon discharge, I went into marketing and media research, working first for ABC-TV and then NBC-TV in New York. I tried to apply my market research skills to financial analysis, and had fair success investing in broadcast stocks. Wanting to diversify, though, I also invested in other industries. I was never as successful with these investments, despite my knowledge of basic financial analysis. As a business major in college, I had studied corporation finance, accounting, and investing principles. My background gave me a great deal more knowledge about investing than the average person has, yet I found it difficult to make money.

When I did my own research, I found my individual efforts handicapped by a lack of essential data. While historical data, as found in *Moody's Industrials*, were readily available, future data were hard to come by. I seldom had timely information on corporate plans, earnings projections, or the countless other facts that go into evaluating a stock correctly.

Moreover, it is difficult to put the facts about unfamiliar industries into perspective if one is isolated from the investment community. I lacked the contacts to discuss ideas with knowledgeable financial analysts. As a result, even if I had good information and evaluated it correctly, sometimes the market didn't act on it as I had anticipated.

It's not surprising that my greatest successes came in my own field—broadcasting. For example, I had a very profitable trade in a company that benefited from a hit ABC-TV program. In December 1965, the American Broadcasting Company invited advertising executives to a breakfast to preview programming that was due to premiere in a few weeks. On this morning, a five-minute demonstrator film of *Batman* was screened. It seemed to me, and others, that this show was going to be a certain hit. Back in the office, several researchers pondered over how to capitalize on this early information. Buy ABC? No. A single program, even a major hit, can't move ABC stock. The production company? A little better, but still the same problem. What about the company that held the merchandising rights, a big thing with hit children's shows. We checked and found they were held by National Periodical, the company holding the rights to *Batman* comic books. We were convinced that it would benefit greatly from the TV hit. The success of the TV show would have a significant impact on National Periodical's earnings.

Less than an hour had elapsed since we had seen the film. A group of us bought National Periodical heavily at what was virtually the bottom. We told our friends, who also bought heavily. We were rewarded by seeing the stock increase by 50% in a few short weeks, and eventually double in the middle of the 1966 bear market. We beat Wall Street on that one.

Here was a case where everything went right. I had analyzed the situation correctly, my information was timely, and I made money for the right reasons. I got a great deal of satisfaction out of that profit. But how often could I do that? This kind of opportunity comes at rare intervals. The truth is that it hasn't happened to me since.

Most of the time, of necessity, I turned to stockbrokers for investment advice. I always viewed the broker as a source of information for making money; I was never the kind of client who made frequent phone calls to brokers primarily for psychic gratification. In part, for this reason, I had only three stockbrokers during my thirteen years of exclusive stock investing. Two of them were good, the third was excellent. Yet despite this, my relationship with them was not truly productive. It took me a long time to understand why.

Incidentally, three brokers in thirteen years is most likely below average. A special nation-wide study by the respected market research firm of R. H. Bruskin Associates found that in November 1971 there were 10.2 million men in the United States who had used the services of a stockbroker in the preceding five years. Of these, 3.2 million—almost a third—had used two or more brokers and 1.4 million had used three or more brokers. Interestingly, the commonest reason for leaving a broker was dissatisfaction with the quality of service provided, not bad advice.

I stuck with my first broker the longest. He was certainly competent and personally likable, yet I never knew how to really "use" him. Should I, as an investor, rely completely on his advice? Should I take some of his advice and disregard other? Should I call him or should I wait for him to call me? I never answered these questions satisfactorily.

Certain questions always nagged me. Was he doing as much for me as for his other clients? Did he have hot stocks or new issues that were going to other customers, but not to me? Did he even remember what stocks I owned? Eventually some of these questions were answered for me. My brother became a stockbroker and, naturally, I switched to him.

For the first time I had confidence in a broker. I also got an education, learning about the broker's problems and the tensions that go into giving advice that may make or lose clients' hard-earned money. I learned that brokers are basically salesmen, working on commission, and are subject to the temptations and pressures of this pay structure. Significantly, for the first time, I fully realized that brokers are not investment counselors. For the most part, they merely pass along recommendations from their research departments. I learned that hot new issues are rarely offered to the small investor and there are wide variations in performance among stocks recommended. My brother explained that brokers diversify their own risks by never recommending the same stock to more than a few of their customers. In that way, if the stock goes down, *they* don't risk losing all.

After several years, my brother left the brokerage profession for another he found more satisfying. My next broker was by far my best. He was a broker who was also research director of a small New York Stock Exchange firm, and he was outstanding. He had few "retail" clients, and took me on only because I was a personal friend. His advice was top-notch and I made money with him. Unfortunately this relationship lasted only a short time. He was too good. Important institutional clients filled his day. Understandably, he didn't have time for me. I didn't leave him, he left me.

I never really went the advisory letter route. I read *Anyone Can Make a Million* by Morton Shulman, which has a devastating chapter on crooked advisory services. After that, I had no desire to become an expert on them.

I did, however, once subscribe to an introductory offer of Standard & Poor's "The Outlook." This advisory letter is generally considered to be one of the best published, and Standard & Poor's is a highly reputable firm. I was sent a report which recommended approximately twelve stocks. The recommendations sounded good, but since I didn't have the time or the resources to check their research, I felt I had to know how S & P's past recommendations had done. When I called up, I found this information was unavailable. When the firm failed to report something this basic, I lost interest in advisory services.

I also had problems with most of the Wall Street research typically available to laymen. For example, my office subscribed to *The Wall Street Transcript,* a weekly newspaper summarizing the published research from major brokerage firms. I once bought a stock because no less than seven firms had recommended it. It bombed. That experience taught me that some brokerage firms copy other firms. How else could so many have been so wrong?

By this time, I was tired of haphazard methods and started looking for a better, more reliable way to invest. In 1967, I began to look seriously at mutual funds as a way to make money.

Heretofore, I had never owned a mutual fund. This was ironic,

since some years earlier I had been a part-time mutual fund salesman. In 1957, I briefly joined the legions of people attracted by
ads promising easy part-time earnings. With my college background and investing experience, I easily passed the licensing test
to become a full-fledged part-time salesman.

Like most part-timers, I sold funds to a few friends and then
quit. Unlike many other salesmen, I never bought funds for
myself. I thought the 8.5% load, not to mention the contractual
plans where half of the first year's investment went to salesmen,
was exorbitant. When a salesman buys a fund for himself, he pays
only about half of what a customer would pay in commissions.
I thought even the 4.25% to 4.5% commission I would have paid
still excessive. And psychologically I felt paying commissions
would lock me into fund investments at times when I should be
selling.

In 1967, I finally decided to limit my investing to no-load
mutual funds, a special type of fund that has no sales commission.
No-load funds are flexible and permit me to switch easily or to go
to cash as investment conditions change. Of course, I also save
hundreds of dollars in commission expense.

Originally, I had avoided mutual funds because I thought fund
investing was too dull for me. I shared the prevailing view that
mutual funds were only for people who didn't understand investing. In addition, my thinking was molded by the training given
new mutual fund salesmen. It is directed toward selling the concept of mutual funds, i.e., as a way to save or to create a nest egg
for retirement. Now, there is nothing wrong in selling long-term
goals—so long as proper fund selection is not disregarded. But
salesmen did ignore fund selection then, and usually do so today.

For example, when I started writing this book, I wanted to find
out if sales training techniques had improved since I had under-
gone training. Accordingly, I again applied for a job as a part-time
salesman with a major fund group and attended an employment
interview. With other prospective salesmen, I listened to a ninety-
minute orientation program. It became obvious from this in-depth
lecture that we would be trained primarily to sell the concept of
mutual funds. When the question of quality arose, it was simply
stated that this group's funds were among the best. Although
other funds could be sold, there was no need to do so.

Furthermore, an incident occurring later that first orientation night perfectly illustrates how fund salesmen become preoccupied with long-term goals to the exclusion of proper fund selection. We were all shown the long-term performance of the group's basic fund, which had made $10,000 grow to $93,000 in twenty-five years. This, the speaker indicated, showed the merits of the fund. I raised my hand and pointed out that the next twenty-five years might be different. "It doesn't matter," said the lecturer, "whether the investment grows to $93,000 or $60,000 or $120,000. That isn't the point. What is important is having an investment program for retirement or for other long-term goals."

Well, I suppose that is the point for people who never save. But it makes a considerable difference to me whether $10,000 grows to $60,000 or $120,000!

To return to my story, I took a fresh look at mutual funds and found that much of what I believed about funds need not be true. Selecting the best-performing funds could be a challenging and rewarding task and yet one that did not require hours of my time.

When I finally rid myself of a lot of conventional "wisdom," I found there were definite advantages to investing in funds instead of in stocks, and that it was easy to properly exploit these advantages. When I concluded that mutual funds were the best way for me—and for the average investor, for that matter—to make money grow, I stopped buying stocks.

I now buy mutual funds exclusively, concentrating on those I expect to turn in superior performances. And while I don't consider myself a trader, I do sell quickly when a fund's performance falters. While I haven't made a million in mutual funds, I am more than satisfied with my investment performance, and, for the first time, know exactly what it is. Most gratifyingly, I am getting more enjoyment, more excitement, more satisfaction, and a greater sense of accomplishment out of investing in mutual funds than I ever did from my stock investments.

Section I
NO-LOAD MUTUAL FUNDS: THE
NEW WAY TO MAKE MONEY GROW

THERE'S NO doubt that no-load mutual funds are big investment news. They are making headlines with increasing frequency:

Section I explains this financial phenomenon. It shows why no-load mutual funds, which are unique in that they are sold without a sales charge, may be the best way for individual investors to profit in the volatile institution-dominated markets of the 1970's.

CHAPTER 1 YOU CAN GET TRAMPLED BY THE INSTITUTIONS

The traditional way to invest is to buy individual stocks and bonds. However, for the small investor, this way has always been risky. Until the thirties, small investors found they were often at the mercy of millionaire speculators, since in a virtually unregulated stock market, manipulation by insiders was commonplace. "Pools" were formed to drive the price of stocks to high levels; at this point, "smart" money got out and the overpriced stocks were unloaded on unwary investors.

In 1934, the Securities and Exchange Commission was formed and new government regulations made the stock market a much safer place for the small investor. Short selling was limited; the advantages of insiders were severely curtailed. When the prospectus came into use, information that had previously been secret was made available to the lay investor. In this new climate, the New York Stock Exchange took steps to broaden the base of stock ownership and began a vigorous campaign to sell shares of corporate America.

THE INSTITUTIONS NOW DOMINATE THE MARKET

However, in recent years there has been a dramatic shift in the character of the stock market. This shift has been a direct result of the increased size and activity of the various financial institutions in the market. Mutual funds, pension funds, and insurance companies moved billions of dollars into the stock market as a result of inflation and the bull market of the sixties. These institutions have become the most important force in the market.

In 1955, small investors accounted for nearly two-thirds of the trading volume, but by 1971 these figures were reversed. Today, the institutions account for more than two-thirds of the dollars publicly traded (this excludes trading by specialists and brokerage firms). Furthermore, big blocks—trades of 10,000 shares or more—have increased dramatically as the institutions have become more active. The number of these block trades has risen from 2,171 in 1965 to 31,207 in 1972. In 1972, these big-block transactions accounted for 18.5% of all New York Stock Exchange transactions, as compared to only 3.1% in 1965.

In an institutionally dominated market the small investor is often at a decided disadvantage. By massive moves in and out of stocks—often based on the timeliest of information—institutions can cause prices to fluctuate sharply. In the process, small investors get hurt. Did this ever happen to you? Well, it happened to me.

I lost a portion of some paper profits almost certainly as a result of institutional power. While I had disposed of most of my stockholdings by 1971, I was reluctant to sell one stock because it had performed well and, with a low price-earnings ratio, seemed solid. Then one day in November 1971, when the Dow was up over 14 points, the stock was abruptly hit for 19%, declining from 26¾ to 21¼ on high volume.

I learned the bad news the next day. Searching for a clue to the sudden decline, I finally found a brief squib buried deep inside *The Wall Street Journal* (on page 32). The *Journal*, noting the unusual activity in this stock, inquired as to its probable cause; the company then allowed as how its soon-to-be-released quarterly earnings just might come in as much as 21% lower than had previously been anticipated.

I am reasonably sure the selling came from institutions since I had at that time a report from Vickers Guide to Investment Company Portfolios. Vickers is a research company which compiles and summarizes mutual fund stockholdings. According to Vickers, about eight funds—including two I personally owned—held this particular stock. These funds, some of which may well have been quick sellers, did not suffer any 19% decline that day. On the contrary, with their diversified portfolios they were up with the market.

On the other hand, I suffered the full paper loss that day. My broker hadn't called me, and even if he had noticed the unusual activity in my stock it is unlikely that he would have known the reason in time to properly advise me.

Since it seemed quite clear that something less than full disclosure had been practiced in this instance, I thought I might possibly obtain recourse by complaining to the company and to the SEC. I wrote to both and promptly got a letter from the company president stoutly disavowing any illegal activity. A reply from the SEC explained that while it made investigations when they were considered appropriate, these inquiries were conducted privately and their outcome was not disclosed unless public enforcement action was to be taken. To my knowledge, the SEC did not act publicly in this particular case.

When this sort of thing happens, it is individuals like you and me who suffer most. Even if it happens only occasionally, who needs it—particularly in the middle of a bull market!

Without any more personal narrative, here are, in some detail, the reasons I feel institutional power threatens the small investor, and why the most practical alternative is to join the institutions via mutual funds.

INSTITUTIONAL AND INDIVIDUAL INVESTORS TRADE WITH EACH OTHER

The institutions now own a substantial percentage of many favored growth stocks. At year's end of 1972, Wiesenberger Services found that mutual funds held 10% or more of the outstanding stock of 422 of our largest corporations. This figure itself is grossly understated since it doesn't include the larger holdings of other institutions such as pension funds and insurance companies. While their portfolios aren't generally accessible to the public, the SEC did conduct a study in 1969 which covered more than 200 major institutions, including the 50 largest bank trust departments. As of September 30, 1969, the study found that these institutions collectively owned 43% of the outstanding shares of

IBM. Other holdings were Xerox, 53%; Avon, 48%; Sears Roebuck, 45%; and Eastman Kodak, 41%—just to name a few.

If you own stock in these companies or in other institutional favorites, you are likely to find yourself competing against the giants. Since the institutions typically trade in big blocks, some people have assumed they are trading mainly among themselves. This is not so. The Securities and Exchange Commission in a major study of institutional investors conducted in 1968 and 1969 found that the institutions do trade against the public, and their trading influences the prices the public must pay.

In essence, the study analyzed the trades of 229 large institutions. It concluded that about one-fourth of their trading activity in the twenty-seven largest common stocks on the New York Stock Exchange was with the public (the other three-fourths was with other institutions). In another analysis of 198 randomly selected New York Stock Exchange stocks, it was found that 55% of the institutions' trades was with the public. When American Stock Exchange stocks were examined, the figure was 38%.

The study also attempted to ascertain whether institutions tended to "gang up" on a stock during a particular month. It was found that when trading the stocks of the twenty-seven largest companies, institutions were on one side of the market (either as buyers or sellers) by a ratio of three to two. On average, thirty-two institutions were on one side while only twenty-one were on the other side.

The SEC looked further at the resulting prices and reported that "net institutional selling is systematically associated with price decreases, and net institutional buying is systematically associated with price increases."

The *Institutional Investor Study* concluded: "Existing institutional volume and patterns of trading could not be maintained if these surveyed institutions were segregated into a separate market and compelled to trade with each other."

Furthermore, New York Stock Exchange studies have corroborated the SEC findings. One 1969 study showed that public customers—other than institutions—participated to some extent in three of every four large-block transactions examined during a two-week period. Public participation on the opposite side of large-block trades (10,000 shares or more) was found to be 34% of share volume.

When the typical investor buys or sells stock, he always believes he is making the right move. What he fails to take into account is that there is another party on the other side of the transaction. And this other party also feels that *he* is making the right move. The kicker is that today this other party is more likely than ever to be a professional money manager.

Now, Mister Typical Investor, what do you think the odds are that *your* decision is the right one?

THE MARKET LACKS LIQUIDITY

In the past, when the market was dominated by millions of small investors, there was always someone to sell to or to buy from. This market was fluid because the small investors had varied investment objectives. They bought and sold for many reasons—they inherited money or they needed cash to pay for a house or a car. Furthermore, small investors received investment advice from many sources, and they didn't respond very quickly to changes in market conditions.

Today, the market is dominated by institutions that are more likely to think and act alike than are individuals. The institutions respond quickly to government economic data and the investment research provided by a relatively few suppliers. They have been the prime beneficiaries of government rulings forcing full and timely disclosure of investment information. This has made matching buyer and seller more difficult and has led to illiquidity—sharp fluctuations in individual stocks and the market as a whole. This is such a common occurrence nowadays that when institutional holders make simultaneous sell decisions and the price of a stock declines 15% to 50% in a single day, the financial scribes shrug it off with the explanation, "The stock hit an air pocket." Colorful airplane terminology, but it worries perceptive individual and professional investors alike.

William McChesney Martin, Jr., the former Federal Reserve Board chairman who has spent much time studying the problems of the securities industry, has stated, "I'm very concerned about the liquidity of the stock market, and I've talked to corporation heads who are worried to death about it."

Small investors who own popular "institutional favorites" should be concerned, too, because they never know when the price of their stocks might fluctuate excessively.

THE PROFESSIONALS HAVE EARLIER INFORMATION

Institutional trading generates millions of dollars of commissions. Money talks, and nowhere does it talk louder or more eloquently than on Wall Street, where institutions use this commission money to purchase earlier and more comprehensive information and better service.

It is obvious to any investor who has seen his stocks rise and fall for no apparent reason that professionals receive and make use of information first. Fluctuations in individual stocks occur every day. And in many cases, it is only after it is far too late to make a profit or to cut a loss that the reasons for the stock's move become public. At this point, the pros have long since bought—or sold.

Every now and then this commonplace event becomes news, as in the Penn Central bankruptcy. Here, apparent inside information made a dramatic difference. Chairman Wright Patman of the House Banking Committee charged that the investing public was "kept in the dark" while banks and other institutional investors unloaded hundreds of thousands of Penn Central shares in the weeks before the railroad's financial collapse.

"It is obvious," said Representative Patman, "that many of these sales were undertaken with either the greatest clairvoyance or on the basis of inside information about the corporation's future prospects."

Despite federal efforts to insure full and equal disclosure, it is a continuing problem. In October 1972, *The Wall Street Journal* investigated these practices, headlining its story "In the Know; Rise Detected in Use of Inside Information to Make Stock Profits." The story reviewed several current cases where the SEC was investigating whether corporate officials had benefited from inside information in selling their stock. The corporations involved included Stirling Homex, ITT, Fabergé, Inc., Liggett & Myers, and Bausch & Lomb.

Former SEC chairman William J. Casey reflected on this problem and noted, "We are finding too many instances where inside information is being passed on in the guise of research analysis. Sometimes," Mr. Casey said, "analysts or salesmen for a securities firm get a peek at a corporation's latest financial results several hours or even days before the information is publicly released. Then," he said, "the information is circulated to the securities firm's preferred clients, usually institutions such as mutual funds, banks, and insurance companies."

Whether the SEC's investigations or the real concern of its chairman will curtail these abuses is problematical. Because of a big case load and a lack of manpower, the SEC has allowed suspected violators merely to enter into an accord in which they admit nothing and agree not to repeat the practice.

Besides getting inside information, institutions often receive brokerage research and analysis well before these data are passed to the broker's smaller customers. With its large high-commission trades, institutional business is generally more profitable to brokers than is retail or small investor trading. Brokers compete avidly for this institutional volume; giving tips to institutions on future research reports is a common tactic. Even if a brokerage report doesn't contain new information, the opinion that the report expresses often affects the price of the stock in question.

The small investor has been placed at such a disadvantage by these practices that *The Wall Street Journal* did a major article titled "The Little Guy, Small Investors Fear Institutions Put Them at Growing Handicap,"* exploring this issue in depth. Following are several cases that were cited, pointing up different aspects of the little guy's plight.

· · · A former official of a big New York securities firm recalled his experience seeking a new institutional sales manager. The prime candidate refused to take the job unless his department could receive the firm's research reports sixty days before they were released to the firm's retail department. The official said he suggested a thirty-day lag. The two men compromised on forty-five days.

· · · Institutions sometimes use pressure to get tips. Equity

---

* Reprinted with permission of *The Wall Street Journal,* February 24, 1971.

Research Associates, a respected New York investment advisory service, reported that it sometimes "got some heat" from institutions because it distributed reports simultaneously to all clients.

· · · Fearing accusations of favoritism toward institutions, other securities concerns are switching to a simultaneous release policy. But even when reports carry identical release dates, advance word on the contents of a major report is often passed on to institutions informally.

· · · One analyst for a big New York securities company said his firm's written reports are indeed distributed simultaneously to all clients—big and small. But he added that "half to two-thirds of the analysis we dispense goes over the phone, and obviously there's a sequence of calling. You tend to favor your best clients."

THE PROFESSIONALS HAVE
BETTER INFORMATION

In addition to receiving earlier information, the quality of research available to professionals is far superior to that available to lay investors. For example, if a security analyst is writing for lay investors, it is thought that brevity is of paramount importance. This often means showing only conclusions, rather than the research that backs it up. It is common to see "research" reports with nothing more than the name of the stock and the advice: buy, sell, or hold.

In contrast, a research report on the telecommunications field intended primarily for professionals was prepared for the use of Coenen & Co., a brokerage firm. Titled *Data Communications and the Specialized Common Carriers,* it ran to 171 pages and thoroughly investigated the investment potential of this industry and the companies in it. The report took two years to prepare and was given free to Coenen & Co. clients, who paid for it in "soft" dollars (i.e., commissions). The charge to nonclients (including, of course, the public) was $500.

While the individual investor can obtain brokerage firm research that says more than buy, sell, or hold, it's most unlikely that he will obtain better research than the institutions receive from those Wall Street firms serving them. The SEC's *Institutional*

Investor Study underscores the disparity between institutional research and the retail research aimed at the public. It was found that in 1968, New York Stock Exchange firms dealing primarily with institutional investors incurred greater research expenses, both absolutely and in relation to total expenses, than did firms dealing primarily with the public. While the median research expense per retail firm was $45,000, the median for institutional firms was $129,000.

Furthermore, even when professionals receive the same information at the same time as the public, they make better use of it. Take annual reports. Despite the promotional character of the typical annual report, professionals take the time to read them, while amateurs often don't. A study by Georgeson & Co., New York, surveying 73 security analysts, found 60% spent over an hour reading each report of companies in which they were interested. But checking 219 small stockholders, Georgeson found 25% spent less than five minutes on annual reports of companies in their portfolios. Another 15% didn't read them at all.

Similarly, intelligent security analysis requires an understanding of corporate earnings statements. Considering the complexity of today's accounting practices, this is now a fine art. It takes time and expertise to properly evaluate earnings statements, often replete with footnotes. Even statements that appear simple can be misleading because they do not detail the methods used to arrive at the end figures.

Can you confidently evaluate the earnings statements on page 26 which appeared in *The Wall Street Journal?*

If these earnings statements stumped you, don't worry—you have a lot of company. According to *Fortune* magazine, one *Wall Street Journal* bureau chief advises his new reporters to turn to senior reporters for help when stumped by footnotes. "They may be just as befuddled as you are, but they hide it better," said the bureau chief.

There is another, even greater problem in evaluating earnings. On occasion, an investor will buy a stock anticipating higher earnings, see his expectations realized, and yet find the price of the stock declining. The reason for this somewhat illogical behavior is that the earnings were not up as much as professional analysts on Wall Street had expected.

CORPORATE EARNINGS REPORTS

GENERAL HOST CORP. (N)

Year Dec 30:	a1972	b1971
cShr earns	$1.21	$1.01
Sales, etc	562,290,000	321,586,000
eNet cnt op	3,617,000	3,038,000
Loss dsc op	1,032,000	841,000
Income	2,585,000	2,197,000
Spec credit	f822,000	g5,459,000
hNet inco	3,407,000	7,656,000
cQuar shr	1.01	.76
Sales, etc	153,256,000	123 761,000
eNet cnt op	2,580,000	2,050,000
Loss dsc op	415,000	417,000
Income	2,165,000	1,633,000
Spec credit	f822,000	j423,000
hNet inco	2,987,000	2,056,000

a-For 53 weeks and 13 weeks. b-For 52 weeks and 12 weeks. Restated and includes results of Cudahy Co. from date of purchase, July 15, 1971. c-On a primary basis and based on income before special credit. e-Equal to $1.69 a share in the year and $1.20 a share in the quarter of 1972, compared with $1.40 a share and 96 cents a share, respectively, in the like periods of 1971. f-Consists of a $5,482,000 gain on the purchase of company's debentures and a $412,000 tax-loss carry-forward credit, less a $3,295,000 provision for losses on discontinuation of operations and disposal of facilities and a $1,777,000 provision to cover additional costs relating to prior year's extraordinary charges. g-Consists of a $5,036,000 gain on sale of Greyhound Corp. securities and a $423,000 tax-loss carry-forward credit. h-Equal to $1.59 a share in the year and $1.39 a share in the quarter of 1972, compared with $3.53 a share and 96 cents a share, respectively, in the like periods of 1971. j-Tax-loss carry-forward credit.

On a fully diluted basis, per-share earnings were 99 cents before and $1.50 after special credit, in the year, and 40 cents before and 91 cents after special credit, in the quarter, of 1972, compared with 88 cents before and $2.57 after special credit, in the year, and 37 cents before and 67 cents after special credit, in the quarter, of 1971.

GREAT EQUITY FINANCIAL (O)

Year Dec 31:	1972	e1971
aShr earns	$.77	$.20
Total revs	37,678,000	20,781,000
Income	932,000	198,000
cCap gns,etc	300,000	22,000
bNet inco	1,232,000	220,000
Avg shrs	1,221,970	973,379

a-Based on income before realized capital gains and other items. b-Equal to $1.01 a share in 1972, compared with 23 cents a share in 1971. c-In 1972, consists of $140,000 realized capital gains plus $160,000 as tax carry-forward credit; in 1971, from $104,000 realized capital gains, less a $82,000 extraordinary charge. e-Results in early 1971 adversely affected by strikes in the automobile industry, the report notes.

LTV CORP. (N)

Year Dec 31:	1972	a1971
Sales	$3,442,296,000	$3,153,091,000
Nt ct op	7,723,000	d19,756,000
Nt dc op	311,000	2,202,000
Income	8,034,000	d17,554,000
Spc item	c804,000	b40,286,000
Net inco	8,838,000	d57,840,00
Quarter:		
Sales	931,665,000	742,830,000
Nt ct op	3,479,000	d16,150,000
Nt dc op		993,000
Income	3,479,000	d15,157,000
Spc item	c512,000	b7,679,000
Net inco	3,991,000	d22,836,000

a-Restated by company. b-Debit; in the 1971 year consists of loss of $32,200,000 from sale of interests in certain subsidiaries, net of $63,850,000 reserves provided in prior years, provision of $9,000,000 for estimated loss on disposition of investments; $915,000 write-off of unamortized discount on debt repaid with proceeds of investment disposals; $1,150,000 provision for loss on investment in unconsolidated subsidiary; less net credits of $2,979,000 for equity in subsidiary net gains from disposition and discontinuance of operations and investments, income tax carry-forward credits and change in inventory method; in the 1971 quarter, consists of $4,115,000 provision for estimated loss on disposition of investments; $1,150,000 provision for loss on investment in unconsolidated real estate subsidiary; and $2,414,000 equity in subsidiary net losses from discontinuance of operations and provision for investment losses, less income tax carry-forward credits. c-Credit; in the 1972 year, consists of gain on disposition of E-Systems Inc. and Altec Corp. of $3,965,000, less provision by subsidiaries for anticipated disposition of facilities and operations of $2,291,000, and write-off of unamortized debt discount and expense applicable to debentures retired of $870,000; and in the fourth quarter, consists of adjustments of previously reported gain on disposition of E-Systems and Altev Corp., of $1,964,000 and adjustments of subsidiary provisions for loss on disposition of facilities and operations of $1,218,000, less write-off of unamortized debt discount and expense applicable to debentures retired of $870,000. d-Loss.

The company reported share earnings of 63 cents before special items and 73 cents after special items in the year 1972, and in the fourth quarter, 34 cents before and 40 cents after special items. Also, net from continuing operations was equal to 59 cents a share in the year 1972. The company is in arrears on its preferred stocks.

On a fully diluted basis, per-share earnings before special items were 57 cents and 66 cents after special items, in the year 1972, and 30 cents before and 36 cents, respectively, in the fourth quarter.

A stock's current price discounts all that is currently known about it, which means its price reflects Wall Street's consensus of its value. If earnings come in as predicted, the price of the stock probably will not change. If earnings come in lower than anticipated, the price may fall; if higher than anticipated, the price may rise.

This puts the lay investor in the difficult position of learning the range of earnings estimates the Street has put on a stock, and ferreting out those stocks which, hopefully, will do even better than the professionals expect.

There's another more clannish and social way in which the professional gets the edge on the lay investor. The Society of Security Analysts, an august group of approximately 3,000 members, has a direct pipeline to management. (As an indication of its influence, the Society's forum was used by Presidential candidate George McGovern to present his revised economic program.)

The Society hosts lunch sessions at which major corporations make presentations to the assembled analysts. The lineup of corporations is impressive. Here, for example, are typical 1973 agenda as reported in *Barron's*.

At the Security Analysts:	
New York	
Texfi Industries	Feb. 5
Whitaker Cable	Feb. 6
Lone Star Gas	Feb. 7
Reichhold Chemical	Feb. 8
Scott & Fetzer	Feb. 9
Baltimore	
RPS	Feb. 8
Denver	
Tidewater Marine Svc.	Feb. 8
Los Angeles	
Western Airlines	Feb. 6
Richmond	
Best Products	Feb. 7
St. Louis	
Beech Aircraft	Feb. 7
San Francisco	
Harrahs	Feb. 8
Wilmington	
Hercules Inc.	Feb. 7

At the Security Analysts:	
New York	
Arrow Electronics	Feb. 26
C.I. Mtg. Group	Feb. 27
Toledo Edison	Feb. 28
Transamerica	Mar. 1
Brown Group	Mar. 1
Northrop	Mar. 2
Atlanta	
Mobile Home Ind.	Feb. 28
Cleveland	
Dow Chemical	Feb. 28
Los Angeles	
Bath Ind.	Feb. 27
San Francisco	
Alberto-Culver	Feb. 27
Washington	
AT&T	Feb. 28

Since what a corporation reports at these meetings can influence the price of its stock, much time and effort are put into its presentation. In many cases, elaborate charts or slides are prepared; the president and major corporate officers are there to explain the company's activities and to answer questions.

Security analysts find these sessions useful. Even though companies habitually put their best feet forward, analysts have the opportunity to personally size up management as it presents its case. The luncheons give analysts additional knowledge of companies and industries with which they are already intimately familiar, as well as research leads on new companies. In addition, there is always the valuable interchange of opinions in a relaxed atmosphere with their professional peers.

The investor doesn't have this face-to-face opportunity to evaluate management. He receives his information filtered by the press or by the analysts.

It's not surprising that professional security analysts have better information and make more use of it. Most have degrees in business, finance, or economics, and, unlike laymen, their full-time job is to evaluate the investment potential of public corporations.

Bernard Baruch stated the case for the professional well:

Success in speculation requires as much specialized knowledge as success in law or medicine or any other profession. It never would occur to anyone to open a department store in competition with Macy's or Gimbels, or to make motor cars against Ford and General Motors, without prior training or preparation. Yet the same man will cheerfully toss his savings into a market dominated by men who are as expert in their line as Macy's and the auto makers are in theirs.

COMMISSION RATES FAVOR THE INSTITUTIONS

Historically, commission rates on the New York Stock Exchange were the same for a given stock regardless of how many round lots (100 shares) were traded. There were no quantity discounts. Then on December 5, 1968, a new rate structure was established, giving a discounted commission rate for trades of 1,000 shares or more. This gave the institutions an advantage over the small investor.

Next, in April 1970, the Exchange made trading even more costly for the small investor by imposing a temporary $15 surcharge on all trades of less than 1,000 shares. The temporary surcharge was lifted on March 24, 1972, only to be replaced by new rates that differed little from the previous surcharge rates. The new commission schedule was devised to pass along to the institutions the economies of scale that result from their big-block buying.

This rate structure continued until September 1973, at which time the SEC, acting in response to a New York Stock Exchange request, authorized commission increases of 10% on orders up to $5,000 and 15% on orders from $5,000 to $300,000. At the time it acted, the SEC stipulated the rate rise would remain in effect until March 31, 1974. It could then be extended for another year if two new rules were adopted by the Stock Exchange.

Furthermore, if the institution buys stocks valued at $300,000 or more, the commission on that portion above $300,000 is now negotiated. Given the large profits from transactions of this size, rates have declined by more than half from previous fixed levels on this portion of the order—and these are Big Board rates. Institutions can do even better if they negotiate commissions off the Exchange. The resulting rate structure places the small investor at a decided disadvantage vis-à-vis the institutions.

With the current rates, if a small investor purchases 100 shares of a $20 stock—a $2,000 order—the effective commission rate is 2.1%. There is another 2.1% commission when he sells. If an institution buys 1,000 shares of a $20 stock—a $20,000 order—the commission rate is only 1.5%. Of course, the bigger the transaction, the lower the rate. The commission for 1,000 shares of a $100 stock is only .7%.

NEW YORK STOCK EXCHANGE COMMISSIONS
Percentage of Amount Invested

Size of Order	PRICE PER SHARE			
	$10	$20	$40	$100
20 Shares	4.6	3.4	2.8	2.0
100 Shares	2.8	2.1	1.6	.7
1,000 Shares	2.0	1.5	1.0	.7

In addition, the investor making the 20-share purchase or sale also pays the odd-lot differential, an eighth of a point (dollar) for stocks selling under $55, a quarter of a point for those selling above $55.

In summary,

· · · The institutions trade directly against the small investor.

· · · The new institutional market lacks liquidity and results in wide price fluctuations.

· · · The institutions generate millions of commission dollars, enabling them to buy more comprehensive and earlier information —and to use it against the small investor.

· · · The institutions have more expertise than the small investor.

There is no doubt that the institutions have made the market a hazardous place for the small investor. Unlike the millionaire speculators of the twenties, institutions cannot be indicted for base and reprehensible motives. Yet, because of their power, the hazard to the small investor is much the same. The market is now less accommodating to the small investor. The message is clear: The new way to financial success is not to fight the institutions but to join them.

CHAPTER 2 BUY MUTUAL FUNDS TO JOIN THE PROS

There are a number of ways to join the institutions, but the best, in my opinion, is the mutual fund—and particularly the no-load mutual fund. The no-load fund, properly utilized, can enable the investor to profit most advantageously in today's volatile markets.

But first of all, for the benefit of those who have never bothered to investigate mutual funds, let's explain what mutual funds are and how well they perform.

Mutual funds are the modern way to make money grow; they provide the investor with a diversified portfolio of stocks and bonds under the continuous supervision of professional management. They seek to do for the individual what he might do for himself if he had time, inclination, background, experience, and sufficient resources to spread his investments among many corporations.

A mutual fund pools the capital of many investors with similar goals and, like other corporations, issues shares of its own stock to investors. Thus, a mutual fund is a single large investment account owned by many individuals who share its income and expenses, profits and losses in proportion to the number of shares owned. Since a mutual fund provides joint ownership of securities that can go either up or down, it cannot guarantee any certain return to its investors. It is thus fundamentally different from a savings account, which does guarantee a fixed rate of return to depositors, who are lenders, not owners.

HOW MUTUAL FUNDS GREW

Mutual funds evolved from investment trusts and investment companies that were founded toward the close of the nineteenth century in Boston, New York, Philadelphia, and other cities. These trusts were established by bankers, brokers, investment counselors, and others who saw the need for making professional financial management available to investors of moderate means.

The first mutual fund, or open-end investment company, was formed in 1924 when the Massachusetts Investors Trust (M.I.T.) granted its shareholders the right to redeem their shares at net asset value less a discount of $2 per share. However, mutual funds did not achieve real growth until after the passage of the Investment Company Act of 1940, which eliminated certain abuses of the 1920's and provided statutory safeguards for investors. This act provided the essential framework for the substantial growth of the mutual fund industry in the last three decades.

And, as the following charts indicate, the industry's growth has been phenomenal. In 1972, approximately 8.5 million Americans had established nearly 11 million mutual fund shareholder accounts, with $60 billion in assets.

FUNDS ATTRACT "UPSCALE" INVESTORS

Significantly, the typical mutual fund shareholder is better educated and has a higher income than the investor who owns only stock. This was the key finding of a special study conducted by the Research Department of the New York Stock Exchange.

The study, based on the Exchange's 1970 "Census of Shareholders," found that "the profile of the mutual fund holder is bent toward the professionals and higher income group" and "the educational level of the adult mutual fund holder is substantially higher than that of the adult who owns stock exclusively."

Specifically, it found that 45% of mutual fund holders had completed college or undertaken postgraduate work, compared to only 29% of the exclusive stockholders.

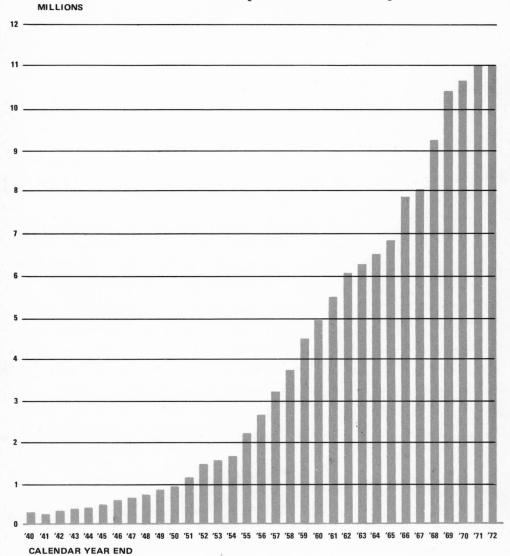

GROWTH OF SHAREHOLDER ACCOUNTS
Open End Investment Companies 1940–1972

MILLIONS

CALENDAR YEAR END

SOURCE: Investment Company Institute, *1973 Mutual Fund Fact Book*

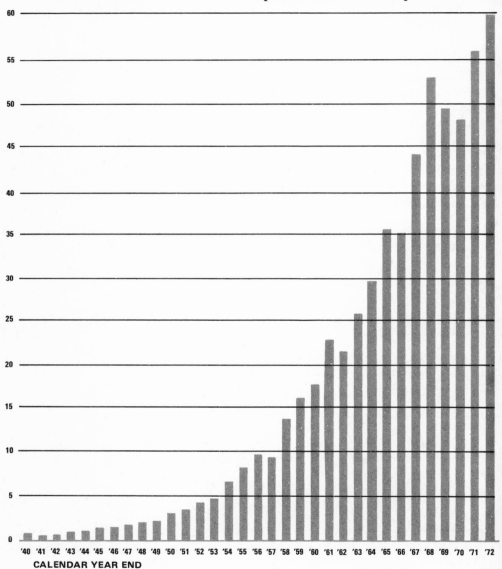

BILLIONS OF DOLLARS

GROWTH OF NET ASSETS
Open End Investment Companies 1940–1972

CALENDAR YEAR END

SOURCE: Investment Company Institute, *1973 Mutual Fund Fact Book*

MUTUAL FUND HOLDERS VS. EXCLUSIVE STOCKHOLDERS BY EDUCATION

Education	Mutual Fund Holders	Exclusive Stockholders
3 Years High School or Less	7.7%	16.1%
Completed High School	27.3%	33.6%
Some College	19.9%	21.2%
Completed College	27.1%	18.9%
Postgraduate Work	18.0%	10.2%

SOURCE: NYSE Research Dept.

Similarly, almost 30% of fund shareholders had incomes of $20,000 or more; only 21% of those holding only stocks were in that income bracket.

MUTUAL FUND HOLDERS VS. EXCLUSIVE STOCKHOLDERS BY HOUSEHOLD INCOME

Household Income	Mutual Fund Holders	Exclusive Stockholders
Under $10,000	25.1%	31.4%
$10,000–$15,000	27.2%	31.2%
$15,000–$20,000	18.5%	16.7%
$20,000 and Over	29.2%	20.7%

SOURCE: NYSE Research Dept.

Finally, what the study called the "most pronounced difference" between fund shareholders and stock shareholders was the size of portfolios. Many of the fund owners also held some stock too. The fund owners held median portfolios of $9,200, much more than the $5,600 median portfolio for stockholders who owned no mutual funds.

While mutual funds were started for investors of moderate means, wealthy individuals and institutions now buy them as a better way to achieve their investment objectives. In 1972, 20% ($9 billion) of reported mutual fund assets were held in 1,119,243 different bank trust department, fiduciary, pension fund, foundation, union, business, and various other institutional accounts.

There are good reasons why these large investors and institutions buy mutual funds, and most of them are even more applicable to small investors. I think the following reasons are particularly compelling for the "sophisticated" individual investor, and although they will be discussed completely elsewhere in the book, I will touch on them here.

· · · Funds have professional management.

· · · Past performance records are readily available for systematic evaluation.

· · · There are prospectuses available in which funds must disclose unfavorable facts.

· · · Funds are diversified.

· · · Funds' risk-reward ratios can be determined fairly accurately, and the ratios are generally acceptable.

· · · The entire field can be adequately researched and mastered by laymen.

· · · There are qualified mutual fund advisory services to make the task of analysis easy.

· · · You can redeem easily.

Mutual fund shareholders receive *professional management* at rock-bottom fees.

The second reason, to my mind, is by far the most important and bears emphasis. There is *easy availability of past performance records.* From the layman's point of view, this is unique and terribly important. There is no way to compare the performance of stockbrokers or, in most cases, even investment counselors. Only mutual funds publish industry-wide performance records that are readily accessible to laymen. With this indispensable data bank, the layman can make optimum investment decisions.

When you buy a mutual fund you will always receive a *prospectus* which may give you unfavorable facts about the fund, as well as the favorable information fund management would like to convey. This makes the prospectus a valuable data source, one not available when you select an investment counselor or buy stock, unless it's a new issue. A prospectus enables you to avoid investment pitfalls. For example, it was when the Penn Central issued a prospectus in early 1970 in order to sell a debenture offering that many Wall Street money managers first found out how badly off the railroad was. Armed with this knowledge, they sold fast and received relatively good prices for their stock.

Diversification, owning a large portfolio of stocks, is a standard reason given for buying funds. However, each year, as the stock market seems to become more volatile, I find this reason more compelling. Every time I read about a stock plummeting on high volume, I am happy my investments are diversified in funds.

Diversity is also a major advantage that funds hold over advisory letters or stockbrokers' recommended lists. There is always great variation in the performances of individual stocks, but with funds it is the portfolio's over-all performance that counts. By way of illustration, an examination of individual stock performance in a fund's portfolio will show why. In its report to shareholders, the New Horizons Fund lists its ten best and ten worst performers. In a typical report, its ten best performers were up 68% or more, and its three worst performers were down more than 50%. With seventy-one stocks in the fund's portfolio, that's a wide range.

I've used the example of New Horizons because it is an outstanding fund. It is the only fund that was in the top ten for the entire decade of the sixties and, despite its large size, still remained in the top ten in 1971 and the top 10% in 1972. It is managed by T. Rowe Price of Baltimore, a firm that advises four funds totaling $1.5 billion of assets (plus double that in individual investment accounts). The firm has an outstanding reputation for investment acumen.

Acumen or no, it, too, has its share of losers, as the chart on the next page indicates. Advisory services and brokerage firms surely pick just as many losers, but their clients do not get the benefits of diversification.

One of the truisms in investing is that greater *risks* and greater *rewards* go hand in hand. Investors are usually advised to seek situations where the probability of profit is greater than the possibility of loss. But with stocks it is hard to apply this generality. I am sure most investors have had the experience of buying a conservative stock, often with a low price-earnings ratio, and yet suffering a substantial loss.

Mutual funds have similar risk-reward ratios. Speculative funds, offering great profit potential, can also be counted upon to decline the sharpest in a bear market. However, with funds the risk-reward ratios are generally acceptable and, for reasons to be explained later, probably significantly more favorable than with stocks. Even more important, the risk-reward ratios are far more easily ascertainable than with stocks. With funds, even a layman

NEW HORIZONS FUND

STOCK PERFORMANCE RECORD—
TWELVE MONTHS ENDED DECEMBER 31, 1972

The ten best and ten worst performers of those common stocks presented in the portfolio as of December 31, 1972 are as follows:

TEN BEST PERFORMERS	Market Change
Extracorporeal	+172.4%
Loctite	+161.5
King Radio	+119.0
MGIC Investment	+114.6
Medtronic	+ 97.5
Farinon Electric	+ 93.1
CMI Investment	+ 88.2
Tropicana Products	+ 83.1
Ionics	+ 80.8
Wal-Mart Stores	+ 68.3

TEN WORST PERFORMERS	Market Change
Minnesota Fabrics	— 71.9%
WTC Air Freight	— 50.7
Science Management	— 50.0
Fred S. James	— 41.9
Airborne Freight	— 41.6
McCulloch Oil	— 40.0
Levitz Furniture	— 32.1
Host International	— 29.0
Fleetwood Enterprises	— 28.3
Thermo-Electron	— 24.6

can assess his risk fairly accurately (this book explains how in Chapter 7), and since there is a wide selection of funds ranging from very speculative to very conservative, he can select the fund or funds best suited to his own investing needs.

I became attracted to mutual funds because I found that as a layman I could do the kind of analysis with funds that only professionals do with stocks. By this I mean *the entire field can be well researched and mastered,* even by a busy layman who has only a limited amount of time to devote to his investments. There are 1,900 stocks listed on the New York Stock Exchange, nearly 1,300 stocks on the American Stock Exchange, and approximately 3,200 unlisted stocks traded by over-the-counter dealers. Few professionals can follow this vast field.

On the other hand, there are only about 600 funds, of which 160 are no-loads. More important, there are uniform data available for all funds (see list starting on page 43 for an example). As a result, you are virtually forced into an organized approach to investing, automatically looking for the best performers and eliminating the rest. You thus have an excellent chance to maximize your profits. In contrast, no layman can know all there is to know about stocks, and as a practical matter most laymen find it exceedingly difficult to compare adequately the relative merits of stocks because data are seldom complete or uniform.

Of course, you need data for analysis. When I turned to mutual funds I started subscribing to introductory offers of *mutual fund advisory services.* Somewhat to my surprise, I found that many were quite factual. They compute mutual fund performance and rank all funds so that the best can easily be spotted. This makes it possible for the investor to achieve good investment results with relatively little energy expended.

It's easy to *redeem* mutual funds. Shares can be sold quickly and easily at fair market value.

HOW PROFITABLE ARE MUTUAL FUNDS?

Until the mid-fifties, most mutual funds followed similar conservative investment policies. As a result, mutual funds were thought of as stodgy investment vehicles, beneficial only to small

investors who were incapable of understanding the basic principles of investing.

In those days, "smart" investors bought stocks. In fact, in 1951,
the entire mutual fund industry had assets of only $3.1 billion—
only slightly more than Investors Mutual, the nation's largest
fund, had in 1972.

Then, performance became an important element in mutual
fund competition. It soon became clear that funds like Dreyfus
and Fidelity were regularly outpacing the market averages. Fund
salesmen, who had once talked retirement goals, began to stress
appreciation. New funds were formed which frankly stated that
their objective was to achieve maximum capital gains. "Smart"
money moved into well-managed aggressive funds. The mutual
fund industry was, in fact, revolutionized.

This industry record has been documented impressively by the
Investment Company Institute (see chart on page 41), the trade
association for all funds (load and no-load). *It found that a
$10,000 investment in the average fund on January 1, 1950, would
have grown to $103,898 by the end of 1972.* There were, of course,
years like 1969 and 1970 when the average fund declined in value;
but over the long term, the number of up years exceeded down
years by nearly 3 to 1—and gains far outpaced losses. (Because of
the many load funds in the average, these results are based on an
actual initial investment of $9,150, after the deduction of an $850
sales charge.) These investment results mean that the average
fund grew at the long-term rate of 10.7% per year, compounded
annually.

I suspect that few people really appreciate the vast difference
that exists between this 10.7% growth rate, compounded annually,
and a lower fixed rate such as the 5% or 6% obtainable from the
savings bank. In the case of the mutual fund performance record,
there was a $93,898 profit (above the original investment). This
is four and a half times the $20,719 gained at the 5% rate, even
though the growth rate itself was approximately only twice as
much. The reason is that the investor's money is compounded.
A table detailing this power of compound growth is on pages
231–232.

Unfortunately, some people, primarily academicians, have deni-
grated this growth record by pointing out that the *over-all* per-

THE MUTUAL FUND RECORD

Year	Initial Investment* $10,000	% Change	Gain	Loss	Compared with 5% interest compounded annually $10,000
1950	$11,089	+10.89	$1,089		$10,500
1951	12,734	+14.84	1,645		11,025
1952	14,166	+11.24	1,432		11,576
1953	14,150	− .11		$16	12,155
1954	20,233	+42.99	6,083		12,763
1955	23,805	+17.65	3,572		13,401
1956	25,604	+ 7.56	1,799		14,071
1957	23,023	−10.08		2,581	14,775
1958	32,088	+39.37	9,065		15,514
1959	36,198	+12.81	4,110		16,290
1960	37,403	+ 3.33	1,205		17,105
1961	46,911	+25.42	9,508		17,960
1962	41,484	−11.57		5,427	18,858
1963	48,519	+16.96	7,035		19,801
1964	54,866	+13.08	6,347		20,791
1965	66,256	+20.76	11,390		21,831
1966	62,785	− 5.24		3,471	22,923
1967	84,294	+34.26	21,509		24,069
1968	99,138	+17.61	14,844		25,272
1969	85,100	−14.16		14,038	26,536
1970	78,616	− 7.62		6,484	27,863
1971	94,008	+19.58	15,392		29,256
1972	103,898	+10.52	9,890		30,719

*Figures in this table are based on annual performance averages of funds listed in the Management Results section of Wiesenberger's *Investment Companies*, except for the categories of bond and preferred stock funds, tax-free exchange funds and international funds. Annual average performance was derived by adding each fund's performance and dividing by the number of funds. New funds were added as they appeared in the Wiesenberger volumes which were used. In 1950, 1961 and 1970, for example, the number of funds was 40, 145 and 307, respectively. Investment results assume initial investment of $9,150 following deduction of sales charge of 8½ percent and subsequent reinvestment of dividends and capital gains. 1972 numbers are preliminary.

formance of mutual funds has been no better than the market as a *whole*. It isn't at all surprising that this is the case since their huge over-all size—$60 billion in assets—mitigates against a radically different performance for the industry. And this will surely continue since the institutions are now in the process of virtually *becoming* the market.

Nevertheless, these studies are seriously misleading many investors because they (1) have never compared institutional results to individual results and (2) fail to focus on the individual investor's basic goal—finding the best single investment, out of many imperfect ones, to meet his needs.

YOU CAN'T BUY ANY FUND AND FORGET ABOUT IT

The above figures are averages, and like many averages, they conceal more than they reveal. You can't buy the average mutual fund any more than you can buy the Dow Jones or Standard & Poor's stock averages.

Top-performing funds, of course, perform significantly better than average. Funds in the top 10% grew at an annual rate of 12% to 15% during the years of the Investment Company Institute's study. T. Rowe Price Growth Fund, the top fund between 1953 and 1972, turned $10,000 into $143,933.

If you have never owned mutual funds and are used to thinking of growth in terms of an occasional stock doubling or tripling in value, 12% to 15% per year may not excite you. For long-term growth, though, the figures are most impressive. They include down years as well as up years, losses as well as gains, cash held, and commissions and management fees paid out. It's a difficult performance to match.

On the other hand, there are many poorly performing funds which even over the long term don't provide their shareholders with the return obtainable from the savings bank.

The most striking fact about individual funds is that their performance varies tremendously from the averages. And it's easy to understand why. Their objectives differ. Individual funds range in size from a few hundred thousand dollars to $2.9 billion, while their portfolios may hold as few as 15 stocks or as many as 536. (In 1972, the average fund held 62 issues.) While they all have "professional" management, some professionals are better than others.

To better illustrate these wide variations in mutual fund performance, here is a ranking of all funds in 1972, courtesy of *Mutual Funds Scoreboard*, a mutual fund advisory service. While 1972 was used primarily because it was the most recent annual data available at the time the list was prepared, it is also a good year to use because it is about as close to typical as a year can be. The average fund was up 10.5% in 1972, the same as the long-term average (+10.7%). Thus, in this "normal" climate, the differences between funds are most meaningful.

Note that "performance," as used in the mutual fund industry and in this book, means the fund's performance, not the investor's. This list does not take into account any sales load. Furthermore, since no-loads will be stressed in this book they are set in boldface type. (LO after a fund means low-load, a fund with a sales charge of less than 3%.) Since December 1972, a number of funds have gone no-load. Other funds—usually the worst performers—have changed their names. In the interests of being as up-to-date as possible, new names and current load status are shown.

1972 MUTUAL FUND PERFORMANCE RANKINGS

Top 10%	% Gain or Loss	Top 10%	% Gain or Loss	Top 10%	% Gain or Loss
Templeton Growth	+67.6	**Cambridge Appreciation**	+26.7	**One William Street**	+22.5
International Investors	+57.3	Transatlantic	+26.7	Keystone K-2	+22.4
American Insurance &		**Harvest Fund**	+26.6	**Growth Industry Shares**	+22.2
Industrial	+44.9	Founders Special	+25.3	New York Venture	+22.0
Omega Fund	+43.8	Landmark Growth	+25.2	Vance, Sanders Common	
Twentieth Century Growth	+42.4	Allstate Enterprises Stock	+24.8	Stock	+21.9
Putnam Voyager	+41.0	**Johnston Mutual**	+24.5	Heritage Fund	+21.9
Putnam Vista	+36.4	**Stein Roe & Farnham**		Oppenheimer Time	+21.9
Charter Fund	+36.1	**Cap. Op.**	+24.4	Sigma Venture Shares	+21.5
Janus Fund	+33.9	**Tudor Hedge**	+24.3	**Rowe Price New Horizons**	+21.4
Life Insurance Investors	+32.3	**American General Growth**	+24.1	BLC Growth Fund	+21.2
Scudder Development	+31.1	Canadian Fund	+24.0	Explorer Fund	+21.1
Magellan Fund	+30.1	Hedberg & Gordon		Mass. Investors Growth	
Channing Venture	+29.8	Lev. (LO)	+23.9	Stock	+21.1
Afortress Fund	+29.3	Independence Fund	+23.7	Putnam Equities	+21.0
Chemical Fund	+29.3	National Investors Corp.	+23.7	**Stein Roe & Farnham**	
Scudder International Inv.	+28.6	Industries Trend Fund	+23.6	**Stock**	+20.9
USAA Capital Growth		Eaton & Howard Growth	+23.4	Keystone S-1	+20.9
Fund	+28.5	Sentry Fund	+23.2		
Nicholas Strong	+28.1	**David L. Babson**	+23.1	**Second 10%**	
Putnam Investors	+28.0	State Street Investment	+23.1		
Alpha Fund	+27.4	**Mairs & Power Growth**	+22.8	**Mairs & Power Income**	+20.8
IDS New Dimensions	+27.0	**Financial Venture**	+22.5	W. L. Morgan Growth	+20.8

Second 10%	% Gain or Loss	Third 10%	% Gain or Loss	Fourth 10%	% Gain or Loss
Investors Variable Payment	+20.7	Southwestern Investors	+16.1	FML Equity Income	+13.4
Investors Research	+20.3	Franklin DynaTech Series	+16.0	Hedberg & Gordon	+13.4
Pioneer II	+20.3	Imperial Capital	+16.0	Keystone S-3	+13.3
Rowe Price New Era	+20.3	AGE Fund (LO)	+15.9	Scudder Special	+13.3
Newton Fund	+20.2	Sigma Investment Shares	+15.9	American Business Shares	+13.2
Brown Fund of Hawaii	+20.0	Edie Special Institutional	+15.9	Armstrong Associates	+13.2
Financial Industrial	+20.0	Founders Mutual	+15.9	Dikewood Fund	+13.2
Franklin Growth Series	+20.0	Mathers Fund	+15.8	Investors Income	+13.2
Century Shares Trust	+19.8	Ziegler Fund	+15.7	Investors Mutual	+13.2
Imperial Growth	+19.8	Fidelity Destiny	+15.6	Sigma Capital Shares	+13.2
Whitehall Fund	+19.8	Hamilton Income	+15.6	Steadman Investment	+13.2
Transwestern Mutual	+19.7	Investment Co. of America	+15.6	AMCAP Fund	+13.2
Sentinel Growth	+19.6	Transamerica Capital	+15.5	Drexel Investment	+13.1
George Putnam	+19.5	Dividend Shares	+15.4	Syncro Income	+13.1
Union Capital	+19.5	Keystone Apollo	+15.4	Safeco Equity Fund	+13.0
Afuture Fund	+19.2	Loomis-Sayles Cdn. & Int'l.	+15.4	Keystone S-4	+13.0
Putnam Growth	+19.1	Massachusetts Fund	+15.4	Vanderbilt Mutual	+12.9
Westfield Growth	+19.1	T. Rowe Price Growth Stock	+15.4	Lexington Research	+12.8
CG Fund	+19.0			First Investors	+12.7
Naess & Thomas Special	+19.0	Commerce Fund	+15.3	Medici Fund	+12.7
Security Ultra	+19.0	Fidelity Fund	+15.3	Paramount Mutual	+12.7
Rochester Fund	+18.9	Travelers Equities	+15.3	Rittenhouse Fund	+12.7
PLIGROWTH Fund	+18.8	Investors Stock	+15.2	John Hancock Signature	+12.6
Ziegler Select	+18.8	Smith, Barney Equity	+15.2	Dreyfus Leverage	+12.5
Pegasus	+18.5	All American	+15.1	United Accumulative	+12.5
E&E Mutual	+18.5	Audax Fund	+15.0	Common Stock of SBM	+12.4
Legal List Investments	+18.4	Hyperion Fund	+15.0	Dodge & Cox Stock	+12.4
Commonwealth Plans A & B	+18.3	Keystone S-2	+15.0	Wade Fund	+12.4
Horace Mann	+18.3	United Income	+15.0	Progress Fund	+12.3
Stein Roe & Farnham Balanced	+18.2	John Hancock Growth	+14.9	Schuster Spectrum	+12.2
Research Equity	+18.1	Pioneer Fund	+14.9	Sigma Trust Shares	+12.2
Corporate Leaders Trust	+18.0	Alpha Investors	+14.8	Affiliated Fund	+12.1
Pace Fund	+18.0	Impact Fund	+14.8	Bayrock Fund	+12.1
Chase Frontier Cap.	+17.9	New World	+14.7	Axe Science Corp.	+11.9
Scudder, Stevens & Clark Com.	+17.9	Leon B. Allen	+14.6	ISI Trust Fund Shares	+11.9
Bayrock Growth	+17.8	Hornblower Growth	+14.6	Research Capital	+11.9
NEL Growth	+17.8	NEA Mutual (LO)	+14.6	Oppenheimer A.I.M.	+11.8
Variable Stock	+17.7	Nelson Fund	+14.6	SoGen International	+11.8
Resources Growth	+17.6	Smith, Barney Inc. & Gr.	+14.6	IDS Progressive	+11.7
Financial Dynamics	+17.5	Fleming Berger	+14.5	Investment Tr. of Boston	+11.7
Mass. Capital Development	+17.5	First Fund of Virginia	+14.5	Ivest Fund	+11.7
Pioneer Enterprise	+17.5	La Salle Fund	+14.5	Washington National	+11.7
Consolidated Invest. Trust	+17.3	Security Equity	+14.5	Colonial Growth Shares	+11.6
Polaris Fund	+17.3	Scudder, Stevens & Clark Bal.	+14.4	Gateway Fund	+11.6
Redmond Growth	+17.3	Providor Growth	+14.3	Keystone B-4	+11.6
Loomis-Sayles Capital Dev.	+17.1	State Farm Growth	+14.3	Twentieth Century Income	+11.6
O'Neil Fund	+17.1	Eaton & Howard Stock	+14.2		
Weingarten Equity	+17.0	Fidelity Trend	+14.2	**Fifth 10%**	
Philadelphia Fund	+16.9	Ivy Fund	+14.1	Barclay Growth	+11.5
Pacific Mutual	+16.8	New England Life Side	+14.1	Country Capital Investment	+11.4
Nassau Fund	+16.7	Over-the-Counter Securities	+14.1	Directors Capital	+11.4
Capital Trinity	+16.6	Wall Street Growth	+14.1	Guardian Mutual	+11.4
Edie Special Growth	+16.5			Dodge & Cox Balanced	+11.1
Aetna Fund	+16.3	**Fourth 10%**		Interfund	+11.1
		Eaton & Howard Balanced	+14.0	Axe-Houghton Stock	+11.0
Third 10%		Farm Bureau Mutual	+13.9	Energy Fund	+11.0
Contrafund	+16.3	First Multifund of America	+13.9	Foursquare Fund	+11.0
Founders Growth	+16.3	EGRET Growth	+13.7	Lutheran Brotherhood	+11.0
ISI Growth	+16.3	Fund for Mutual Depositors	+13.7	Mass. Investors Trust	+11.0
Broad Street Investing	+16.2	R. S. Hershey Fund	+13.6	Pilgrim Fund	+11.0
Companion Fund	+16.2	Viking Growth	+13.6	Sun Growth	+11.0
Sentinel Trustees	+16.2	BLC Income	+13.5	Argonaut Fund	+10.8
MidAmerica Mutual	+16.1	Lexington Growth	+13.5	American Investors	+10.7
		Commonwealth Plan C	+13.4	Bullock Fund	+10.7
				Fund of the Southwest	+10.7
				Life Fund of Boston	+10.7
				Nation-Wide Securities	+10.7
				American Mutual	+10.6

Fifth 10%	% Gain or Loss	Sixth 10%	% Gain or Loss	Seventh 10%	% Gain or Loss
Magna Income Trust	+10.6	Anchor Income	+8.5	Enterprise Fund	+6.4
Puritan Fund	+10.6	Mut. Inv. Found.—MIF Gr.	+8.5	National Growth	+6.4
Financial Industrial Inc.	+10.5	Washington Mutual Inv.	+8.5	Supervised Investors Gr.	+6.4
MagnaCap Fund	+10.5	American Express Income	+8.4	Channing Special	+6.2
Wellington Fund	+10.5	American Leaders	+8.4	**Davidge Early Bird**	+6.2
Value Line	+10.5	**Continental Mutual**	+8.4	First Investors Fund for Gr.	+6.2
American Express Inv.	+10.4	Eagle Growth Shares	+8.4	**Selected American Shares**	+6.2
Crown Western—Dallas	+10.4	Hamilton Funds HDA	+8.4	Decatur Income	+6.1
Evergreen Fund	+10.4	Investors Selective	+8.4	Knowledge Communication	+6.1
Foundation Growth Stock	+10.4	Channing Bond	+8.3	Lord Abbett Bond Deb.	+6.1
Loomis-Sayles Mutual	+10.4	Crown Western—Diver.	+8.3	United Continental Income	+6.0
Mass. Financial		Knickerbocker	+8.3	**Columbia Growth**	+5.9
Development	+10.4	MONY Fund	+8.3	National Preferred	+5.9
North Star	+10.4	American Growth	+8.1	Constellation Growth	+5.8
Putnam Income	+10.4	Axe-Houghton Fund B	+8.1	**Bridges Investment**	+5.7
Diversified Fund of SBM	+10.2	**Burnham Fund**	+8.1	**Concord Fund**	+5.7
Supervised Investors Inc.	+10.2	Heart of America Growth	+8.1	Hornblower Equity	+5.7
Westwood Fund	+10.2	National Stock	+8.1	**Neuwirth Inc. Devel.**	+5.7
Willow Fund	+10.2	Rinfret Fund	+8.1		
Fund of America	+10.1	**Alliance Growth**	+8.0		
Berkshire Capital	+10.0	Composite Bond & Stock	+8.0	**Eighth 10%**	
Oppenheimer Fund	+10.0	Lincoln National Capital	+8.0		
Americare Growth	+9.9	Sentinel Income	+8.0	Fund for U.S. Gov't.	
Boston Mutual Equity		Southwestern Investors Gr.	+8.0	Sec. (LO)	+5.6
Growth	+9.9	Wisconsin Fund	+8.0	Hamilton Growth	+5.6
Colonial Fund	+9.9	**Elfun Trusts**	+7.9	Mutual Benefit	+5.6
Combined Securities	+9.9	Group Securities—Balanced	+7.9	**No-Load Selected**	+5.6
Freedom Fund	+9.9	Mutual Benefit Growth	+7.8	**Reserve Fund**	+5.6
Capamerica Fund	+9.8	Trustees' Equity	+7.8	Chase Fund of Boston	+5.5
Channing Growth	+9.8			Mass. Income Devel.	+5.5
Eaton & Howard Income	+9.8			National Dividend	+5.5
Challenger Investment	+9.6	**Seventh 10%**		American Equity	+5.4
PLICO Fund	+9.6			Mutual of Omaha Income	+5.4
Sovereign Investors	+9.6	Delaware Fund	+7.7	Paul Revere Courier	+5.4
Cumulo Fund (LO)	+9.5	Safeco Equity Western	+7.7	**One Hundred and One**	+5.3
		Fundamental Investors	+7.7	Fairfield Fund	+5.2
		Westfield Income	+7.7	**Investment Guidance**	+5.2
Sixth 10%		Admiralty Insurance	+7.6	Franklin U.S. Gov't.	+5.1
		Istel Fund	+7.6	ISI Income	+5.1
Income Fund of America	+9.4	American Express Stock	+7.5	**Aberdeen Fund**	+5.0
State Farm Income	+9.4	Channing Balanced	+7.5	Tower Capital	+5.0
S&P/InterCapital Dyn.	+9.4	Keystone B-1	+7.5	First Investors Fund	
Wellesley Income	+9.4	Keystone K-1	+7.5	for Inc.	+4.9
Mutual Inv. Found.—MIF	+9.3	**Penn Square Mutual**	+7.5	**Inverness Fund**	+4.9
Pacific Standard	+9.3	Providor Investors	+7.5	**Neuwirth Century**	+4.9
Inverness Growth	+9.3	Vance, Sanders Special	+7.5	Dreyfus Special Income	+4.8
Windsor Fund	+9.3	**American Enterprise**	+7.4	Harbor Fund	+4.8
Northeast Investors Trust	+9.2	Delchester Mutual	+7.3	Planned Investment	+4.8
Technology Fund	+9.2	Security Investment	+7.3	American Birthright Trust	+4.7
Keystone B-2	+9.1	**Consultant's Mutual**	+7.2	Security Bond	+4.7
Ocean Technology	+9.1	National Bond	+7.2	Pilot Fund	+4.6
Colonial Income	+9.0	**Steadman Associated**	+7.2	Everest Fund	+4.5
Dreyfus Fund	+9.0	Fidelity Bond—Debenture	+7.1	United Continental Growth	+4.5
Unified Mutual Shares	+9.0	National Income	+7.1	**Beacon Investing Corp.**	+4.4
Pine Street	+9.0	Shearson Income	+7.1	Compass Income	+4.4
Boston Foundation	+8.9	**Beacon Hill Mutual**	+7.0	United Science	+4.4
Group Securities—		Capital Shares	+7.0	Admiralty Income	+4.3
Common Stk.	+8.9	**East/West Fund**	+7.0	Composite Fund	+4.3
INTEGON Growth	+8.9	FML Growth	+7.0	**United Services**	+4.3
Transamerica Investors	+8.9	Fundpack (LO)	+7.0	Central Mutual	+4.2
Bank Stock	+8.8	NEL Equity	+7.0	Franklin Income Series	+4.2
Fidelity Capital	+8.8	Supervised Inv. Summit	+7.0	Phoenix Fund	+4.2
Mutual Trust	+8.8	Unified Growth	+7.0	Technivest Fund	+4.2
National Industries	+8.8	Axe-Houghton Fund A	+6.9	Liberty Fund	+4.0
Oceanographic Fund	+8.8	United Bond	+6.8	**Sequoia Fund**	+3.9
PRO Fund	+8.8	CG Income Fund	+6.7	Eaton & Howard Special	+3.8
Value Line Income	+8.8	Channing Income	+6.7	First Sierra	+3.8
Anchor Venture	+8.7	Franklin Utilities Series	+6.7	Financial Fund	+3.7
Vance, Sanders Investors	+8.7	**Viking Investors**	+6.5	Income Fund of Boston	+3.6
Acorn Fund	+8.5	American Diversified Inv.	+6.4	Colonial Convertible	+3.5

Eighth 10%	% Gain or Loss	Ninth 10%	% Gain or Loss	Bottom 10%	% Gain or Loss
American National Income	+3.4	United Vanguard	0.0	Convertible Securities	
JP Growth	+3.0	Clarence M. Whipple (LO)	−0.1	Mutual	−5.5
Lighthouse Fund B	+3.0	Shearson Appreciation	−0.2	Conglomerate Fund of Amer.	−5.6
Channing Common Stock	+2.9	Hawick Fund	−0.2	Pine Tree	−5.7
Salem Fund	+2.8	Compustrend Fund	−0.3	American Inv. Counseling	−5.8
AID Investment	+2.7	Astron Fund	−0.4	Falcon Fund	−5.8
American National Growth	+2.6	Selected Special Shares	−0.4	Delta Trend	−6.0
Samuel Greenfield	+2.4	Surveyor Fund	−0.5	Fundex	−6.2
Bondstock Corporation	+2.3	Eberstadt Fund	−0.6	Competitive Capital	−6.4
Colonial Ventures	+2.2	Mates Investment Fund	−0.6	Compass Growth	−7.2
		Equity Progress	−0.9	Centurion Fund	−7.6
Ninth 10%		Contrails Growth (LO)	−1.0	Milwaukee Equity	−8.1
		Twenty Five	−1.0	Side Fund	−8.3
Shearson Investors	+2.1	Comstock Fund	−1.1	Eldorado Fund	−8.8
Spectra Fund	+2.1	Columbine Fund	−1.1	Hartwell and Campbell	−9.5
Varied Industry Plan	+1.9	Advisers Fund	−1.2	Churchill Fund	−9.7
Equity Growth Fund of Am.	+1.9	Unifund	−1.7	Counselors Investment	−9.9
Puerto Rican Investors	+1.8	Group Securities—Apex	−1.8	Chesapeake Fund	−10.5
Anchor Capital	+1.8	Summit Capital	−2.0	Drexel Hedge	−10.5
American Express Capital	+1.7	American Express Special	−2.5	Value Line Special Sit.	−11.0
Essex Fund	+1.6	Neuwirth Fund	−2.7	St. Regis Growth	−11.7
Founders Income	+1.5	Able Associates	−2.9	I-M-A Fund	−11.8
Comsec Fund	+1.5	Sagittarius Fund	−2.9	Western Industrial Shares	−12.2
Old Dominion Inv. Tr. (LO)	+1.4	Mutual of Omaha Growth	−3.0	Hedge Fund of America	−12.9
Provident Fund for Income	+1.4	Manhattan Fund	−3.3	TMR Appreciation	−13.6
Syncro Growth	+1.4	Industry Fund of America	−3.3	Ithaca Growth	−13.8
Knickerbocker Growth	+1.4			Seaboard Leverage	−14.2
One Hundred	+1.3	**Bottom 10%**		Washington Inv. Network	−14.3
Selected Opportunity	+1.2			Kaufmann Fund	−16.0
Berkshire Growth	+1.2	Colonial Equities	−3.4	Ling Fund	−16.7
Pax World	+1.0	Doll Fund	−3.4	Sherman, Dean	−18.9
Revere Fund	+1.0	First Investors Discovery	−3.4	Hartwell and Campbell Lev.	−20.7
de Vegh Mutual	+0.8	Pennsylvania Mutual	−3.5	Growth Fund of America	−20.8
Lincoln National Income	+0.8	Decathlon Fund	−3.8	Convertible Technique	−21.3
Anchor Growth	+0.7	Herold Fund (LO)	−4.0	Vanguard Fund	−21.8
Emerging Securities	+0.7	General Securities	−4.1	Admiralty Growth	−22.1
Chase Special	+0.5	Pension Equity	−4.1	California Venture	−24.4
Mutual Shares Corp.	+0.5	Steadman American Ind.	−4.2	New York Hedge	−24.8
Drexel Equity	+0.4	Capital Investors Growth	−4.6	Ted Warren	−31.7
Fulton, Reid & Staples	+0.3	Chandler Fund	−5.0	Mutual Securities Fund	
Shareholders' Trust of		Shearson Capital	−5.0	of Boston	−32.7
Boston	+0.2	Lenox Fund	−5.2	Israel-American Diver.	−32.9
Fletcher Fund	+0.2	44 Wall Street	−5.3	Market Growth	−34.2
Venture Securities	0.0	First Spectrum	−5.3		

SOURCE: *Mutual Funds Scoreboard* The Hirsch Organization, Inc.

As you can see, the differences are extreme. The best-performing fund was up 68% in 1972. Funds in the top 10% were up at least 21%, but on the other hand the worst fund showed a 34% *loss!*

In future years these funds will perform differently.

For various reasons, which will be discussed in detail in the chapters on mutual fund selection, it is highly unlikely that any fund will maintain an outstanding growth record over a long period of time. Even more important, few funds manage to perform consistently over even relatively short periods of time. It is a myth that you can find a fund that gives consistently outstanding performance.

"Experts" frequently give this advice: "Don't try to select the number-one fund (which everybody knows won't stay number one for long); you'll be far better off buying a fund that just performs in the top 10% year after year."

This advice is fallacious; no such fund exists. It is impossible to buy a fund that is a consistent top performer. *FundScope,* a comprehensive mutual fund advisory service that over the years has greatly increased investor understanding of mutual funds, made a landmark study of mutual fund consistency, covering the performance of 470 funds over an eight-year period—1964 through 1971. Out of all these funds, the study found that not one performed in the top 10% for all eight years. It went further and found that not one fund made the top 10% for even six or seven of the eight years, and only one fund made the top 10% for five of the eight years.

Other experts, thinking that the tortoise and the hare fable is in some way analogous, say, "Don't buy the hot fund that's exciting all the investor interest this year; just buy a good solid fund that is in the top *half* year after year. Over the long run, this is the way to build your nest egg."

These experts are also giving impossible advice. According to the same *FundScope* report, *not one single fund was above average (in the top 50%) each year for all of the eight years covered.*

There are good reasons why funds don't turn in outstanding performances year in, year out. Some are victims of their own success. They become overly large, fat, and complacent, losing the aggressiveness that originally distinguished them. Others are casualties of the market's cyclical ups and downs, for it is axiomatic that the aggressive, performance-oriented funds that surpass all others in bull markets are, by their very nature, the funds that decline the most when the inevitable bear market arrives.

WHAT TO DO

The implications are clear. It is no trick at all to buy a fund that has been an above-average performer in the past. Moreover, with the knowledge this book imparts it is often possible to select funds that will perform substantially better than average for periods of perhaps one to two years. But if you want to maintain above-average performance year after year, *you are going to have to switch funds from time to time.* Since owning above-average funds is measurably more profitable than owning average or below-average funds, that should be the involved investor's goal.

The fund industry has always correctly pointed out that the greatest rewards come to the long-term investor. However, this is not to say that the investor should "marry" any particular fund. Holding a fund for an investing lifetime is definitely not the way to maximize profits.

Once this basic fact is recognized, you must then consider the cost of buying and selling mutual funds—the sales charge—and its effect on your investment program. I think you will agree that a sales charge, while legitimately compensating salesmen, becomes an entrance fee which constrains people from making optimum investment decisions.

As this book goes to press, there is only one way to avoid this entrance fee—by buying no-load mutual funds, a type of fund unique in that it is sold without any sales commission. For the sophisticated investor, the absence of any entrance costs gives greater liquidity and greater flexibility, and removes the psychological restraints that lock investors into holding when they should be selling. With no-loads, it's easy to switch from poorly performing funds to better performers. It's easy to sell a fund if you feel a bear market looms and easy to buy back in better times.

Load funds, with their traditional 8.5% sales commission, don't offer this flexibility. However, this may possibly change. The SEC has questioned the load fund's practice of levying a high fixed commission, and the Justice Department has instituted an anti-trust suit that could reduce this commission in some cases. In the event this suit or other legislation results in commissions declining to 1% or 2% (or roughly the same as stocks), the load would become academic. For all practical purposes, load funds would then become as desirable as no-loads. In that eventuality, Section II of this book, which shows how to select the best-performing funds—and sets up criteria for disposing of poorly performing ones—would apply to all funds, not just no-loads.

Until such time, though, the way to make mutual fund investing realize its fullest potential is to *buy no-load mutual funds.*

CHAPTER **3** DEFINING NO-LOAD MUTUAL FUNDS

No-load funds are a special category of mutual funds. They are exactly like their more expensive counterparts, the load funds, in every single respect except one. No-loads are sold without a sales commission (which the industry terms a "load"). This is possible because there are no salesmen involved in their purchase. The initiative to buy them lies solely with the investor.

No-loads were started about the same time as load funds, usually by investment counseling firms as a depository for accounts too small for individual handling. The biggest no-load fund group, T. Rowe Price, had such a start, as did Boston's Scudder, Stevens & Clark. These counseling firms now view their mutual funds as a "showcase" for their investment acumen and expertise.

Later, brokerage firms set up their own no-load funds, seeing in them vehicles that would provide a steady flow of new commissions from their portfolio transactions. Today, many well-known brokerage firms sponsor no-load funds—Smith, Barney; Drexel, Burnham and Co. with its Burnham Fund and Consultants Mutual Investments; Lehman Bros. with its One William Street Fund; and Merrill Lynch, Pierce, Fenner & Smith through its Lionel D. Edie investment counseling subsidiary.

Because no-loads enable the involved investor to save substantial sums, they have grown rapidly in recent years. At the beginning of 1967 there were 61 such funds. By the end of 1972 more than one in four funds was a no-load; their numbers had grown to 160, and they held $7.4 billion in assets in approximately 1.3 million shareholder accounts. The industry has recognized this dramatic growth of investor interest; more than 30 load funds have responded by becoming no-load. More are expected to abandon their commission structures.

Sophisticated investors have recognized the outstanding values that no-loads provide. In 1971, the Investment Company Institute studied 2,500 families that had heard of mutual funds. Of those families that had incomes of less than $12,500, only 17% had heard of no-load funds, but 40% of the $20,000-plus earners knew about no-loads. Even more important, these upper-income wage earners preferred no-loads to loads by almost 4 to 1.

Still, no-loads are an unknown quantity for most people. There are no salesmen to proclaim their advantages. Their advertising does not reach many of the people who would most benefit from owning them.

HOW TO IDENTIFY NO-LOADS

It's easy to tell the difference between no-load and load funds. If you turn to the financial pages of a daily newspaper, there is usually a listing of mutual fund quotations. (I've shown *The Wall Street Journal's* listings on the accompanying page.)

After the name of each fund, there are two price quotations. In *The Wall Street Journal* the first column is titled "N.A.V." The second column is titled "Offer Price." In other papers the columns are titled "N.A.V." and "Offer"; "Sell" and "Buy"; and a few still use the old OTC terminology, "Bid" and "Asked."

Notice that for most funds the quoted offer price is higher than the N.A.V. Notice also that there are some funds where the N.A.V. and the offer prices are the same. The funds with the higher offer price are load funds; the difference between the N.A.V. and the offer prices is the maximum commission that goes to the mutual fund salesman and his selling organization.

The funds that show the same N.A.V. and offer prices are NO-LOADS. There is no sales commission.

EXPLAINING THE DIFFERENCE

To understand fully the difference between loads and no-loads, you must understand how funds are sold, managed, and valued.

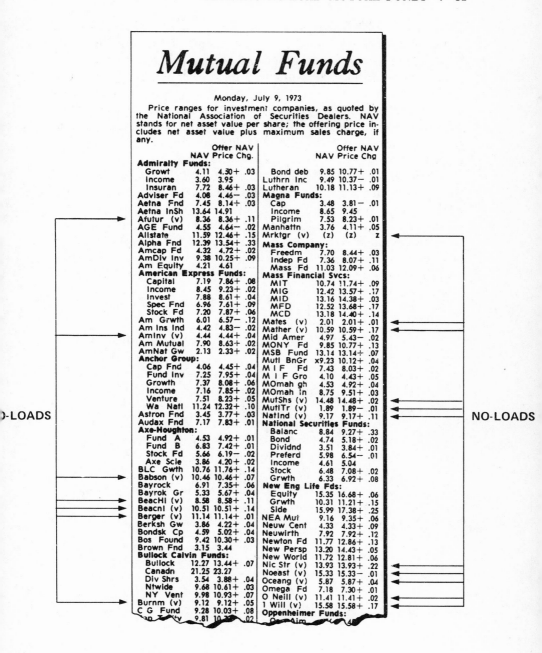

NOTE: *The Wall Street Journal* identifies no-loads with the symbol "V" after the name.

First of all, let's explain what the N.A.V. or net asset value per share is. The N.A.V. price is what a share of the fund is really worth. It is derived by computing, each day, the total market value of the fund's portfolio plus any cash on hand and then dividing this sum by the total number of shares outstanding. The net asset value may also be defined as the liquidation value of the fund if it were able to sell everything at the end of the day and divide the proceeds among its shareholders. In sum, it is what you get when you sell your shares back to the fund.

On the other hand, the offer price is what you pay to buy shares in the fund. In the case of the load fund, it includes a sales charge; in the case of the no-load, it does not.

Both load and no-load mutual funds are managed by professional investment advisers who are paid fees for selecting the right stocks, for providing judgment in timing the buy and sell orders, and for safeguarding the investors' money. The fee for this service does *not* come out of the sales commission paid to load funds. It is a common misconception that some—or all—of the sales charge goes to pay management. This is not true at all. In the case of the load funds, the sales charge goes *solely* to the salesman and his selling organization.

But don't grieve for management. Management, for both the load funds and the no-load funds, is paid by a separate fee. In both cases, this management charge is typically one-half of 1% (.5%) of a fund's net asset value paid annually. For example, the management of a mutual fund with $100 million of assets usually gets about $500,000 per year for providing investment counsel to the fund. In the case of load funds, this is in addition to the sales charge. The fact is that none of the sales commission goes to management, or benefits existing or new shareholders; it is solely a distribution expense.

CHAPTER 4 NO-LOADS AND LOADS PERFORM EQUALLY WELL

Performance should always be paramount in fund selection. If no-loads don't perform as well as the more familiar loads, an investor would be penny-wise and pound-foolish to buy an inferior fund simply to save a sales charge. It can be shown that poor performance costs many times more than any sales commission saved.

However, no-load funds are indeed as good as load funds. Independent research has consistently shown no difference in performance, on average, between no-loads and loads. This means there are good and bad no-loads and there are good and bad load funds.

One of the best comparative studies in this area was an exhaustive comparison of no-loads versus loads covering income, growth, and stability. It was conducted by *FundScope* in 1971 and concluded: "In the end, because so many no-load and so many load funds perform above average and so many below average, you must reach the conclusion there just is no relationship, no correlation, between load and results."

The *FundScope* study is only one of many over the years. As far back as 1962, a special study prepared by the Wharton School of Finance for the Securities and Exchange Commission found "no evidence that higher sales charges go hand-in-hand with better investment performance. Indeed, the study showed that fund shareholders paying higher sales charges had a less favorable investment experience than those paying less."

Similarly, in June of 1961, *Dun's Review* analyzed no-load funds, saying, "The 8% savings in sales commission involves no sacrifices in quality of management."

In 1971, the noted economist Paul Samuelson, in his *Newsweek* column, had this to say on the subject of mutual funds:

A small man—anyone with a portfolio of, say, under $100,000—is unlikely to do as well investing his own money as he can do in a no-load mutual fund. Commissions are getting to be higher on his own small transactions. . . . There is no evidence that buying a load fund —i.e., one sold to you by a broker, insurance agent, or fund salesman— brings you anything for your five to nine per cent commission charge in the way of superior performance or safety.

Let's see for ourselves whether there is any difference between no-loads and loads. Rather than show many pages of statistical tables, I have used the annual *Forbes* magazine ratings to make the comparison. *Forbes* rates mutual funds on the basis of their performance over the last three up and down markets (i.e., bull and bear markets)—approximately a ten-year period of time. In up markets, the funds are rated from a high of A+ to a low of D. In down markets, the ratings span from A to F.

Forbes's 1972 study rated 38 no-load and 153 load stock funds (balanced funds were excluded). Classifying these funds by grade, it was found that roughly the same proportion of the no-loads received top ratings as did the loads. For example, in up markets 21% of both no-loads and loads were rated A or A+. Defensively, results were also similar. In down markets, 5% of the no-loads were rated A as compared to 4% of the loads.

HIDDEN COSTS

The sales charge is not the only fee paid. In addition, there are management fees and other administrative costs, and in some cases reinvestment and redemption fees.

As was previously noted, the management fee is typically one-half of 1% (.5%). In some cases it is higher, but the funds that charge a higher fee are equally likely to be loads or no-loads. There is no relationship between the load and the management fee.

Besides the management fee, there are other expenses of run-

DISTRIBUTION OF STOCK FUNDS SIX YEARS OR OLDER

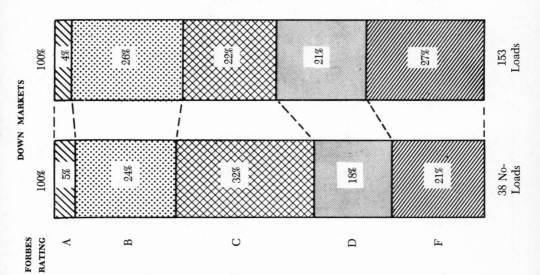

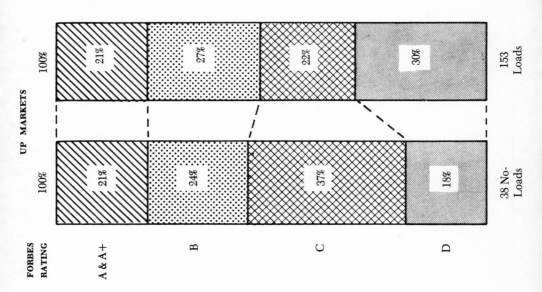

SOURCE: 1972 *Forbes* Mutual Fund Ratings

ning a fund. Some of these are legal and auditing fees, taxes, prospectus printing costs, and directors' fees. These expenses and the management fee are totaled and percentaged against net assets. The resulting figure is called the fund's expense ratio.

These expense ratios vary widely from fund to fund. They commonly range from as low as .20% to more than 2%. While there are many reasons why expense ratios vary, the size of the fund is the most significant. Since many expenses are fixed, they account for a smaller portion of the cost of running a large fund than a small fund.

When funds are classified by size, expense ratios of no-loads are generally comparable to those of load funds. Among funds with assets of more than $5 million, the annual differences in 1972 were no more than .18%. *These differences are insignificant compared to the wide range of performance results between funds.* For funds under $5 million, the expense-to-asset ratio of the average no-load was .76% higher; however, there were great differences between these small funds. One no-load with assets of $300,000 had an expense ratio of 13.5%; another $200,000 fund had an expense ratio of 12.0%. Discounting these funds, the differences between most small load and no-load funds were not meaningful. In fact, a close examination of these small funds revealed that 39 of the 67 no-loads had expense ratios lower than the average under $5 million load fund.

AVERAGE EXPENSE RATIOS
Year ending December 31, 1972

Assets in Millions	NO-LOADS		LOADS	
	No. Funds	Expenses % Avg. Assets	No. Funds	Expenses % Avg. Assets
$300+	6	.54%	41	.54%
$200–300	4	.69%	16	.65%
$100–200	10	.72%	35	.78%
$ 50–100	14	.88%	40	.80%
$ 25–50	11	1.01%	57	.93%
$ 10–25	27	1.15%	63	1.05%
$ 5–10	13	1.37%	49	1.19%
Under $5	67	2.30%	67	1.54%

NOTE: Analysis based on expense data from Wiesenberger's *Mutual Fund Panorama*, Dec. 31, 1972. Low loads excluded.

REDEMPTIONS

Redemptions are the bane of the mutual fund industry, and the negative publicity surrounding industry net redemption statistics suggests to some that mutual fund ownership is out of fashion. Nothing could be farther from the truth. Let's put redemptions in proper perspective, see what's happening to loads and no-loads, analyze why, and see how it affects you as a mutual fund investor.

The industry ended 1972 in a net redemption position—the first time ever for a whole year. In 1972, investors cashed in $1.7 billion more fund shares than were sold. Why? The answer is complex, but probably centers on two facts.

First of all, the industry is older now, and many long-term shareholders are redeeming to achieve their investment goals. The larger, older funds are most affected by redemptions for this reason.

The second reason is probably more critical: there are now fewer fund salesmen. They quit the industry in droves during the 1969–70 bear market, and many never returned because the industry's most lucrative sales practices have mostly been wiped out. Funds can no longer order give-ups (kickbacks) on brokerage commissions to reward brokers selling their shares, and the profitable sale of contractual plans has been severely limited. Despite these difficulties confronting the industry, 1972 was still the fourth-best year ever for gross mutual fund sales—and no-loads have continued to avoid the net redemption problem.

Actually, it's not surprising that no-loads, which have no salesmen to begin with, have never been in net redemptions. In 1972, no-loads had net sales of $323 million, as contrasted to approximately $2 billion in net redemptions for the load funds. (While $2 billion net redemptions is a large figure, it should be noted that brokers also sold $1.2 billion of closed-end funds, mostly conservative income and bond funds, in 1972. Closed-end sales have always been excluded from mutual fund statistics, though many now feel they should be taken into account.)

In every year for which separate statistics have been computed, no-loads, as a group, had better sales-to-redemption ratios than did load funds. I think this clearly demonstrates that no-load investors have greater loyalty to funds they selected themselves than do load investors to their holdings. Significantly, this loyalty doesn't weaken with the market. Even in May 1970, at the low point of the 1969–70 bear market, no-loads had net sales of $14.9 million; the loads, only $1 million.

Up to now we have been discussing industry statistics. Like many other mutual fund averages, they really have little bearing on the individual investor. The only way total industry redemptions could become the investor's problem is if they were large enough to cause wholesale price declines (and if this happens, both stockholders and fundholders are in trouble). The fact is that the roughly half-billion dollars of redemptions in 1972 (taking into account closed-end sales) can't begin to affect the value of the nation's trillion dollars of publicly held stock and $950 billion of net corporate debt.

What is significant to the investor is whether *his* fund has net sales or net redemptions since this does have a bearing on performance. (This is discussed in detail in Chapter 9.)

But when you look at individual funds, you quickly see that their sales and redemptions are affected by performance. Some poorly performing no-loads are in net redemptions, but they are outweighed by the flood of money pouring into top-performing no-load funds. In 1971, the top-performing Rowe Price New Horizons Fund had net sales of $69 million. The Rowe Price Growth Fund had net sales of $131 million and followed this up with net sales of approximately $215 million in 1972.

Nicholas Strong started 1971 with only $6.4 million in total assets and attracted $31.1 million in new money as a result of its outstanding performance that year. Similarly, the Janus Fund, 1972's top-performing no-load, started the year with $3.5 million and received $35 million net new money by December.

Many top-performing load funds did well, too. The Chemical Fund added approximately $68 million net new money in 1972; Putnam Investors, $30 million.

As expected, poor performers were more likely to suffer redemptions. Value Line Special Situations Fund, which saw its net asset value decline 11% in 1972, had net redemptions of approximately

$23 million. Many long-suffering Manhattan Fund investors (off 3% in 1972) finally bowed out. The fund started 1972 with $168 million in total assets, but then had $29 million in net redemptions. (I regard this development as salutary. If this becomes a trend, it might even improve average fund performance.)

Therefore, don't be concerned with publicity over industry redemptions; it's their problem, not yours. Eventually you're going to redeem, too, and when you do you'll receive net asset value— and that's the important consideration.

REDEMPTION FEES

Approximately forty no-load and low-load funds charge a redemption fee. This is a fee, typically 1% and never more than 2% of net asset value, which is paid when the fund's shares are redeemed. Since the purpose of the fee is to prevent "trading," in many cases it is rescinded after the fund has been held six months to a year. If a fund is sufficiently desirable, this becomes a minor cost. If not, these funds are easily avoided.

To sum up, all the facts show that a sales charge—or lack of it— is not a factor in achieving performance. The conclusion is inescapable: load or no-load, the basic product is the same. So it's only logical to go no-load and save the commission expense.

CHAPTER 5   EVALUATING THE LOAD

IS THE LOAD EXCESSIVE?

The sales charge, or load, has traditionally been considered 8.5% because this is the maximum commission for most funds. But over the years people have questioned whether this commission rate is excessive. After all, stock commissions are considerably lower. If you invest $3,000 in a mutual fund with the traditional 8.5% load, the sales charge is $255, while to buy and sell 100 shares of a $30 stock costs only $108. (The round-trip comparison is used because there is generally no charge to sell a fund.)

Furthermore, the sales charge actually paid has always been understated because it is expressed as a percentage of the total purchase price (net asset value plus sales charge) rather than as a percentage of the amount actually invested in a fund as is the case with stock commissions. The stated 8.5% sales charge is really 9.3%, or about 9% higher than most investors believe. That's because it is 8.5% of the money paid out but 9.3% of the money actually invested. For example, if $10,000 were paid into a load fund, $850 would go to the sales organization; the balance—$9,150 —would actually be invested in stocks and bonds. Divide the $850 by $9,150 and you get 9.3%. Put another way, if you want $10,000 working for you in a load fund, you must pay $10,930 total.

CHANGES MAY BE IN THE OFFING

As this book goes to press, the mutual fund industry is in ferment because the government is attempting to lower the sales charges. In 1972, the National Association of Securities Dealers (NASD) proposed that the maximum sales charge be limited to

8.5% (one in five funds in 1972 charged more) and be scaled down to 6% if three services are not provided. Specifically, these services are: reinvestment of dividends at net asset value, rights of accumulation, and quantity discounts.

Then, former SEC Chairman William J. Casey urged the repeal of Section 22(d) of the 1940 Investment Company Act; 22(d) is government jargon for the retail price maintenance (fair trade) clause which forces all salesmen to charge the commission set by fund management. The SEC feels that if 22(d) is repealed by Congress, competition will reduce sales commissions substantially. Hearings were held in Washington in early 1973 to reconsider the need for 22(d) and to learn the industry's view. (The industry said it prefers the status quo.)

At the same time the SEC was investigating 22(d), the Justice Department dropped a bombshell. It filed an antitrust suit against NASD, several large funds, and broker-dealers (including Fidelity; Wellington; Vance, Sanders; Merrill Lynch; Bache; and Walston) charging conspiracy to prevent the development of a secondary market in mutual fund shares. If a secondary market is established, fund owners would no longer have to buy and sell at prices fixed by the funds. Instead, they could trade fund shares on the open market just as over-the-counter stocks are bought and sold. Again, this would probably result in the commissions of many, if not all, fund shares being reduced.

If either the SEC or the Justice Department prevails, the entire load fund distribution system will almost certainly undergo radical changes to the investors' benefit. This is certainly desirable. The sales charge should be less, and fair trade laws of any sort are anachronisms that should be eliminated. However, as of this writing, it is far from certain whether these proposed changes will ever come to pass.

To put these proposals and hearings into proper perspective, here is a short history of these efforts. The Securities and Exchange Commission, which regulates the fund industry, has always felt the charge excessive and for years has attempted to lower it. As long ago as the late 1930's, the SEC studied the infant mutual fund industry and found "sales charges disturbingly high." Then, the Investment Company Act of 1940 empowered the National Association of Securities Dealers and the SEC to make rules precluding "unconscionable or grossly excessive" sales loads on mutual fund shares.

The SEC again studied the question of mutual fund sales charges in 1966 and, as a result, introduced legislation in 1967 that would have limited the load to 5%. However, when the bill finally became law, in December 1970, this provision had been stricken. Thus, thirty years of governmental effort through 1972 has produced no meaningful change in the commission rates.

Furthermore, even if 22(d) is repealed or is by-passed by the establishment of a secondary market, it is hard to foresee what impact this would have on the industry. Knowledgeable fund people think commissions for purchases under $1,000 would be virtually unchanged. For purchases up to the $5,000 to $7,500 range, there are differences of opinion. Some think the changes would be minimal; others foresee a decline to near the same commission rates as those for stocks. For purchases larger than $7,500, supply and demand might well reduce the commissions to the same levels as stock commissions—which for the average investor aren't low at all! And with funds, this entrance fee is in addition to the day-in, day-out commission expense incurred when the fund trades its portfolio stocks.

However, if the rates were to drop significantly, the industry would almost certainly find itself in a terrible predicament. A lower commission rate would make load funds more desirable for the investor, but there would then be few salesmen willing to push them for the simple reason that they would not be adequately compensated for their efforts. This is Catch-22 for the load funds.

It is not generally realized but, by and large, fund salesmen employed by independent dealers who concentrate on selling mutual funds (who account for approximately three-fourths of all fund sales) do very poorly at this pursuit even now with the high fixed commissions. Calling on clients at home or in the office is the most costly and inefficient of all selling methods. In 1970, these salesmen netted, on average, only $1,800, while two-thirds made less than $2,500 that year. Even in prior years with rising markets, half still made less than $2,500.

These income figures just cited are based on data supplied to the SEC by the funds. They are for full-time salesmen who supposedly spend most of their working hours selling funds. (The SEC found that part-timers averaged $616 in 1970 and $1,219 in

1969.) However, since nobody can live on $2,500 per year or less, it is obvious that the data need clarification. According to the SEC study the answer appears to be that since these salesmen are independent contractors, not employees, the funds don't really know how much time they spend selling funds. The firms themselves spend very little to maintain these salesmen, who are almost always required to bear such expenses as telephone calls, gasoline, et cetera. Most fund organizations figure any sales, no matter how few and far between, are productive. Thus, many salesmen reported as full-time are really part-time, and the averages are understated accordingly.

The SEC's report recognized the dilemma of adequately compensating salesmen by stating:

The repeal of 22(d) would have little, if any, immediate impact on the no-loads. The relative importance of the no-load group might grow. This would happen if an appreciable number of load fund adviser-underwriters decided that sales loads just weren't worth bothering with under a competitive regime and that if investors were to be appealed to on a price basis, they might as well go all the way by eliminating the sales charge altogether.

In other words, more loads would become no-loads and investors would benefit even more from knowing how to buy a professionally managed mutual fund portfolio without the help of a salesman.

In view of the current uncertainty, it is particularly interesting to examine the traditional 8.5% sales charge in order to see its impact on the small man's investment. Perhaps the realization of how significant the load really is will in some small way assist in lowering the sales charge so that the average investor can economically avail himself of the best-performing load funds as well.

WHY THE 8.5% LOAD IS EXCESSIVE

With increased competition from the no-loads, mutual fund salesmen now have to justify the load. They offer many arguments; the most common of all is that over the long run the fund's shares will double and triple in value and the 8.5% load becomes insignifi-

cant in comparison. But the load does make a considerable difference, particularly if the difference is measured in terms of the
most valuable commodity of all: time.

Most male wage earners have a working life of approximately
forty-five years. By the time the typical worker reaches retirement
age, the likelihood is that he wants a nest egg, an estate. And
forty-five years is not really a great deal of time to build an estate
that will provide an income over and above social security and
a pension.

First of all, in the early working years, earnings are relatively
low. Typically, approximately three-fourths of savings go solely
for homes and automobiles until the age of 35. From 35 to 49,
earnings and savings rise, but it's at 45 that most wage earners
reach the peak of their earning power. Statistics show that the
45-to-54 age group saves at least one-third more than any other
age group. Thus, it is the number of years that a man's savings and
investments actually grow for him that is of critical importance.

As was noted previously, mutual funds have been growing
approximately 10% annually. This means that in the long run,
under average conditions, the investor who purchases no-loads is
a *year ahead* of an investor who buys the same performance but
pays a load.

Some people argue that over the long run, the load fund will
make up this difference. They reason that over a period of nine
years the charge is amortized to only 1% per year. They then con-
clude that 1% a year doesn't make any real difference.

Again, there is a difference. The longer the fund is held, the
greater is the difference, since commission money saved by the
no-load fund buyer compounds each year. This constant compounding increases the spread between the no-load and the load
fund return.

Let's illustrate this difference more fully with some hypothetical
examples. Take two funds, one load versus one no-load, each with
a long-term growth rate, through bull and bear markets, of 10%
annually. In each fund, $10,000 is invested in a lump sum. In the
case of the no-load fund, the whole $10,000 goes to work immedi-
ately. With the load fund, $9,150 is actually invested.

At the end of year one, the no-load investor's fund has grown
10% and now has a cash-in value of $11,000. The load fund has

also grown 10%, but its cash-in value is only $10,065, or slightly more than the amount originally invested the year before.

At the end of year two, the no-load is worth $12,100 while the load is worth $11,072, or $1,028 less. The performance spread between the two is widening. Where the load investor was $850 behind at the beginning, he is now more than $1,000 behind. The load investor lost the $850 and will also lose forever the 10% a year growth on this portion of his investment. Over the years, the spread will continue to widen. By the end of ten years, still assuming equal growth rates, $10,000 in the no-load fund will have grown to $25,939. The no-load investor will be $2,204 ahead. *This is the real difference the load makes.*

If you follow the advice in this book, you will be able to select a no-load fund that is as good as any load fund. However, suppose for a moment that there is a load fund that will grow 50% faster than any available no-load. This load fund certainly has more long-term potential. But when we compare a no-load fund growing 10% a year with a load fund growing 15% per year (or 50% faster) we find that even with a vastly superior fund, it will take two years for the load fund investor to make that 9.3% differential disappear.

COMPARISON OF $10,000 INVESTMENT IN TWO MUTUAL FUNDS

	NO-LOAD FUND	LOAD FUND
	Growing 10% per Year	*Growing 15% per Year*
Initial Capital Working	$10,000	$ 9,150
End Year 1	11,000	10,523
End Year 2	12,100	12,101

Similarly, a load fund appreciating 25% more per year than a no-load will take four years to catch up; a load fund appreciating 10% more per year than a no-load will catch up in approximately ten years.

The above comparisons presume growth in a bull market. But there are also bear markets. And, of course, here the no-load investor doesn't suffer the instantaneous 8.5% loss on top of declining net asset values.

**COMPARISON OF $10,000 INVESTMENT
IN TWO MUTUAL FUNDS
EACH GROWING 10% PER YEAR, COMPOUNDED ANNUALLY**

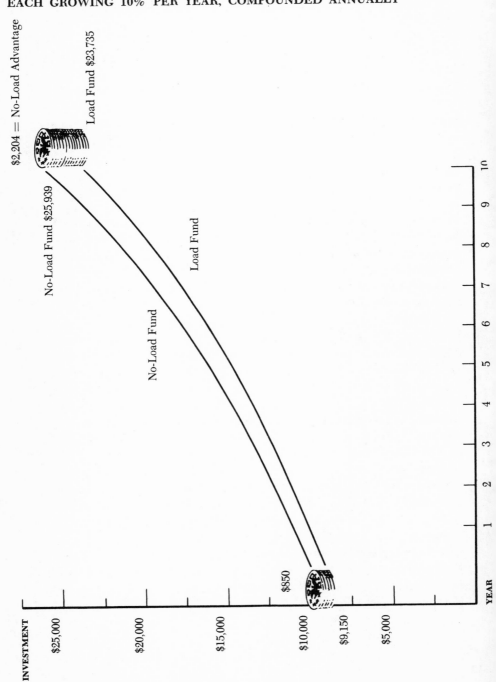

CHAPTER 6 YOU *CAN* SELECT A NO-LOAD FUND YOURSELF

On November 24, 1972, *Wall Street Week,* a unique television program for investors, questioned George Putnam about the latest mutual fund developments. George Putnam is eminently qualified to discuss mutual funds. He is chairman of the Investment Company Institute and chairman of Boston's Putnam Group of load funds, which handle about $2.5 billion of assets. He is a Boston "Brahmin," distinguished as a descendant of Justice Samuel Putnam, who in 1830 laid down the "prudent man" rule that all good trustees now follow.

Commenting on the industry's redemption problem, Louis Rukeyser, the program's host, noted, "George, don't you think it's significant that one kind of fund that has done very—relatively well in this period . . . is the no-load fund, the kind that doesn't carry a sales charge. . . . Why *should* anyone buy a load fund?"

"Well, that's a very good question," responded Putnam. "It's a question of whether you like to have a professional help you or whether you like to do things yourself. If you have the facilities and the know-how to find the funds for yourself that's best suited to you, by all means you should do that. You can buy a fund that does not have a sales charge. Sales charge is the commission for your broker or financial expert who helps you find what *you* need and what fund is best suited for these needs."

Putnam is essentially right, but it's not only a question of whether you *like* to have professional help or *like* to do it yourself; it's also a question of whether you *can* select the best-performing funds yourself without devoting an inordinate amount of time to the task.

The ability to select properly is critical. There are now 600 different funds to choose from, offering a wide range of objectives and varying greatly in quality. Poor selection will cost the investor far more than paying any load charge.

The fact is that the typical investor—and certainly you—can select top-performing funds without the assistance of a salesman. This can be proved by comparing past selections made by no-load and load investors. As was noted earlier, there are both good and poorly performing load and no-load funds—and money is invested in all of them. In the case of load funds, the investor is assisted in his choice by a salesman. With no-loads, the investor is the sole decision maker.

In order to determine how well no-load investors have done as compared to load investors (as distinct from the performance of the funds themselves), I analyzed the funds on the basis of the 1972 *Forbes* ratings to see where the money is now invested. I wanted to determine what proportion is in the top-rated funds and what proportion is in the lowest-rated funds. To do this, I totaled the assets of the A-rated funds, the B funds, down to the F funds, added them all together, and computed a percentage distribution.

Earlier it was shown that there is roughly the same proportion of good versus bad funds for both loads and no-loads. Nevertheless, I found a far greater proportion of the money in no-loads is invested in top-rated funds than is the case with the loads. *Unassisted investors patently demonstrate a greater ability to put their dollars in the best performers.*

With no-loads, I found that 68% of the dollars is invested in funds rated B or better in up markets. Conversely, only 4% of the no-load investors' dollars is in funds rated D.

For money invested in load funds, different results were obtained. Here, only 52% of the money is invested in funds rated B or better in up markets. A full third, or $12.3 billion, is invested in the lowest-rated D funds.

Even in down markets no-load investors fared better; 44% of the dollars invested in no-load funds is in funds rated B or better versus only 29% for money invested in load funds.

Since most fund money has been invested for years, it could be argued that some of these funds were better at the time they were

STOCK FUNDS SIX YEARS OR OLDER
Distribution of Assets

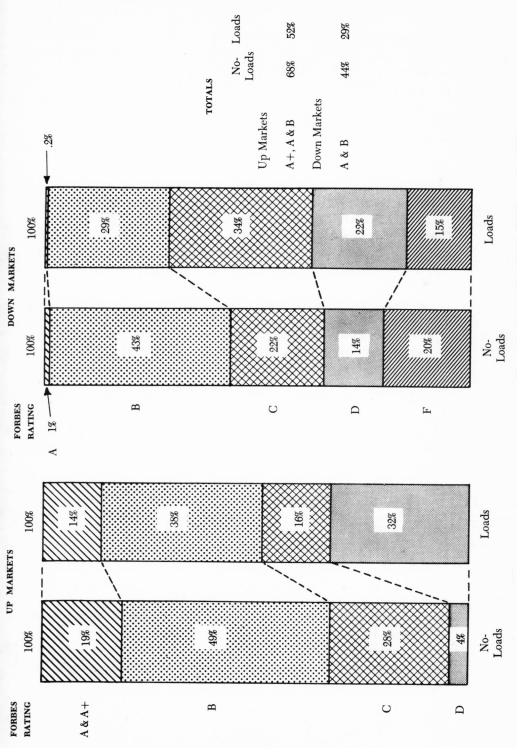

Based on $4.4 billion no-load and $38.9 billion load assets in 1972.

bought than they are now. Possibly, but if this is the case, the load has obviously inhibited many investors from selling when the performance of their funds faltered. How else could so much money remain invested in the lowest-rated load funds?

TRY NO-LOADS

No-loads aren't for everybody. Only people who have the inclination to learn how to evaluate mutual funds and are prepared to make their own investment decisions will profit from no-load mutual funds. Not everybody wants to or has the ability to do this. Some people who have no interest in financial matters will always prefer to rely on a trained salesman and will consider his fee worth the expenditure. Nevertheless, if you are willing to spend some time learning about mutual funds and do some work evaluating them, you, on your own, can do a good job picking top mutual funds. Other no-load investors are doing it right now. So can you.

Now, only 27% of all stockholders own mutual funds and there are many reasons for this relatively low figure. Many investors have rejected the benefits of fund ownership because they think the sales commission is unreasonable; many, too, are unaware of no-load funds, or don't know how to obtain them. Others who did well on their own until 1968 confused luck with skill. Having lost in 1969 and 1970, they are now willing to settle for a small inflationary loss each year in return for the safety of the savings bank.

There are many ways of investing in the stock market; however, for the layman, buying no-load mutual funds can be an eminently desirable way to achieve success in the market. No-load mutual funds can make your money grow and perhaps will do it more conveniently and more consistently than other investment approaches.

The conventional wisdom offered by all experts is to buy the best fund regardless of sales charges. This advice, while valid, doesn't take into account that today—in contrast to even a few years ago—there are so many good no-load funds that there is no longer any reason to buy a load fund in order to achieve superior performance. In 1972, there were nineteen no-loads in the upper

10% of all funds and seventy-six no-loads in the upper 50%. Since few investors need more than three or four funds, the selection is more than adequate.

Finally, no-load mutual funds are not an all-or-nothing choice. Any portion of your savings can be channeled into no-loads and can be compared to your other investments. So give them a try. All that's required is your initiative and your time. And as far as I've been able to discover, there is no sales charge on either. Besides, the rewards can be great.

Section II
HOW TO INVEST IN
NO-LOAD MUTUAL FUNDS

BUYING NO-LOAD funds is a challenging do-it-yourself program in which the investor exercises the initiative. Like most do-it-yourself programs, it requires time and know-how. But in the case of no-loads, once you've learned the fundamentals, periodic evaluation shouldn't take more than one hour per month. Of course, there is the quick check, at least once a week, of your funds in the paper. But it's well worth the effort. When success is yours—and the chances are good when you follow a logical plan—the psychic and monetary rewards of investing in no-loads are great.

Here are the steps necessary to initiate a no-load investment program. Each will be discussed in detail in subsequent chapters.

1. Analyze your specific investment objective. How much risk are you willing to take? Will you accept great risks for maximum gains, or would you prefer a more conservative course of investing with less risk and less potential?

2. Learn to recognize which mutual funds are designed to meet your specific investment objective. This is the most important step and the one most neglected. Far too many investors have unknowingly bought funds either too speculative or too conservative for them—and their investment programs suffered as a result.

3. Obtain a directory of no-load funds whose objectives coincide with your own. The easiest way to do this is to buy an introductory offer of a mutual fund advisory service.

4. Analyze past performance to determine the best two or three funds among those that meet your objective. Performance figures can be obtained from advisory services or from newspapers.

5. Learn the criteria for selecting those funds that are most likely to perform well in the future.

6. Write or phone for prospectuses of two or three top-performing funds. You need the prospectuses to eliminate funds that are undesirable for reasons other than performance. For example, you can learn from the prospectus if the fund is being sued or if expenses are abnormally high. In addition, the prospectus usually has an application blank, making it convenient to purchase the fund.

7. After examining the prospectuses, make a decision and buy one or more funds.

8. Continue to follow the performance of these and other top-ranked funds.

With this plan of action you can blueprint your own financially rewarding investment program. Now, read on for the details.

CHAPTER 7 MATCH FUNDS TO INVESTMENT OBJECTIVES

As in any carefully planned investment program, the first step that must be taken in selecting mutual funds is to establish the investment objective. Once this has been determined, the next step is to identify those funds—out of hundreds catering to a wide range of objectives—that satisfy the investor's goals.

Young investors need to build up their savings for a variety of reasons—emergencies, a new house, eventual retirement. Older investors, who already have an estate, need income to live on in retirement. Typically, the young investor is looking for growth; in the latter case, the investor needs income. Since there are funds available to serve both needs, the first order of business is to classify mutual funds by their investment objective.

ANALYZE THE FUND'S OBJECTIVES

At one end of the spectrum, there are no-load funds committed to a policy of conservative investing, specifically to produce income. At the other extreme there are funds that lean to speculative investing for maximum capital gains. There are funds spread across every segment of the investment horizon, and it is often difficult to determine minor differences in their investment philosophies.

However, for purposes of illustration, funds putting some or all of their money into common stocks can be classified into three categories—maximum capital gains, quality growth, and growth-income funds. In addition, there are funds that primarily buy bonds. Their usual objective is income.

THE WIDE SPECTRUM OF FUNDS

600 + Funds

TYPES:	Maximum Capital Gains	Quality Growth	Growth–Income
TYPES OF STOCK HELD:	Speculative	Middle-of-the-Road	Conservative
OBJECTIVE:	Maximum Growth	Long-Term Growth	Growth, Income, Stability
RISK:	High	Average	Low

MAXIMUM CAPITAL GAINS FUNDS

These funds are also called "go-go" funds, "performance" funds, "speculative" funds, and "aggressive growth" funds. Maximum capital gains funds are the most common type of no-load mutual fund. More than 40% of all no-loads are MCG funds as compared to 33% in the quality growth group and 25% in the growth-income category. MCG funds predominate among the no-loads because without salesmen to push them, no-loads need outstanding performance records to attract new investors and to grow.

The principal characteristics of the maximum capital gains funds are:

1. They are growth-oriented.
2. They are risk-oriented.
3. They are volatile. They will do very well in bull markets and very badly in bear markets.

The objective of a maximum capital gains fund is to grow faster than all the other funds because top growth means top returns for management. Money pours into funds that have achieved outstanding performance in a given year—or even in a given quarter. Since management fees are determined basically by the size of the fund, growth is the primary way for fund management to increase its income.

This is especially true for the no-loads, which do not have salesmen calling on prospects. An impressive growth record is, therefore, the surest, and by far the best, way of becoming bigger and more profitable to management. With no-loads, all the advertising in the world is not as effective as a top-ten performance record for the year.

BIGGER RISKS FOR GREATER REWARDS

The men who run maximum capital gains funds are not afraid to take risks in order to grow rapidly. They attempt to call the turns in the market. They buy stocks that have the potential to double in six months to a year, and they are quick to sell stocks that don't measure up to expectations. Most aren't traders, but they do turn over their portfolios at a far faster rate than do managers of less speculative funds. These portfolio managers usually have the authority to act on their own. Since they have to act too quickly to make investment decisions by committee, the approval of their board of directors is not required before they buy or sell. Furthermore, they may borrow money from banks on margin to obtain "leverage," and in some cases they may "sell short" and buy "puts and calls." As a further incentive, some funds provide for additional compensation to management for superior performance.

There is tremendous profit potential for those investors who are willing to accept the risks these funds are taking. In a bull market, the best MCG funds provide sufficient action for even the most profit-conscious of investors. Here is the performance of some better-than-average MCG funds in the bull market that started on May 26, 1970.

No-Load Fund	Increase from May 26, 1970, Lows to December 31, 1972*
Nicholas Strong	+258%
Afuture	+231%
New Horizons	+170%
Janus	+163%
Neuwirth Century	+143%
Edie Growth	+116%
Edie Institutional	+113%
Stein Roe & Farnham Capital	+107%
Loomis-Sayles Capital Dev.	+100%
Smith, Barney Equity	+94%
Columbia Growth	+88%
Fleming Berger	+87%
Hartwell & Campbell	+81%
Hyperion	+81%
New York Stock Exchange Industrial Average	+80%
Dow Jones Industrial Average	+62%

* Adjusted for all distributions.
SOURCE: *FundScope*

It's better to look at mutual fund performance in terms of percent changes; however, if you prefer more conventional measures, the top-ranked Nicholas Strong went from $7.37 to $26.40 a share in this period.

Now, some investors who had individual stocks that performed well in this period might not be impressed by this performance. Nevertheless, I submit that this performance is excellent and that few lay investors were able to duplicate it. This growth was achieved over an entire portfolio, including all cash reserves held along the way. In contrast to the popular averages, it represents net growth after management fees, expenses, and brokerage commissions have been deducted.

If you "do-it-yourself" you might make a comparison on equal terms with your own investment results in this period. This means computing the value of your entire portfolio as of May 26, 1970, and adding to this figure all the cash that would normally have been earmarked for the market but had been withheld because of fear and uncertainty. Next, compute the value of your portfolio as of December 31, 1972, remembering to include cash still not invested and also cash received for stocks sold in late 1970, 1971, and 1972, if not reinvested. Add it all up; divide by your May 26, 1970, total and you will obtain your percent gain (or loss). Now compare this to the performance of the funds. Chances are you didn't come close.

On the other hand, it must be emphasized that in the case of MCG funds, performance variations are particularly wide because the managers are taking great risks. Here is the performance of the bottom five no-load funds, as reported by *FundScope*, in this same period of time.

THE BOTTOM FIVE FUNDS
Rising Market Period
May 26, 1970 to December 31, 1972

No-Load Fund	
Pennsylvania Mutual	+21%
Hedge Fund	+ 5%
Sagittarius	− 9%
Market Growth	−20%
Washington Investment Network	−33%

Because this wide variation in performance exists, an investor must take great care in selecting MCG funds, and must watch them carefully afterward.

MAXIMUM CAPITAL GAINS FUNDS ARE VOLATILE

A principal characteristic of maximum capital gains funds is that they are volatile, that is, their price fluctuates rapidly in *both* directions. In a bull market many MCG funds appreciate one to two times as fast as the New York Stock Exchange's Composite Index.

In a bear market, MCG funds' performance will be worse than the Index's; again, many MCG funds can lose one to two times the Index. And the very worst MCG funds can turn in disastrous performances. One declined 72% in the 1969–70 bear market. Another declined 51% in the first half of 1973 versus a 15% decline for the Composite Index. As a group, MCG funds will decline more in a bear market than will more conservative funds.

The following chart shows how an outstanding maximum capital gains fund performed in the 1969–70 bear market and the rising market in 1971. The Nicholas Strong Fund was started in August 1968, just as the long bull market was drawing to a close. It exhibited the volatility typical of an MCG fund, declining precipitously in the bear market. Then, in the subsequent bull market, it recouped all its losses and went on to new highs. It was the top-performing fund in the country in 1971 and the eighteenth best in 1972.

MCG FUNDS DON'T ACT DEFENSIVELY
IN BEAR MARKETS

MCG funds have little ability to anticipate bear markets and act defensively. They don't switch their multimillion-dollar portfolios from aggressive stocks to defensive stocks or cash effectively enough to ride out bad markets.

Their problem was explained succinctly by George Chestnutt of the American Investors Fund (a no-load MCG fund) in a September 1969 interview in *Forbes*. At the time of the interview, the market had already declined for nine months. Chestnutt is a master chartist. Why didn't he sell when his charts told him the

ASSETS IN MILLIONS

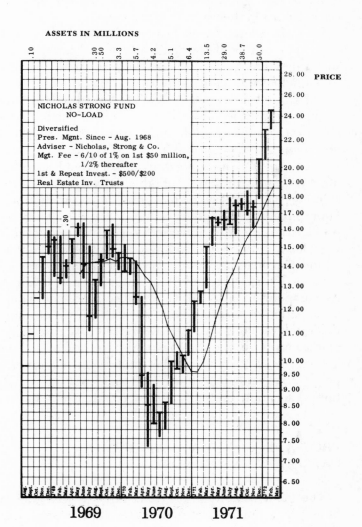

NICHOLAS STRONG FUND
NO-LOAD

Diversified
Pres. Mgmt. Since - Aug. 1968
Adviser - Nicholas, Strong & Co.
Mgt. Fee - 6/10 of 1% on 1st $50 million,
1/2% thereafter
1st & Repeat Invest. - $500/$200
Real Estate Inv. Trusts

PRICE

1969   1970   1971

SOURCE: *Growth Fund Guide*

roof was caving in? Why didn't he sit on cash until the market hit the bottom and then start to buy again?

Said Chestnutt, "In the process of selling out, I would probably depress the price of the fund by 10%. I'd probably bid the same stocks up a bit getting back in. But if the market dropped 25% and I handled it right, I'd be way out in front."

The trouble is Chestnutt didn't follow his own advice. Why not? He blamed the SEC and its concern about portfolio turnover rates. However, there are additional reasons that may have weighed heavily in Chestnutt's thinking.

According to Chestnutt, the market would have to decline 25% for a move to cash to be profitable. Other portfolio managers, considering the inability to recognize tops and bottoms, think the figure may be even higher, around 30%. But, it is very difficult to predict the extent of a market decline. Since World War II, only the 1962 and 1969–70 bear markets declined more than 25%. Thus, a fund's inclination is to ride out what may be a minor dip.

Secondly, even though it is wrong, a fund is affected by what its competition does. If Chestnutt's fund had gone to cash in anticipation of a serious bear market and was wrong, the price of the fund would have been depressed 10% in selling. When the market went up, the stocks would have had to be bought back at higher prices. As a result the fund would have performed more poorly than its competitors. This may well have caused redemptions. Chestnutt probably felt he couldn't take these risks.

PROS AND CONS OF MAXIMUM CAPITAL GAINS FUNDS

The great advantage of MCG funds is that they are now the best vehicle for buying the high-multiple stocks that often have the best prospects for outstanding long-term growth. Because funds are diversified, it's not as risky for MCG funds to buy stocks like Levitz or Winnebago, which can quintuple in a year, but can then retreat abruptly if their earnings prospects decline to anything less than outstanding.

In today's institutional market, the individual is taking an enormous risk if he speculates in these stocks on his own. The only logical way to participate is through no-load MCG funds. This way, even a 100% decline in a high-flying stock isn't catastrophic if that stock accounts for only 2% or 3% of a diversified portfolio.

The principal disadvantages of MCG funds are their extreme price fluctuations, lack of defensive strengths in a bear market, and their inconsistent performance (discussed in detail in the next chapter). However, these disadvantages can be greatly minimized by diversifying investments into two, three, or four funds, then following performance closely and being prepared to sell if a downturn occurs.

Moreover, while the MCG fund's volatility can be a disadvantage in the short run, it has definitely been an advantage in the long run, since the postwar experience has been for bull markets to last longer and go farther than bear markets. In the 1960's, when bull markets predominated, maximum capital gains funds were easily the best type of fund for investors seeking growth. In the decade from 1961 to 1970, seven out of the top ten funds were maximum capital gains funds. If, in the future, bull markets continue to predominate, the maximum capital gains funds will still be the best way for investors to profit.

The following chart graphically illustrates how growth funds in general (including both MCG and quality growth categories) outperformed growth-income and income funds in the 1960's.

HOW TO IDENTIFY MCG FUNDS

In the 1960's, MCG funds were bought by investors who didn't realize the risks they were taking. Many investors were led to believe that all mutual funds were safe because they offered diversification, had professional management, and—decades ago— had conservative goals.

By their nature MCG funds aren't safe. Diversification of a speculative portfolio is a distinct advantage in a bull market because while individual stocks are unpredictable, gainers will usually outnumber losers. On the other hand, diversification is of little help in a bear market since the MCG funds typically hold many illiquid stocks of small companies that are virtually impossible to sell in a declining market.

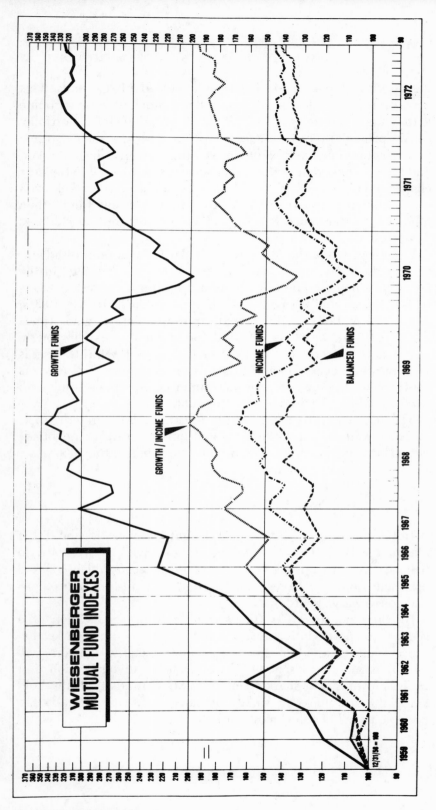

WIESENBERGER
MUTUAL FUND INDEXES

GROWTH FUNDS

GROWTH / INCOME FUNDS

INCOME FUNDS

BALANCED FUNDS

12/31/58 = 100

SOURCE: Wiesenberger Services, Inc.

It is, therefore, most important to know whether a fund under consideration is a maximum capital gains fund or not.

There are three basic tests:
1. Measure volatility.
2. Analyze the fund's objectives as stated in the prospectus.
3. Check its portfolio.

HOW TO MEASURE VOLATILITY

Several of the mutual fund advisory services measure volatility. One of them, available in many libraries, is Wiesenberger's *Investment Companies*. In the 1972 issue, Wiesenberger computes each fund's performance in eight rising and falling markets and shows it as a percent of the New York Stock Exchange's Composite Index's change in the same period of time. For example, a fund with a ratio of 1.00 would be moving at the same rate as the NYSE Index. While there are great variations from fund to fund and in different periods, volatile MCG funds will have the highest indexes in the report.

FundScope, in its *Mutual Fund Guide* published each April, appraises volatility with word descriptions ranging from "generally low" to "average" to "high." The funds appraised "high" are MCG funds.

The annual *Forbes* ratings can also be utilized to determine volatility. In *Forbes,* the typical MCG fund will receive an A or A+ in up markets and a D or F in down markets.

For those investors who do not have ready access to this reference material, here is a shorthand way to check volatility. Examine mutual fund prices in a daily newspaper on any day there has been a significant movement of the Dow Jones Average. Select a day the Dow has moved at least five points in either direction.

Let's assume the Dow rose nine points one day. If the Dow Jones Index was around the 900 level, this would mean an increase of 1%. Next, scan the mutual funds section of the newspaper; see which funds outpaced the Dow and by how big a margin. This quick analysis must be made in terms of percent since the dollar or cents changes will not provide a meaningful comparison.

Specifically, if a fund with a net asset value of $10 increased its value by 10¢ this same day, the fund also increased 1%, the same as the Dow. If it was up 20¢, that's 2%, or twice the percentage increase of the Dow. Similar comparisons can be made when the market is declining.

On a day like this, you will find some funds moving from one and a half to four times as fast as the market indices. These funds are *maximum capital gains funds.* Any one day's price action may be a typical; however, a check of these prices over a period of several days should give you a very good idea of which funds are the most volatile.

One caution: This is not a method of selecting which fund to buy or is it a method of predicting future growth. The most volatile funds aren't always the biggest gainers over a long period of time.

Wall Street professionals now have a new, sophisticated means of measuring the volatility of individual stocks and entire portfolios. It is called the beta coefficient. It provides a statistically precise measurement of volatility and investment risk by means of complex computations which isolate how a stock performs in relation to the market as a whole. As of this writing, the beta's usefulness as an analytical tool has not been completely established. However, the financial press has discussed it extensively and the popular press is beginning to cover it too. For those of you who wish to become as knowledgeable as the pros—well, almost—betas are explained in Appendix I.

ANALYZE THE FUND'S OBJECTIVES

The second test of a maximum capital gains fund is to see what the fund considers its "objectives" to be. Every sale of a mutual fund must be made by prospectus, and in every prospectus there is a section labeled "Objectives." Maximum capital gains funds will describe their funds' objectives in the following manner:

"The fund is designed for investors who, aware of the risks, seek the possibility of greater than average capital appreciation over a period of years."

"The fund is not intended to present a complete investment program, and shares of the fund should not be purchased by those who cannot afford the unusual risks involved in investing in the fund."

"The fund may employ speculative techniques of borrowing for leverage, short-term trading, and investing in securities of unseasoned companies, securities of foreign companies, and restricted and other nonliquid securities."

"A substantial portion of the fund's assets may be committed to one industry which management believes offers unusual investment opportunities."

"The investment policy may entail risk proportionate to or greater than potential gains."

"Current income, if any, will be incidental."

EXAMINE FUND PORTFOLIOS

Another way to determine the fund's attitude toward growth and risk-taking is to examine the stocks in its portfolio. The portfolio of the Edie Special Growth Fund, a no-load fund oriented toward maximum capital gains, follows on pages 88–89.

There are no staid blue chips in this portfolio. In fact, only 45% of the fund's stocks are listed on the New York Stock Exchange. The small emerging growth stocks that Edie specializes in are traded elsewhere. Of the balance of Edie's portfolio, 34% are listed on the American Stock Exchange, 20% are traded over-the-counter, and 1% are on the Midwest Stock Exchange.

ARE MAXIMUM CAPITAL GAINS
FUNDS FOR YOU?

Yes . . . if you are interested in making your money grow as fast as possible and are young enough to sustain losses without worrying.

EDIE SPECIAL GROWTH FUND
March 31, 1973

Shares Held	COMMON STOCKS	Cost	Market Value	Percent of Total Net Assets
ADVERTISING (.7%)				
24,000	WELLS, RICH, GREENE, INC. .... A creative and rapidly expanding advertising agency.	$ 555,209	$ 345,000	.7%
APPAREL & TEXTILE (1.0%)				
47,000	SUAVE SHOE CORP. .... Manufacturer of sneakers and casual footwear.	834,218	458,250	1.0
AUTOMOBILE (10.7%)				
35,000	*BANDAG, INCORPORATED .... A retreading process designed to maximize tire life.	1,300,960	2,056,250	4.5
47,000	MONROE AUTO EQUIPMENT .... Manufacturer and distributor of automatic shock absorbers and ride control products.	1,519,651	1,304,250	2.8
25,000	EARL SCHEIB, INC. .... National chain of automobile paint shops.	505,714	412,500	.9
33,000	ECHLIN MFG. CO. INC. .... Producer of automotive replacement parts.	1,194,811	1,138,500	2.5
BUILDING PRODUCTS (5.0%)				
40,000	PAYLESS CASHWAYS, INC. .... Mid-western supplier of lumber and building materials.	1,026,894	660,000	1.5
29,500	SCOTTY'S HOMEBUILDERS SUPPLY, INC. .... Florida discount retailer of building materials.	506,734	711,687	1.5
20,000	STANDARD BRANDS PAINT COMPANY .... Western chain retailing "do-it-yourself" items to the home improvement market.	484,517	915,000	2.0
CHEMICAL PRODUCTS (2.7%)				
50,500	AIRWICK INDUSTRIES, INC. .... Producer of odor control chemicals and disinfectant products.	462,793	940,562	2.0
22,000	LEA-RONAL CORP. .... Developer of electroplating processes primarily for the electronics industry.	346,040	310,750	.7
CONSTRUCTION (8.8%)				
40,000	MASCO CORPORATION .... Maker of single handed faucets and other plumbing supplies.	1,191,197	1,960,000	4.3
47,250	*TOOL RESEARCH & ENGINEERING CO. .... Producer of lightweight specialty metal products.	2,240,713	986,344	2.1
20,000	*BRASS-CRAFT MANUFACTURING CO. .... Manufacturer of valves, fittings and flexible copper tubing.	509,900	400,000	.9
46,000	†OVERHEAD DOOR CORPORATION .... Upward-acting doors for commercial and residential use.	786,779	701,500	1.5
COSMETICS (2.3%)				
32,000	JOHNSON PRODUCTS INC. .... Manufacturer of hair care products and cosmetics for the black consumer.	539,265	1,056,000	2.3
EDUCATION & LEISURE (7.8%)				
15,000	A. T. CROSS CO. .... Manufacturer of quality pen and pencil sets.	637,695	834,375	1.8
8,000	JOSTEN'S INC. .... Manufacturer of student jewelry, yearbooks, and awards.	252,909	163,000	.4
40,000	*STERNCO INDUSTRIES, INC. .... A leader in breeding and distributing tropical fish and related supplies.	1,070,950	1,645,000	3.6
7,000	STURM-RUGER COMPANY .... Manufacturer of custom sporting firearms.	139,898	70,000	.1
34,000	BIC PEN CORPORATION .... Leading manufacturer of low priced pens.	951,071	858,500	1.9
ELECTRONICS (2.6%)				
40,000	AUGAT, INC. .... Producer of high precision connecting devices.	1,050,746	1,180,000	2.6
FOOD & BEVERAGES (2.6%)				
15,500	G. HEILMAN BREWING COMPANY .... A brewery operating primarily in the Mid-western states.	370,879	209,250	.5%
10,000	LAWRY'S FOODS, INC .... Producer of specialty seasonings and food products.	180,725	82,500	.1
23,000	†*TROPICANA PRODUCTS, INC. .... Leading producer and marketer of chilled juices.	979,075	925,750	2.0

Shares Held	COMMON STOCKS — Continued	Cost	Market Value	Percent of Total Net Assets
FOOD SERVICE (5.1%)				
13,000	HICKORY FARMS OF OHIO, INC. . . . . $ Nation-wide system of specialty food stores.	443,550	$ 559,000	1.2
44,500	*CHURCH'S FRIED CHICKEN . . . . Operator of take-home food outlets in the Southern states.	1,509,413	561,813	1.2
50,000	SAMBO'S RESTAURANTS, INC. . . . . A western chain of coffee-shop type restaurants.	1,170,046	1,243,750	2.7
HOME FURNISHINGS (4.1%)				
80,000	*LEVITZ FURNITURE CORP. . . . . A furniture retailer pioneering warehouse-showroom outlets.	2,657,710	1,080,000	2.4
18,000	KNAPE & VOGT . . . . Manufacturer of specialty hardware and fixtures for the home improvement market.	696,438	369,000	.8
12,000	†LA-Z-BOY CHAIR COMPANY . . . . Manufacturer of upholstered reclining and rocker chairs.	484,237	432,000	.9
INSURANCE (.9%)				
15,000	MERCURY GENERAL CORP. . . . . Automobile insurance specialists for the California market.	453,188	423,750	.9
MEDICAL RESEARCH (.6%)				
7,500	*CHARLES RIVER BREEDING LABS. . . . . Breeder of laboratory animals for scientific purposes.	97,537	256,875	.6
PRINTING & PAPER PRODUCTS (1.5%)				
11,500	BOWNE & COMPANY . . . . Major financial and corporate printer.	252,553	196,938	.4
29,000	PAPERCRAFT CORP. . . . . A leading producer of gift wrapping and related consumer products.	984,871	493,000	1.1
RESORT & HOTELS (2.4%)				
57,000	*HYATT CORPORATION . . . . Nation-wide operator of premium hotels and motels.	1,115,400	1,097,250	2.4
RETAIL TRADE (12.1%)				
23,920	*GREENMAN BROTHERS, INC. . . . . Wholesale and retail distributor of toys, games and sporting goods.	574,932	304,980	.7
30,000	LONGS DRUG STORES, INC. . . . . Self-service drug chain serving California and Hawaii.	1,443,034	2,062,500	4.5
32,000	REVCO D.S. INC. . . . . Discount drug chain operating in mid-western and southern states.	1,462,779	1,312,000	2.8
26,200	*BEST PRODUCTS CO. . . . . Catalog retailer of general merchandise through warehouse and showrooms.	1,406,831	1,126,600	2.5
40,000	*DOLLAR GENERAL CORP. Discount retailer serving the Southeastern states.	1,093,737	370,000	.8
36,000	*FAMILY DOLLAR STORES INC. . . . . Self-service retailer of general merchandise in Carolina Region.	730,998	396,000	.8
SERVICE (2.3%)				
20,000	AMERICAN APPRAISAL ASSOCIATES, INC. . . . . . . Provides asset and property valuations.	480,200	310,000	.7
50,000	BANKERS UTILITIES . . . . Specialized courier service for commercial and industrial customers.	1,085,283	768,750	1.6
MISCELLANEOUS (2.8%)		1,693,876	1,283,750	2.8
TOTAL COMMON STOCKS (76.0%)		$39,475,956	34,972,924	76.0
CASH, SHORT TERM CORPORATE NOTES & RECEIVABLES LESS LIABILITIES (24.0%)			11,071,510	24.0
NET ASSETS — Equivalent to $23.94 per share on 1,923,519 shares outstanding (100%)			$46,044,434	100.0%

*Non-income producing.   †Addition to portfolio during past quarter.

Yes . . . if your income is substantial enough to sustain a "businessman's risk."

Yes . . . if you currently buy volatile stocks on the American Exchange or the over-the-counter market, or maintain a margin account, or sell short, or are a serious student of the market.

Yes . . . if you are willing to take the necessary time needed to follow the fund.

Yes . . . if you can discipline yourself to sell when performance falters.

Performance funds aren't for everyone, but if you fall into any of the above categories, you should consider putting some of your capital into no-load MCG funds.

QUALITY GROWTH FUNDS

Quality growth funds are also called "growth" funds, "long-term growth" funds, and "middle-of-the-road" funds. They put their primary emphasis on long-term growth. Quality growth funds do not attempt to win the performance derby each year. On the contrary, their aim is to make the money entrusted to them by investors grow *prudently*. Some of these funds were "go-go" funds in their early years but have since grown too big to maintain the percentage increases needed to stay in that performance league.

Typically, quality growth funds are less volatile than MCG funds and are rated accordingly by *FundScope*. While MCG funds receive a "high" volatility rating, quality growth funds are usually designated "above average." In terms of the *Forbes* ratings, they would ideally be rated with a pair of B's. That is, they are not the best performers in up markets but are far from the poorest in down markets.

ADVANTAGES

The principal advantages of quality growth funds are greater stability, less volatility, and more consistent performance than

MCG funds. Even though they are basically common stock funds, they don't hesitate to buy bonds or defensive stocks if they anticipate trouble ahead. In bull markets, they grow fast enough to do a superior job of combating inflation, but they are certainly not in the league of the go-gos.

The following chart shows the performance of the Weingarten Equity Fund from its inception in 1969 through February 1972. Note that its decline in the 1969–70 bear market was not nearly as steep as those of the maximum capital gains funds.

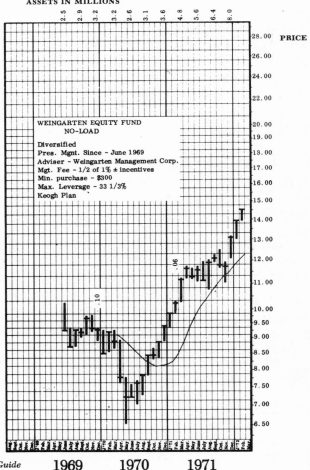

ASSETS IN MILLIONS

WEINGARTEN EQUITY FUND
NO-LOAD

Diversified
Pres. Mgnt. Since – June 1969
Adviser – Weingarten Management Corp.
Mgt. Fee – 1/2 of 1% ± incentives
Min. purchase – $300
Max. Leverage – 33 1/3%
Keogh Plan

SOURCE: *Growth Fund Guide*   1969   1970   1971

HOW THE QUALITY GROWTH FUNDS DESCRIBE THEMSELVES

The prospectuses of the quality growth funds describe their objectives in the following terms:

"The fund's objective is long-term growth of capital; sensible risks will be taken in that direction."

"The fund's goal is to seek capital growth consistent with what it considers prudent risks."

"The fund will try to secure long-term capital appreciation if management considers opportunities favorable. It will seek liquidity and defensive strength if in the opinion of its management events suggest the wisdom of such a course."

"The fund management believes that an essential objective of investment policy must be to preserve the true value of capital (i.e., purchasing power) from the persistent underlying inflationary trend."

"The fund is flexible in the proportions of the various types of securities and cash in which it may be invested at any one time. While the fund's investments will be primarily in common stocks, the fund may also invest in bonds, preferred stocks, both long- and short-term government and municipal securities if market conditions so warrant."

"The fund takes into consideration fundamental investment factors in arriving at an estimate of the value for any security."

"Most of the fund's investments will be in companies listed on the New York Stock Exchange."

"While current income is not a primary objective, it is hoped that growth in income will accompany growth in capital."

WELL-KNOWN STOCKS IN THEIR PORTFOLIOS

The portfolios of quality growth funds typically include the IBM's, the Xerox's, and other popular Big Board growth companies whose names are easily recognizable by any investor. Following is the portfolio of the Johnston Mutual Fund, a typical no-load fund in this group.

ARE QUALITY GROWTH FUNDS FOR YOU?

Yes . . . if you don't want the risk inherent in a maximum capital gains fund.

Yes . . . if you do want your money to grow, keeping you ahead of inflation.

Yes . . . if current income from capital is not your most pressing need.

The fact is that quality growth funds are suitable for almost all investors. And almost all investors should consider putting some, or all, of their investment dollars into quality growth funds.

A WORD OF WARNING

It is difficult to differentiate some quality growth funds from the MCG's. If there is still doubt after applying the three tests (volatility, stated objective, and portfolio), rely on the test of volatility. The reason: some funds change their tactics with market conditions and at times can be out of phase with their stated objective.

An interesting case in point is the no-load USAA Capital Growth Fund, whose prospectus states, "The Fund's principal investment objective is long-term growth of capital." That sounds like the objective is quality growth. However, Wiesenberger calls it G-I-S (growth-income-stability), while *FundScope* goes to the other extreme, calling it a performance fund.

Let's check these judgments. In 1972's generally rising market,

PORTFOLIO OF INVESTMENTS – March 31, 1973

(Unaudited)

Par or No. Shs.		Market Value
COMMON STOCKS (80.5%)		
Automotive (3.7%)		
90,000	General Motors Corporation	$ 6,502,500
94,600	Purolator, Inc.	5,486,800
		$ 11,989,300
Business Equipment (10.1%)		
100,000	*Digital Equipment Corp.	$ 8,037,500
30,000	International Business Machines Corp.	12,945,000
350,000	Rank Organisation Ltd., ADR "A"	3,981,250
200,000	*Wang Laboratories, Inc.	3,900,000
25,000	Xerox Corp.	3,781,250
		$ 32,645,000
Business Services (1.3%)		
110,000	Brink's, Inc.	$ 1,540,000
100,000	Browning-Ferris Industries, Inc.	2,525,000
		$ 4,065,000
Chemicals (0.8%)		
85,000	Cabot Corp.	$ 2,550,000
Drugs & Toiletries (4.4%)		
100,000	Baxter Laboratories, Inc.	$ 5,150,000
40,000	Squibb Corp.	4,080,000
40,000	Tampax Inc.	4,820,000
		$ 14,050,000
Electronics and Electrical Equipment (1.2%)		
60,000	General Electric Co.	$ 3,870,000
Food & Beverage (5.1%)		
100,000	Anheuser-Busch, Inc.	$ 5,112,500
280,000	*Tropicana Products, Inc.	11,270,000
		$ 16,382,500
Forest Products (1.0%)		
200,000	Mead Corporation	$ 3,075,000
Household Products (6.2%)		
200,000	Clorox Co.	$ 8,175,000
60,600	Colgate-Palmolive Co.	5,810,025
250,000	*Crown Cork & Seal Co., Inc.	5,906,250
		$ 19,891,275
Industrial Equipment (4.4%)		
150,000	Avery Products Corporation	$ 6,562,500
200,000	Gardner-Denver Co.	4,525,000
150,000	Sundstrand Corp.	3,000,000
		$ 14,087,500
Insurance (6.0%)		
150,000	Continental Corp.	$ 6,056,250
80,000	Crum & Forster	2,320,000
50,000	MGIC Investment Corp.	3,675,000
150,300	Travelers Corp.	5,128,987
50,000	U.S. Fidelity & Guaranty Co.	2,031,250
		$ 19,211,487
Merchandising (7.4%)		
200,000	Broadway-Hale Stores, Inc.	$ 7,850,000
150,000	Federated Department Stores, Inc.	7,237,500
56,085	S. S. Kresge Company	2,215,358
100,000	Standard Brands Paint Co.	4,575,000
100,000	Stop & Shop Companies, Inc.	1,875,000
		$ 23,752,858

Mining & Metals (4.1%)

195,500	*Eastern Gas & Fuel Associates	$ 5,107,437
100,000	Pittston Company	2,962,500
60,000	Utah International, Inc.	5,265,000
		$ 13,334,937

Oil & Gas (13.8%)

110,000	Amerada Hess Corp.	$ 3,767,500
240,000	*Dome Petroleum Ltd.	9,840,000
70,000	Exxon Corp.	6,606,250
200,000	Imperial Oil Ltd.	8,400,000
45,000	Kerr-McGee Corp.	3,251,250
140,100	Marathon Oil Company	4,938,525
75,000	Mobil Oil Corp.	5,240,625
50,000	Santa Fe International Corp.	2,381,250
		$ 44,425,400

Public Utilities (1.1%)

100,000	Florida Power & Light Co.	$ 3,412,500

Publishing & Education (2.5%)

160,000	Knight Newspapers, Inc.	$ 8,140,000

Recreation & Leisure (4.4%)

150,000	*Hyatt Corp.	$ 2,850,000
205,000	*Marriott Corp.	7,072,500
101,300	*Sternco Industries, Inc., Class A	4,165,963
		$ 14,088,463

Specialty Technology (0.7%)

50,000	*Damon Corp.	$ 2,156,250

Textile & Apparel (0.7%)

170,000	Angelica Corp.	$ 2,146,250

Transportation (1.6%)

79,600	Emery Air Freight	$ 5,283,450
	Total Common Stocks	**$258,557,170**

Par or No. Shs.		Market Value

PREFERRED STOCKS (3.8%)

70,000	American Express Co. $1.50 Cum. Conv. Pfd.	$ 12,250,000

CONVERTIBLE BONDS (6.6%)

$ 431,000	Baxter Laboratories, Inc. Conv. Sub. Deb. 4%, 3/1/87	$ 1,280,070
2,800,000	Philip Morris, Inc. Conv. Sub. Deb. 6%, 9/1/94	13,387,500
1,000,000	Hyatt Corp. Conv. Sub. Deb. 6%, 2/1/95	920,000
1,080,000	Xerox Corp. Conv. Sub. Deb. 6%, 11/1/95	1,900,800
3,000,000	Standard Oil Co. (Indiana) Conv. Sub. Deb. 5%, 4/1/96	3,825,000
	Total Convertible Bonds	**$ 21,313,370**
	Total Investments (90.9%)	**$292,120,540**

CASH AND EQUIVALENT (9.1%)
Short-Term Notes (8.8%)

$ 3,000,000	C.I.T. Financial Corp.	$ 2,982,812
7,500,000	General Electric Credit Corp.	7,457,052
10,000,000	Grant (W.T.) Financial Corp.	9,945,833
8,000,000	J. C. Penney Financial Corp.	7,954,167
		$ 28,339,864
	Cash and Receivables (Net) (0.3%)	1,047,732
	Total Cash and Equivalent	**$ 29,387,596**
	Net Assets (100%)	**$321,508,136**

*Non-Dividend Paying

the fund was a strong performer, ranking seventeenth among all funds. It was up 29%, or twice the Dow. Then in the first quarter of 1973, a period of declining stock prices, the fund was off 16% as compared to a 7% decline in the Dow. As a result, it ranked 410 among all funds. In short, the fund exhibited the volatility expected of an MCG fund. In early 1973, the USAA Capital Growth Fund should have been conservatively classified as an MCG fund regardless of what the prospectus says.

The ultimate purpose in examining objectives and measuring volatility is to ascertain your exposure to market risk. In my opinion, this is the single most important aspect of fund investing. If you can forecast market trends accurately, you are most unusual. What you can do—and do easily—is determine mutual fund risk-reward ratios. If you make it a rule to always do this, you will get the utmost out of fund investing.

GROWTH-INCOME FUNDS

The third major category among funds is growth-income. Growth-income funds are conservative, giving their investors a reasonable return based on a combination of growth and income. These funds would probably prefer to satisfy their investors with income alone, but in an era when the median New York Stock Exchange stock had a dividend yield of 3.0% (in 1972), this is not possible. They, therefore, need moderate capital gains growth to supplement the dividend yield and make the investment attractive in inflationary times. Growth-income funds provide their investors with *growth, income,* and *stability.* In terms of volatility they can be described as "sluggish on the up side, sluggish on the down side."

There is also a subcategory called income funds. With these funds, income and stability take precedence over growth. Many income funds are bond funds.

In the early 1970's growth-income funds were popular and for good reason. Despite the wrenching 1969–70 bear market, investors holding them long term did very well indeed. According to the Arthur Lipper Corporation, which computes fund performance with dividends reinvested, the average growth-income fund gained 65% in the six years between 1967 and 1972. This is an average annual return of 8.7%. It far surpasses the interest paid by savings banks in this period, not even taking into account that the capital gains portion of the growth was taxed at cheap long-term capital gains rates.

On the other hand, a growth-income fund is certainly more erratic than a bank. The Lipper Corporation also computed performance for the five years between 1968 and 1972. Without 1967 in the averages, growth-income funds gained only 31%, or 5.6% per year. It's still a good return vis-à-vis the bank, but it dramatizes the fact that there are no guarantees when you buy equities.

Here's another comparison for holders of blue-chip stocks. In the decade of the sixties, the average growth-income fund outperformed twenty-one of the thirty blue-chip stocks that comprise the Dow Jones Industrial Average. Growth-income funds are ideally suited for conservative investors, older investors at or near retirement age, and even for young, aggressive investors in times of uncertainty.

The David L. Babson Fund, a no-load growth-income fund with conservative goals, ranked in the top ten of all funds in the five-year period ending September 1973. The chart on page 98 shows how it performed from the end of 1968 to early 1972.

GROWTH-INCOME OBJECTIVES

In their prospectuses, growth-income funds state their objectives as follows:

"Our objective is to provide long-term growth of capital and of income without excessive fluctuations in market value."

"The fund's primary objective is to provide current income consistent with reasonable risk. In pursuit of this objective, there is the possibility of moderate capital growth."

"The fund invests principally in dividend-paying issues of seasoned, well-established companies."

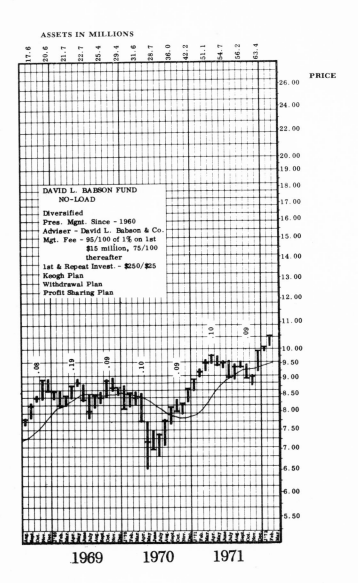

ASSETS IN MILLIONS

DAVID L. BABSON FUND
NO-LOAD

Diversified
Pres. Mgnt. Since - 1960
Adviser - David L. Babson & Co.
Mgt. Fee - 95/100 of 1% on 1st
            $15 million, 75/100
            thereafter
1st & Repeat Invest. - $250/$25
Keogh Plan
Withdrawal Plan
Profit Sharing Plan

PRICE

1969   1970   1971

SOURCE: *Growth Fund Guide*

EXAMINING A TYPICAL GROWTH-INCOME PORTFOLIO

Let's examine the Guardian Mutual Fund portfolio on pages 100–101, since its investments typify no-load growth-income funds.

ARE GROWTH-INCOME FUNDS FOR YOU?

Yes . . . if financially or psychologically you cannot risk your capital.

Yes . . . if dividends are essential to your present income.

Yes . . . if you are retired, widowed, or conspicuously conservative.

Yes . . . if you have been investing yourself—not too successfully—in income-producing stocks.

IRRELEVANT CLASSIFICATIONS CAUSE CONFUSION

The only relevant classification of mutual funds is by objective. There are, however, many other ways of classifying mutual funds which will obscure investment goals. While these other ways have some importance in the industry, and are significant in an academic textbook, the investor should reclassify these funds by objective. There are a number of terms which the investor will run across; I have indicated their relevance to the investment objective.

Open-end and closed-end funds. Open-end funds, also called mutual funds, create new shares when an investor buys; they take back shares when the investor redeems. The number of shares outstanding in an open-end investment company is variable. All the funds discussed in this book are open-end funds.

The opposite of an open-end fund is a closed-end fund. It has a fixed number of shares and does not sell its shares to investors or buy them back. The original investment trusts were closed-end. Both open-end and closed-end funds are available with all types of objectives—either speculative or conservative. Closed-end funds, such as Tri-continental Corporation, are usually traded on

Guardian Mutual Fund, Inc.

No. of Shares		Market Value
COMMON STOCKS (87.39%)		
Aerospace & Airline (1.75%)		
4,300	*Eastern Air Lines, Inc.	$ 53,750
21,000	Flying Tiger Corp.	564,375
10,000	*Trans World Airlines, Inc.	343,750
		$ 961,875
Automotive (5.48%)		
20,000	Ford Motor Co.	$ 1,227,500
25,000	General Motors Corp.	1,784,375
		$ 3,011,875
Banking & Financial (3.95%)		
30,000	C.I.T. Financial Corp.	$ 1,267,500
39,000	Federal National Mortgage Assoc.	575,250
27,000	*Narragansett Capital Corp.	327,375
		$ 2,170,125
Building & Construction (3.27%)		
23,400	PPG Industries, Inc.	$ 789,750
40,000	Presidential Realty Corp.— Cl. B	485,000
35,000	Skyline Corp.	520,625
		$ 1,795,375
Chemical (1.51%)		
20,000	Union Carbide Corp.	$ 830,000
Diversified (5.85%)		
40,000	FMC Corp.	$ 655,000
30,000	Houdaille Industries, Inc.	393,750
11,500	Loews Corp.	322,000
14,300	Pittston Co.	370,012
23,000	Roper Corp.	511,750
40,000	Tenneco Inc.	960,000
		$ 3,212,512
Electrical & Electronics (4.15%)		
20,000	General Electric Co.	$ 1,185,000
26,214	*General Instrument Corp.	455,468
20,000	Westinghouse Electric Corp.	637,500
		$ 2,277,968
Forest Products (2.89%)		
20,000	Crown Zellerbach Corp.	$ 532,500
20,000	Georgia-Pacific Corp.	637,500
30,000	Scott Paper Co.	416,250
		$ 1,586,250

No. of Shares		Market Value
Insurance (2.80%)		
26,000	Associated Madison Companies	$ 208,000
15,000	Lincoln National Corp.	525,000
26,000	Travelers Corp.	806,000
		$ 1,539,000
Machinery & Equipment (10.23%)		
80,000	Allis-Chalmers Corp.	$ 730,000
8,700	Ametek, Inc.	117,450
40,000	Babcock & Wilcox Co.	1,110,000
12,400	Chicago Bridge & Iron Co.	883,500
25,000	Garlock Inc.	421,875
10,000	Ingersoll-Rand Co.	587,500
40,000	International Harvester Co.	1,115,000
58,000	*White Motor Corp.	652,500
		$ 5,617,825
Metals & Mining (5.13%)		
5,000	Aluminum Co. of America	$ 278,125
20,000	American Smelting & Refining Co.	387,500
12,000	Dome Mines Ltd.	1,065,000
40,000	Kennecott Copper Corp.	1,090,000
		$ 2,820,625
Oil & Gas (8.56%)		
10,000	Mobil Oil Corp.	$ 667,500
13,000	Skelly Oil Co.	851,500
10,000	Standard Oil Co. (Indiana)	863,750
700	Superior Oil Co.	180,950
40,000	Texaco Inc.	1,585,000
15,000	Union Oil Co. of California	551,250
		$ 4,699,950
Railroad (6.34%)		
10,800	Burlington Northern Inc.	$ 422,550
100,000	Canadian Pacific Ltd.	1,750,000
20,000	Southern Railway Co.	725,000
10,000	Union Pacific Corp.	583,750
		$ 3,481,300
Steel (4.35%)		
40,000	Bethlehem Steel Corp.	$ 1,180,000
37,000	U.S. Steel Corp.	1,211,750
		$ 2,391,750

Investments *April 30, 1973*

No. of Shares		*Market Value*
	Textile Products & Marketing (3.40%)	
14,300	Indian Head Inc.	$ 300,300
30,000	Marcor, Inc.	656,250
43,300	Phillips-Van Heusen Corp.	617,025
3,000	Sears, Roebuck & Co.	291,000
		$ 1,864,575
	Tire & Rubber (2.33%)	
50,000	Goodyear Tire & Rubber Co.	$ 1,281,250
	Utilities (14.60%)	
47,100	American Natural Gas Co.	$ 1,725,038
10,000	American Tel. & Tel. Co.	517,500
32,000	Arizona Public Service Co.	672,000
50,000	Arkansas Louisiana Gas Co.	1,131,250
7,500	Communications Satellite Corp.	348,750
20,000	Florida Power Corp.	750,000
52,000	Peoples Gas Co.	1,748,500
37,500	Public Service Co. of Colorado	745,312
19,000	Virginia Electric & Power Co.	377,625
		$ 8,015,975
	Miscellaneous (0.80%)	
59,500	Bekins Co.	$ 438,813
	Total Common Stocks (87.39%)	**$47,997,043**

Face Amount	**U.S. GOVERNMENT SECURITIES (6.66%)**	
$1,000,000	U.S. Treasury Bonds, 4⅛%—2/15/74	$ 981,875
$1,000,000	U.S. Treasury Bonds, 4¼%—5/15/74	975,625
$2,000,000	U.S. Treasury Bonds, 4%—2/15/80	1,697,500
	Total U.S. Government Securities (6.66%)	**$ 3,655,000**

Face Amount		*Market Value*
	CORPORATE BONDS (5.16%)	
$ 445,000	City Investing Co. 7½% Cv. Sub. Debs.—12/1/90	$ 445,000
$ 500,000	El Paso Natural Gas Co. 8½% Cv. Sub. Debs.—8/1/95	546,250
$ 600,000	Federal National Mortgage Assoc. 4⅜% Cv. Sub. Debs —10/1/96	523,500
$ 500,000	General Telephone & Electronics Corp. 6¼% Cv. Sub. Debs.—9/15/96	490,000
$ 300,000	Otis Elevator Co. 6½% Cv. Sub. Debs.—10/1/95	288,000
$ 295,000	Southern California Edison Co. 3⅛% Cv. Debs.—8/15/80	226,413
$ 323,000	Tenneco Corp. 6¼% Cv. Sub. Debs.—10/1/92	316,540
	Total Corporate Bonds (5.16%)	**$ 2,835,703**

Investments at Market Value (99.21%)	**$54,487,746**
Cash and Receivables—Net (0.79%)	**433,439**
Net Assets at Market Value (100.00%)	**$54,921,185**

*Non-income producing securities.

an exchange in the same way that common stocks are. Brokers receive the usual commissions for selling them. Interestingly, they may sell for more or less than their net asset value, depending on investor demand.

Common stock funds. If a fund invests primarily in common stocks, as more than 90% of all funds do, it is a common stock fund. This broad classification has no meaning in terms of risk.

Balanced funds. These are funds that, as a matter of policy, keep a certain percentage of their assets in bonds and preferred stocks. This differentiates them from the common stock funds, which do not have this requirement. Balance is a policy, not an objective, per se. Many common stock funds buy bonds when the occasion demands. Most balanced funds should be thought of as growth-income funds. Investors Mutual and Wellington are two well-known balanced funds.

Bond and preferred stock funds. These funds have income as their primary objective. They involve some risk since the bonds in their portfolio fluctuate with interest rates. Bond funds have to be considered individually; they aren't all the same. Some hold high-grade bonds while a few others are less conservative and specialize in buying low-grade debentures or convertible bonds. In addition to diversification, a bond fund provides the investor with far greater liquidity than can be obtained by buying bonds directly in odd lots. Shares in a bond fund can always be sold at net asset value, while the small investor may incur deep discounts from the round-lot bond price when he sells.

For the upper-income investor, there are tax-exempt municipal bond funds, which have been in existence since 1961. These funds do not make a continuous offering of shares like a mutual fund. Instead, they sell "units" that represent an interest in a fixed, existing portfolio of tax-exempt bonds. An example of a no-load bond fund is Northeast Investors Trust. The Nuveen Tax Exempt Bond Fund is an example of a municipal.

Industry funds. An industry classification is another label put on mutual funds. The Oceanographic Fund is a no-load fund primarily investing in the "development and use of the ocean and its resources." The Energy Fund buys energy stocks; the Chemical Fund buys stocks in the chemical industry. The Bank Stock Fund concentrates its investments in bank stocks. There are also five insurance funds specializing in the investment of insurance stocks.

The principal advantage of concentrating a fund's investments in a given industry, perhaps surprisingly, is in selling the fund to investors. These funds adopted their policies primarily as a sales gimmick. When there are 600 funds vying for the investor's attention, prospective fund managers look for ways to stand out from the crowd.

Industry funds can be grouped into two categories: those heavily concentrated in their industry and those whose names perhaps suggest more of a concept than true specialization. The Bank Stock Fund is an example of the former. Other industry funds do not tie themselves too closely to the fates and fortunes of the industry they are supposedly specializing in. For example, the prospectus of the Chemical Fund hedges its industry concentration with the following disclaimer:

"Over the years scientific endeavors have increasingly tended to cut across individual areas of specialization so that clear boundaries no longer exist between chemistry and other sciences. . . . The following table gives examples of fields which may be represented in Chemical Fund's portfolio:

Drugs	Plastics
Nutritional Products	Computer Soft Ware
Toiletries & Cosmetics	Paper
Electronics	Petroleum Products
Office Equipment	Synthetic Fibers
Computers	Analytical & Process
Photographic Materials	Control Equipment
Hospital Supplies	Minerals

The Fund's Charter defines the 'chemical' field broadly to include companies (i) engaged in a business in which the science and technology of chemistry plays an important role, including the manufacture, refining, processing, compounding, mining, extraction, developing or distribution of one or more chemicals or of products in which any chemical forms a constituent part or which are created or developed in whole or in part by means of any chemical reaction, or (ii) engaged in a business in which the use of chemicals or of chemical processes or formulae or the interplay of the various scientific disciplines play an important role."

That's pretty broad!

The important thing is to determine these funds' objectives. The Oceanographic Fund is a maximum capital gains fund. Energy, Chemical, Bank Stock, and the five insurance funds are all quality growth funds. If the fund's assets really are concentrated, you also need to know the investment potential of the particular industry.

Geographic funds. Then there are the geographic funds. The best known is the Canadian Fund, and as the name implies, it invests in Canadian stocks. While it is actually a growth fund, an investor who hadn't checked might well have assumed it was a maximum capital gains fund, considering the reputation Canadian stocks enjoy in this country.

Multifunds. These are funds that invest in other funds. Multifunds currently offering their shares to the public are Fundpack, Hyperion Fund, First Multifund of America, No-Load Selected Funds, and Interfund. The same rules that apply to all the funds previously discussed also hold true here: what is the objective?

In its prospectus, Interfund states that its objective is to "achieve long-term capital appreciation." Both Hyperion and No-Load Selected Funds say only that their funds will "seek capital appreciation."

These stated objectives, while vague, might indicate that these funds are quality growth funds. However, an analysis of their portfolios found Interfund and Hyperion owning MCG funds, while No-Load Selected Funds held quality growth funds.

There is an interesting lesson here. Sometimes the fund's objectives are not obvious. At the time their portfolios were analyzed it would have been logical to classify Interfund and Hyperion as MCG funds and No-Load Selected Funds as a quality growth fund.

Hedge funds. A hedge fund is defined as a fund that as a matter of policy always keeps a portion of its portfolio in a "short" position. Thus, if the market goes up, they will profit from their "longs"

—i.e., stocks they own outright; if the market goes down, the stocks they are "short" on will show a profit. They have, in this way, hedged the future. Most hedge funds are private funds, but there are some available to the public. In terms of objectives, most hedge funds are maximum capital gains funds. One no-load hedge fund is the Tudor Hedge Fund.

Social-conscience funds. The First Spectrum Fund is one of a half-dozen new funds with a social conscience. It seeks to achieve capital appreciation by investing in companies that "comply fully with their legislative and administrative responsibilities in certain areas of corporate social concern and can, at the same time, be financially profitable and a sound investment selection." While this is certainly commendable, it also has to be pointed out that this makes sales sense for the same reasons as were noted for the industry funds.

Like the industry funds, the social-conscience funds can be flexible in their investment policies. The First Spectrum Fund bought into Norton Simon, Inc., because a subsidiary, Hunt-Wesson Foods, has a policy of hiring ex-convicts. The fund shrugged off the fact that another Simon subsidiary, Somerset Importers, has a different claim to fame with its Johnnie Walker Scotch. The two owners of the fund explained, "We decided it would be hypocritical to exclude the company just because it sells Scotch. We both drink."

A closer look at the prospectus of the First Spectrum Fund reveals that "this investment policy may entail risk proportionate to or greater than the potential gains and . . . the fund should not be considered as a complete investment program." The objective as stated in the prospectus would indicate that the fund is a maximum capital gains fund.

Funds for special-interest groups. There are many ways to be different. Ten funds are known not by what they are but to whom they sell the fund. The NEA Mutual Fund is so named because it sells its shares to teachers who are members of the National Educational Association. While it must be flattering to teachers to have a fund all their very own, they still have the other 600 to choose from. The NEA Mutual Fund is a growth fund.

Other funds in this group sell only to doctors, lawyers, military personnel, union personnel, airline pilots, farmers, or members of religious organizations. For example, the Lutheran Brotherhood Fund is a growth-income fund sold to Lutherans.

The prospectus of the PRO Fund states that "it was organized primarily to offer shares to participants in retirement programs for self-employed persons, generally professional men and women. Hence the name PRO Fund, Inc." Nevertheless, shares are now being sold to individuals, institutions, and retirement programs. The fund is listed in the daily papers, which means it has a minimum of 2,000 shareholders. With total net assets of $37 million, it is prospering. The PRO Fund is a growth fund.

A fund considerably more limited in ownership than the PRO Fund is the 39-year-old Elfun Trusts. This no-load fund has 18,500 shareholders, all of whom are past or present employees of the General Electric Company.

Dual-purpose funds. These funds are really two funds in one. The fund's shareholders are divided into two groups, one receiving all the dividend income and the other group receiving all the capital gains. They thus offer two completely different objectives. They are closed-end funds and the price for each is calculated independently of the other. They have not been particularly successful because fund managers find it difficult to fulfill two goals simultaneously.

FOCUS ON YOUR INVESTMENT OBJECTIVE

When you have a clear picture of your own mutual fund objectives, the trade jargon should pose no problem. To summarize, the most important thing to consider when selecting a fund is its investment objective. The greater the orientation toward growth, the greater the volatility and the risk. Young people or people with substantial investments in the market should consider putting a portion of their money into maximum capital gains funds. Quality growth funds are suitable for almost all investors, regardless of age or income. Older and more conservative investors will find growth-income funds to their liking.

There is considerable difference of opinion in classifying funds by objective. Nearly every advisory service or fund guide has a different classification system. What one service describes as a maximum capital gains fund, another service may consider a growth fund. Keep in mind that it is only by looking at a fund's stated objectives and the volatility of its past performance that you will know for certain what you are buying.

CHAPTER 8 HOW TO SELECT TOP
MAXIMUM CAPITAL GAINS FUNDS

To select the maximum capital gains funds that promise outstanding future performance is a challenge to any investor. It is a task as intellectually stimulating and as profitable as selecting a portfolio of the best growth stocks but, in my opinion, far easier.

Since the greatest reward potential is found in MCG funds, this book has devoted the most space to the selection of these specific funds. For the more wary investor, Chapter 10 discusses the simple steps needed to select more conservative funds.

PAST PERFORMANCE AS A CRYSTAL BALL

The first step in selecting a mutual fund is to examine past performance. This is a major determinant of future performance. But it's an art to determine just what periods of time to consider since a fund's performance over the past year might indicate one future growth rate and its performance over the previous five years might indicate another. It is critical to select relevant periods of time in these evaluations.

The fact is that funds do not maintain superior performance over long periods of time. Many MCG funds—not unlike growth stocks—go through periods of exceptional growth and then reach maturity, at which point their growth rate slackens. The most common error in looking at past performance is to examine a too-long track record. Here is how the leading funds in the decade of the sixties fared in 1971 and 1972. (All but Fidelity Trend, First Sierra and Istel are classified as MCG funds by Wiesenberger.)

TOP TEN FUNDS OF THE SIXTIES
Performance Rank Among All Funds

	1961–70	1971	1972
Enterprise	1	133	378
Fidelity Trend	2	272	166
Ivest	3	163	222
Oppenheimer	4	221	268
Penn Square	5	481	350
Axe-Houghton Stock	6	330	234
Rowe Price New Horizons	7	5	51
First Sierra	8	307	438
Istel	9	182	345
Scudder Special	10	196	185

NOTE: No-loads are in boldface type.
SOURCE: *Mutual Funds Scoreboard, Fund Scope*

Only New Horizons stayed in even the top 10% of all funds in 1971 or 1972. The other "best of the sixties" funds were not even in the top 20% in 1971 or 1972. Some of these funds made the top ten list by turning in exceptional performances in one or two years, often in the early part of the decade. For example, the last time Fidelity Trend or Ivest made the upper 10% of all funds was in 1965. Therefore, the first rule of MCG fund selection is never make a buy decision solely on the basis of a fund's long-term record. How funds performed five to ten years ago is just not significant.

The MCG fund is the pre-eminent investment vehicle for a bull market, yet the top performers in one bull market almost never excel in the next one. Not one of the top twenty performers in the bull market year of 1968 made the top twenty in 1971. Furthermore, only two of these twenty placed in the upper 10% in 1971, three in 1972. Therefore, as a general rule, MCG funds should be evaluated essentially within the framework of the current bull market. When a new bull market starts, the funds that will lead are those that correctly anticipate what stocks or industries will be the new winners. Funds that guess wrong or cling to the favorites of the preceding bull market will trail in the new bull market performance race.

If you wish, you can examine a fund's performance over the preceding bear market, but this does not provide any real clues to bull market performance. The only point in looking at the bear market data is to see how volatile the fund is; that is, how much risk you are taking.

There are two ways to analyze a fund's past performance in order to predict its future performance:

1. Compare it to other MCG funds.
2. Compare it to market averages.

To compare funds, take relevant time spans, check the funds' performances and rank them to see which are best. The time spans to be examined are the most recent short-term up and down periods of the market and accumulations of past periods. The short periods can be anywhere from one week to six-to-eight weeks in length. The accumulated periods go back six months, one year, two years, and the span of the current bull market.

Recent performance—the last one-to-three months—most accurately reflects current portfolio momentum. Longer-term performance best shows management skill and the fund's ability to deliver consistently good performance. Both measures are important. The goal is to find funds that perform well under both criteria.

The following chart is taken from *Growth Fund Guide*, an advisory service that closely follows a select list of outstanding funds. *Growth Fund Guide* starts with monthly performance rankings. It then groups these monthly data into relevant up and down periods. In its December 1972 report, performance is shown for three rising periods and one falling period within the 1970–72 bull market.

The funds have been ranked within objective (aggressive growth and growth) by their performance over the period titled "A to F" (the first column). This is the longest bull market span available. The second column, "B to C," then measures the six-month up cycle from November 1971 to April 1972 to show medium-term performance. The next column, "D to E," provides a meaningful indication of the fund's downside risk, and the final column, "E to F," identifies those funds with the best recent performance.

This kind of analysis is then repeated in subsequent up and down periods. It is an ongoing process that should be continued as long as you own MCG funds.

Keep in mind that the up and down periods should be evaluated

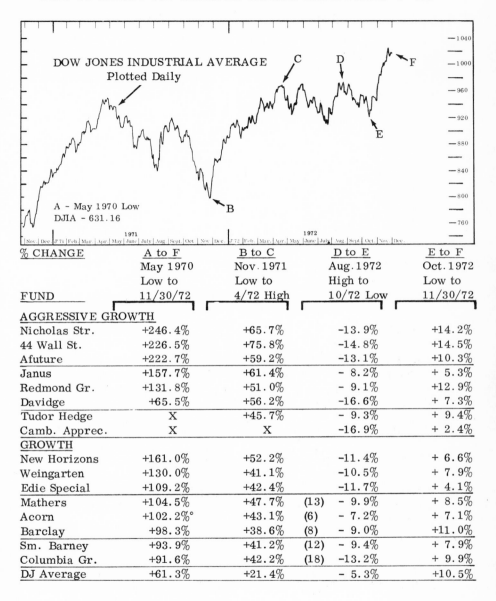

DOW JONES INDUSTRIAL AVERAGE
Plotted Daily

A - May 1970 Low
DJIA - 631.16

% CHANGE	A to F May 1970 Low to 11/30/72	B to C Nov. 1971 Low to 4/72 High		D to E Aug. 1972 High to 10/72 Low	E to F Oct. 1972 Low to 11/30/72
FUND					
AGGRESSIVE GROWTH					
Nicholas Str.	+246.4%	+65.7%		-13.9%	+14.2%
44 Wall St.	+226.5%	+75.8%		-14.8%	+14.5%
Afuture	+222.7%	+59.2%		-13.1%	+10.3%
Janus	+157.7%	+61.4%		- 8.2%	+ 5.3%
Redmond Gr.	+131.8%	+51.0%		- 9.1%	+12.9%
Davidge	+65.5%	+56.2%		-16.6%	+ 7.3%
Tudor Hedge	X	+45.7%		- 9.3%	+ 9.4%
Camb. Apprec.	X	X		-16.9%	+ 2.4%
GROWTH					
New Horizons	+161.0%	+52.2%		-11.4%	+ 6.6%
Weingarten	+130.0%	+41.1%		-10.5%	+ 7.9%
Edie Special	+109.2%	+42.4%		-11.7%	+ 4.1%
Mathers	+104.5%	+47.7%	(13)	- 9.9%	+ 8.5%
Acorn	+102.2%°	+43.1%	(6)	- 7.2%	+ 7.1%
Barclay	+98.3%	+38.6%	(8)	- 9.0%	+11.0%
Sm. Barney	+93.9%	+41.2%	(12)	- 9.4%	+ 7.9%
Columbia Gr.	+91.6%	+42.2%	(18)	-13.2%	+ 9.9%
DJ Average	+61.3%	+21.4%		- 5.3%	+10.5%

SOURCE: *Growth Fund Guide*

separately. If a fund's performances over both up and down spans
are lumped together, the results can be seriously misleading. For
instance, take a hypothetical time span covering a down and an up
period where two funds posted identical over-all price changes
of +2%. If the up and down periods had been analyzed separately,
the following differences would have become apparent.

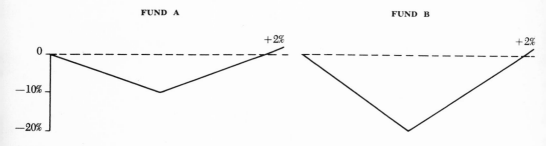

FUND A   FUND B

Fund A went down 10% and recovered. Fund B went down 20%
and also recovered. Even though they both ended up +2%, there
is a tremendous difference between the two. If the market con-
tinues up, Fund B might very well grow at twice the rate of
Fund A. Conversely, if the market turns down, Fund B will probably decline faster than Fund A.

Despite the logic of this approach, it is honored mostly in the
breach. The time spans used for comparison by most advisory
services correspond to their publication dates. This doesn't matter
for weekly or monthly reports; however, when it is done on an
annual basis, the data are susceptible to serious misinterpretations
if used for predictive purposes. A glaring case is the calendar year
1970. Many funds ended the year roughly even, but the final
number completely concealed the depth of the roller-coaster ride
that ensued between January and December.

While annual data are useful in showing what a fund has done
in the past, they are of little value as a predictive tool.

While there are 160 no-load funds available to the investor, in
actual practice the list of funds to be followed can quickly be
narrowed down to a range of from six to ten by eliminating from
consideration all but the very best performers. The relative posi-

tions of these top funds are then continually watched to see whether they are maintaining their lead or are being outpaced.

WHERE TO OBTAIN PERFORMANCE RECORDS

There are essentially three ways of obtaining the mutual fund performance records needed to properly evaluate and select the best funds. You can post or clip fund prices from the newspapers and then compute percent changes. But this method requires a substantial amount of work, and data would still be unavailable for many small but worthwhile funds not listed in the papers.

Another method is to analyze prospectuses. This is inferior for two reasons. Performance data in the prospectus are not provided in a convenient form for comparison to other funds; the data are usually outdated and subsequent quarterly reports issued by the fund must be studied. As a result, examining prospectuses is a most cumbersome method of comparing mutual fund performance.

Furthermore, each prospectus has to be obtained individually, which means you need a comprehensive list of funds with addresses. There are some pitfalls here. For example, it's not possible to develop this list from mutual fund advertising. Only a small percentage of funds advertise, and the SEC doesn't allow their ads to say much more than that they are no-loads and are "seeking possible growth." Moreover, the funds that advertise aren't necessarily the best-performing funds. In fact, it's likely that a heavy advertiser may be a laggard in the performance race. This is particularly true of many of the old-line load funds that recently went no-load in an effort to spur sales by offering the no-load "discount" in lieu of good performance.

The third—and best—method, in my opinion, is to obtain needed performance data from mutual fund advisory services. They compute performance and rank and compare various funds over identical periods of time. In addition, they obtain the amounts of any distributions and include them in their performance computations. This is most important. In order to assess performance accurately, any capital gains and dividend distributions in the measured period must be added to the latest net asset value since the fund's per share price is automatically lowered by the exact amount of these payouts. These figures are not readily available for funds you don't own (assuming you'd rather not read *The Wall Street Journal's* Dividend News each day). As a result, the advisory services can save you much time and effort.

However, if you want to do your own charting, the simplest way is to clip the mutual fund section out of the daily or Sunday paper and file it until you are ready to compute your fund's performance over a recent period. Pull out the applicable days and find the percentage changes over that period. Be sure to check whether there have been any distributions to shareholders in the period. You can tell if a fund has paid a distribution since there will be an x—for ex-dividend—before the fund's price that day. This method is much easier than posting prices every day.

PERFORMANCE VERSUS THE MARKET AVERAGES

The next step is to compare the fund's performance to market averages. As an illustration, take the time span between May 26, 1970, and December 29, 1972. This time span includes periods in which the market rose strongly, marked time, and had several substantial sell-offs—all within the framework of a bull market. As examples, I selected the Nicholas Strong and Afuture funds because they did all the right things and ended up first and second, respectively, among all funds. Their performance in this period is a model to look for when selecting an MCG fund.

I compared these funds to the New York Stock Exchange Industrial Index, a broad-based indicator preferable to the Dow Jones Industrial Average as a bench mark for MCG funds. Furthermore, since MCG funds invest heavily in AMEX and OTC stocks, additional insights can be gained by comparisons to these indices.

For the illustration, I selected periods of time corresponding to the short-term ups and downs of the market. The length of the periods varied; in one case it was less than a week. However, where there were strong continuing up trends (fourth quarter of 1970 and first quarter of 1971), spans over a month were used.

The following table reads that from May 26 to June 19, 1970, the New York Stock Exchange Index was up 14%. In the same period, Nicholas Strong increased 21% while Afuture increased 23%. Then, from June 20 to July 6, the NYSE Industrial Average declined 8%, while Nicholas Strong and Afuture declined 13% and 15%, respectively.

MCG FUND PERFORMANCE VS. NYSE INDUSTRIAL INDEX

PERCENT CHANGES

	Market Days	NYSE Ind. Average	Nicholas Strong	Afuture
May 26–June 19, 1970	18	+14%	+21%	+23%
June 19–July 6	10	−8%	−13%	−15%
July 6–July 30	18	+9%	+7%	+16%
July 30–Aug. 13	10	−5%	−5%	−7%
Aug. 13–Oct. 7	38	+19%	+31%	+32%
Oct. 7–Nov. 18	30	−6%	−7%	−5%
Nov. 18–Feb. 16, 1971	60	+21%	+34%	+34%
Feb. 16–Feb. 22	4	−3%	−4%	−3%
Feb. 22–Apr. 28	47	+11%	+37%	+26%
Apr. 28–June 22	38	−7%	−4%	−4%
June 22–July 12	13	+3%	+13%	+10%
July 12–Aug. 9	20	−8%	−12%	−12%
Aug. 9–Sept. 8	21	+9%	+12%	+12%
Sept. 8–Nov. 24	55	−12%	−10%	−9%
Nov. 24–Apr. 12, 1972	96	+27%	+66%	+59%
Apr. 12–May 9	19	−6%	−9%	−10%
May 9–May 26	13	+6%	+15%	+12%
May 26–July 20	37	−5%	−9%	−11%
July 20–Aug. 14	17	+7%	+3%	+5%
Aug. 14–Oct. 16	43	−7%	−14%	−13%
Oct. 16–Dec. 29	52	+10%	+18%	+13%
Entire Period		+80%	+258%	+231%

Incidentally, some of the advisory services chart fund performance, typically using a separate chart for each fund. These charts are more effective for depicting over-all trends of the individual funds than for comparisons between funds. A more precise way to analyze relative fund performance is to use numerals, as in the preceding table.

Some lessons can be learned from the price action of the two funds. For example, both funds exhibited consistent performance throughout the period. In up markets they performed significantly better than the averages in virtually every instance. Even more important, *they didn't give it all back during short-term declines.* In many cases, their losses in periods of correction did not exceed that of the NYSE Industrial Index.

Other high-volatility MCG funds performed as well as Nicholas Strong and Afuture in up periods, but tended to be equally volatile in down periods, often losing the bulk of their gains. The fact that Nicholas Strong and Afuture were less vulnerable when the market corrected itself was a major factor in making them winners.

It is interesting to see how the performance of these two MCG funds varied during the different phases of the bull market. From May to October 1970, investor interest centered on the depressed blue chips and cyclicals on the NYSE. Even though both Nicholas Strong and Afuture were heavily invested in AMEX and OTC stocks, they outperformed the NYSE average by approximately 50% to 60%. Then investor interest switched to smaller companies and in many up periods between November 1970 and April 1972, both funds performed two to three times better than the NYSE average.

After the extended rally ended in April 1972, the market went into another prolonged period of relatively minor swings. Many growth stocks started to correct, and the long-neglected cyclicals began to attract attention. As a result, these funds' performances weakened vis-à-vis the NYSE Industrial Index. Furthermore, if the comparison had been made to the Dow, their relative performances would have been even poorer since it was in this period that the laggard Dow finally gained the momentum needed to break 1,000. Nevertheless, even in this period, both funds outperformed the NYSE Index in two of three up periods.

Note that the selection of Nicholas Strong and Afuture as examples in no way constitutes a buy recommendation. Future performance may be different. Furthermore, a fund's performance record should be evaluated in conjunction with other guidelines which will be described in the next chapter.

It is a common misconception that money in a mutual fund grows as surely and as steadily as does bank interest. This false idea probably comes from examining the "mountain"—the pictorial growth chart in the prospectus, which is always shown on an annual basis. As the previous chart makes clear, *mutual funds achieve most of their gains in fairly short periods of time when the market is moving strongly upward.* For example, Nicholas Strong rose 37% between February 23 and April 28, 1971, alone— a period of little more than two months. To make money in funds, you have to be invested during these strong upward moves. Otherwise your money will be simply marking time, at a risk far greater than in the bank.

One final word about comparing fund performance to the averages. You will find funds that on some days move contrary to the market indices. Typically, they are small funds with a limited number of stocks in their portfolios. I have found it best to avoid these funds, since they are often inconsistent performers.

FORGET PRICE PER SHARE

In the preceding material, I have consistently analyzed growth in terms of percent changes, not in terms of change in per share value—i.e., the fund went from $7 to $10. With mutual funds, the price per share is virtually an irrelevant statistic. Price per share is not a consideration in the purchase or sale of a fund. Mutual funds are basically purchased in dollar amounts, and most funds issue fractional shares to round out purchases to the exact dollar ordered. You buy $500 worth of a fund, not 100 shares of a $5 fund.

A discussion of growth in terms of price per share as listed in the papers can be misleading if there has been a distribution, which lowers the apparent price. In this case, it would be similar to comparing the price of a stock after it has split to its pre-split price. It can't be done. In evaluating a fund, the percent increase *with distributions included* is the only thing that matters.

In addition, unlike stock, the per share price is not an indication of quality. There is no inherent quality difference between a fund selling at $3 per share and one selling at $50 per share. Incidentally, some banks, which lend money on quality stocks but not on very low-priced stocks, occasionally apply the same policy to mutual funds. These banks don't understand mutual fund pricing.

WATCH OUT FOR THIS KIND OF PERFORMANCE

Here's an actual performance record that's almost too good to be true. In succeeding months in 1968, this fund bettered the NYSE Industrial Index by a ratio of twenty times or more.

PERFORMANCE COMPARISON

	NYSE Ind. Index	No-Load Fund
April 1968	+10%	+32%
May	+2%	+14%
June	No Change	+5%
July	−3%	+20%
August	+1%	+20%
September	+4%	+14%
October	+1%	−1%
November	+5%	+12%

The fund's name is Mates. One reason it grew so spectacularly is that it acquired substantial holdings of restricted "letter" stock between April and July 1968. Letter stock is unregistered stock purchased directly from issuing companies at a discount from the market price. Contrary to the usual practice, Mates valued the stock at the market price for corresponding unrestricted securities or at a small constant dollar discount. This resulted in a large, almost instantaneous, paper profit on these newly acquired securities. It enabled the fund to achieve record growth in a bull market that had virtually topped out.

Then on November 20, 1968, Fred Mates and the fund were sued by certain individuals who alleged violations of the securities laws in connection with the fund's acquisition of certain other securities. As a result of the ensuing publicity, the accountants resigned and on December 19, 1968, the fund's board of directors lowered the value of the letter stock. Next, on December 20, the SEC suspended trading in Omega Equities—Mates's largest letter stockholding—and the fund then immediately suspended redemptions. Mates's shareholders were locked into the fund in a time of declining prices and were unable to sell until July 22, 1969, when the redemption privilege was restored.

In December 1968, the Mates Fund declined 36% as compared to a 4% decline in the NYSE Index. From January to July 22, 1969, the fund declined another 29%, and, of course, it dropped even farther as the bear market continued.

There's a moral to this story. When a fund performs three to five times better than the averages, that's genius; when it performs twenty times better, it should suggest that you check further.

CHAPTER **9**　GUIDELINES FOR FUTURE PERFORMANCE

The analysis of past and current performance is the primary method for selecting funds. However, performance is really the end product. It is the net result of several factors, all of which contribute to a fund's performance—or lack of it. Since the goal is to obtain top future performance, the investor must understand the factors that explain why some funds outperform others.

These factors are guidelines that will enable you to pick funds that offer the best likelihood of outstanding future performance. While these guidelines, like the criteria used for selecting growth stocks, won't guarantee success, they will greatly increase your chances of selecting the funds that will be among the best performers in the future.

SIZE OF FUND

Size is an important criterion in determining the potential for growth. Small funds are more likely to achieve greater percentage gains than large funds.

In 1971, eight of the top ten performing funds started the year with less than $12 million in assets. Their gains ranged from 47% to 86%.

In 1972, all the top ten funds began the year with assets of less than $90 million. They were up 32% or more.

In direct contrast, the table (page 122) shows the slower growth over the same period of time for the ten largest quality growth and MCG funds. (Growth-income and balanced funds have been

1971 PERFORMANCE
Top Ten Funds

Rank	Fund	Total Net Assets in Millions 12/31/70	Gain
1.	**Nicholas Strong**	$ 6.4	+86%
2.	**44 Wall Street**	.3	+71%
3.	**Afuture**	11.6	+68%
4.	Channing Venture	.4	+61%
5.	**Rowe Price New Horizons**	187.1	+53%
6.	**Redmond Growth**	.6	+49%
7.	IDS New Dimensions	118.3	+48%
8.	GAC Growth	.1	+48%
9.	R. S. Hershey	.2	+47%
10.	**S & P/InterCapital Dynamics Fund**	3.9	+47%

NOTE: No-loads are in boldface type.
SOURCE: *Mutual Funds Scoreboard*

1972 PERFORMANCE
Top Ten Funds

Rank	Fund	Total Net Assets in Millions 12/31/71	Gain
1.	Templeton Growth	$ 7.9	+68%
2.	International Investors	4.0	+57%
3.	American Insurance and Industrial	.9	+45%
4.	Omega	39.5	+44%
5.	Twentieth Century Growth	11.5	+42%
6.	Putnam Voyager	33.1	+41%
7.	Putnam Vista	80.9	+36%
8.	Charter	1.4	+36%
9.	**Janus**	3.5	+34%
10.	Life Insurance Investors	86.7	+32%

NOTE: No-load is in boldface type.
SOURCE: *Mutual Funds Scoreboard*

excluded.) These funds range in size from $611 million to $2.2 billion. Besides being large, they have one other thing in common—top-notch management. Their management had to be good or they would never have grown so large. Yet despite this advantage, their performances ranged between +13% and +31% in 1971 and between +9% and +24% in 1972.

TEN LARGEST GROWTH AND MCG FUNDS
Ranked by 12/31/70 Asset Value

Rank	Fund	Total Net Assets in Millions 12/31/70	1971 Gain	1972 Gain
1.	Dreyfus	$2,232	+14%	+9%
2.	Mass. Investors Growth Stock	1,165	+23%	+21%
3.	United Accumulative	1,141	+18%	+13%
4.	Fidelity Trend	996	+16%	+14%
5.	Investors Variable Payment	893	+26%	+21%
6.	National Investors	747	+28%	+24%
7.	Putnam Growth	684	+20%	+19%
8.	**Rowe Price Growth**	658	+31%	+16%
9.	Technology	618	+15%	+9%
10.	Fidelity Capital	611	+13%	+9%

NOTE: No-load is in boldface type.
SOURCE: *Mutual Funds Almanac, Mutual Funds Scoreboard*

Confirming this conclusion, a broad comparison of the performance of 433 funds in the bull market period, May 1970 to April 1972, found that the proportion of funds with less than $100 million in net assets making the top 10% was 75% higher than for funds with more than $100 million in assets.

There are good reasons why small funds can perform better than large ones. For one, small funds can invest in small emerging growth companies. Big funds can't take meaningful positions in these small companies, either because there is not enough stock available or because they are limited by law to owning no more than 10% of the voting stock of any one company.

Consider the case of a promising industrial corporation with only $10 million of stock outstanding. No single fund can buy more than $1 million of its stock. Suppose a $1 billion fund acquires $1 million worth of the company's stock. If the stock doubles, its value is increased only $1 million, and the large fund's total assets are increased to $1,001,000,000, up only one-tenth of 1%.

On the other hand, if a $20 million fund has $1 million of the same stock, a doubling in stock price will increase the small fund's total assets to $21 million, and the net asset value will increase a very substantial 5%.

If the $1 billion fund specialized in these small growth companies, putting no more than $1 million in each, it would need to evaluate and buy 1,000 different stocks. This would be an awesome job, even if it were an economically sound undertaking.

As a result, the larger growth funds prefer substantial holdings in major corporations. Among the large holdings of the $2+ billion Dreyfus Corporation have been $87 million of Polaroid, $50 million of Philip Morris, $49 million of AT&T, and $34 million of Sears Roebuck. These large corporations typically have less growth potential than small emerging companies.

Equally important, large funds can't dispose of huge holdings quickly. If a large fund wanted to sell $10 to $20 million of a stock, this sale would almost certainly depress the stock's price. If the fund decided to sell a quantity of a $40 stock on an exchange, it might receive $40 for the first few thousand shares, but then the price would fall as the supply of buyers dried up. The fund could very well finish selling at prices as low as $34, averaging perhaps $37 for the lot. Even though today the fund has the alternative of selling the stock by means of a private placement, often to another institution, the buyer, here too, may demand a discount for any large block.

Small funds don't have this problem. They can dispose of their holdings on the exchanges without disrupting the price almost as readily as individual investors.

Because of the advantages of being small, some growth funds stop selling shares when they reach a predetermined size—$100 million, for example. Investors who own shares of these funds are fortunate. Their funds are likely to perform well for an extended period of time.

When you examine long-term performance records, you will find many large funds among the top performers. Don't be misled by this. These large funds grew to their present size because they performed well in their early years when they were still small.

The Dreyfus Fund is a classic example of a fund that made its greatest gains when it was small. In the fifties and early sixties, the Dreyfus Fund regularly outpaced the NYSE's Index by margins of two or more times. The Dreyfus Fund started 1957 with $10 million in assets and appreciated 139% in the next five years; the market, as recorded by the NYSE's Composite Index, grew 58%. Now, with more than $2 billion in assets, the Dreyfus Fund lags behind the averages. In the five years ending in 1972, it gained 15% as compared to a 20% increase for the NYSE's Composite Index.

One point should be made clear if you opt for a small fund to maximize performance. Small funds perform better primarily because they are able to buy stocks that are inherently riskier, not because their management is superior. Large growth funds own the stocks of multibillion-dollar growth companies such as IBM and Xerox, which are not likely to go bankrupt in any recession. On the other hand, some emerging growth companies favored by the small performance funds did go bankrupt in the 1969–70 market.

In summary, one guideline for achieving top performance is size. Small funds are more likely to achieve outstanding performance than are large ones.

NEW-MONEY INFLOW

Size is not the only criterion for achieving maximum performance. After all, many small funds fail to outperform the old giants of the industry. One reason why some small funds are top ranked and others are not is *new-money inflow.*

The concept of new-money inflow is not difficult to understand. Open-end mutual funds, unlike closed-end funds or stocks, attract new money by selling additional shares. If a fund is selling more shares than it is redeeming, it is said to be experiencing a positive new-money, or cash, inflow. Conversely, if more shares of a fund are being redeemed than sold, the fund is said to be experiencing a negative cash flow, or outflow. Reinvested distributions and dividends are not counted as capital inflow.

For many years it was thought that new-money inflow or outflow was a function of performance. If a fund did well, it attracted new money; if it did poorly, many investors might redeem their shares, causing a negative outflow.

However, another school of thought emerged that holds that the reverse is true—that a positive cash flow produces superior performance and a negative cash flow causes inferior market performance. The person who popularized this latter theory is a mutual fund buff and amateur chartist, Alan Pope of Albuquerque, New Mexico. (At the time, Pope was an aeronautical engineer directing aero projects for Sandia Corporation, the government nuclear-weapon engineering laboratory.)

Pope's findings came after observing that no fund, however well managed, ever maintained front-rank performance for more than a few years. Size, while one factor, was not sufficient explanation for relinquishing its superior performance. After all, there are many small funds that achieved superior performance for only a short period of time without growing to unmanageable size.

The question is, Why did these funds slow down? Pope concluded that new-money inflow was a key variable. The reasoning behind this was:

· · · With new money coming into the fund, management can buy securities on market dips.

· · · A positive cash flow means the fund need not sell good or promising equities in order to meet redemptions, or to raise cash for defensive purposes.

· · · With fresh money coming in, a fund need not sell existing holdings to take advantage of new or special market situations. By the same token, the fund can easily increase its position in the best performing stocks already in its portfolio. In these cases, decision-making is simpler; only one decision has to be made—not two.

· · · A positive cash flow allows a fund to minimize its investment mistakes since the bad investment is being spread over an increasingly larger asset base. In effect, a cash flow dilutes losses.

· · · With more money to spend, the fund can attract the advice of the best analysts.

· · · With ample cash, fund managers are more alert to the whole market rather than just to their own portfolio.

Another leading authority on cash flow is Melvin Roebuck, president of Roebuck & Company, Managers of Mutual Fund Shares, a company that manages fund accounts for individual and institutional investors. Mr. Roebuck came to the following definitive conclusions:

If a fund nets, in new-money flow over a year, 200% or more of its assets at the start of the year, that fund—in 95% of the cases—will wind up in the top 25% of its group. If the net new-money flow is between 30% and 200% of assets, the fund will probably outperform the average of its group. With a flow of −5% to +30% it can go either way. If the flow is below −5% (i.e., in net redemptions) the fund will probably never again turn up among the top 25%.

Cash inflow also explains why big funds inevitably slow down. They cannot maintain the same rate of growth over a long period of time. For new-money inflow to contribute materially, a fund needs new-money inflows of 200% or more annually. Not even considering a fund's per share growth, this means a $500,000 fund would need only $1 million the first year, but by the end of the fifth year it would need $81 million. A large fund starting with $200 million would require $32 billion in new money by its fifth year. That's more than half the money invested in the entire mutual fund industry.

Cash inflow typically starts after investors note a small fund is turning in an outstanding performance. Cash flow then enables a fund to maintain superior performance until such time as it is no longer meaningful in relation to the size of the fund. Buy funds that have large cash inflow.

HOW TO DETERMINE CASH INFLOW

Cash flow can be determined by obtaining a fund's per share performance and total net asset figures. It is calculated by measuring the per share gain for the year, applying it to net assets at the beginning of the year, then calculating the net inflow of capital over and above this gain.

Here are the specific calculations. Assume a fund started the year with $1 million in net assets, increased its per share value 40%, and ended the year with $3 million in total assets. The 40% per share gain alone would have increased total net assets to only $1.4 million. The balance—$1.6 million—represents new-money inflow. The new-money inflow percentage would be 60%. It was obtained by dividing the $1.6 million inflow by the net assets at the beginning of the period, $1 million.

The advisory service *Growth Fund Guide* provides cash inflow data, already computed and charted, on a quarterly basis. In addition, the data can be computed from successive quarterly reports, which show total net assets.

It is somewhat better to examine cash inflow monthly. This can be done by subscribing to one of several advisory services that show total net assets monthly and then do the required computations yourself. This can be done very roughly. For example, if a fund has increased its per share price 5% and its total net assets 30%, you know there has been good cash inflow.

Unfortunately nothing is clear-cut in mutual fund investing. Occasionally new-money inflow is so great it becomes difficult to control. It is possible to grow too fast, particularly if a fund's objective is to invest in the small emerging growth companies.

An interesting case in point involves the Rowe Price New Horizons Fund. With a policy of investing in small companies, New Horizons found that the only way to maintain growth was to cut off sales from time to time. Curran W. Harvey, the president of the fund, made these comments to *FundScope*.

The New Horizons Fund had an outstanding performance record in 1966 and, as a result, we were inundated with new money as 1967 progressed. This imposed an intolerable burden on our Research Department which was responsible for identifying companies in which the new money could be prudently and productively invested. When it became obvious that money was coming in faster than we could do a thorough job on each company considered for investment and faster than we could find good companies whose stocks were selling at what we regarded as reasonable prices, we suspended sale of Fund shares to reduce the inflow of cash.

New Horizons opened up the fund for sales again in June 1970 when it felt that the emerging growth stocks it wanted were again priced right. However, its minimum investment was increased to $25,000 for new shareholders; previously it had been $2,500. This was done primarily to put a brake on the fund's growth rate. Later, in March 1972, the fund was closed completely to new investors.

Here's another example of what uncontrolled growth can do to a fund. David O. Ehlers, whose Gibraltar Fund was one of the best performers in 1968 and one of the worst in the next three years, told *Forbes:*

Gibraltar grew by itself, not by plan. We started with $100,000 in 1968. Suddenly it became the tail that wagged the dog. We went up over 70% our first year—that was 1968—and the money cascaded in. In a little over a year, we had $100 million—a thousand-fold jump. It was more than I could handle, more than anyone could handle. There were some weeks when we'd get $5 million to $7 million in new money. It ruined my life.

With this kind of money to invest and with the prices of the go-go stocks jumping, Ehlers succumbed to the temptation to invest too quickly. Ehlers reasoned that people weren't buying Gibraltar to enable the fund to build a large cash balance. Today, he wonders if he would have made certain investments if he had not been under pressure to invest with such speed.

NET REDEMPTIONS HURT PERFORMANCE

While excessive cash inflow occasionally presents problems, no fund wants a net cash outflow. Net redemptions always hurt performance. Allan B. Hunter, whose One William Street Fund had suffered net redemptions in the sixties, explains:

Redemptions hurt, in that performance might have been better. The things we sold first were those having the least hope for gain, but you can't be as aggressive as you might want to be. You might be forced to sell things on balance that you might not want to, and how can you be 98% invested with redemptions running at 14%.

One William Street's record reflected the problem of excessive redemptions. Its growth was below average in those years.

AN APPROPRIATE CASH POSITION

The next guideline to analyze is the fund's cash position. This is the portion of a fund's assets that are not invested. These data can best be obtained from the various advisory services. They can also be obtained from the prospectus or the quarterly reports by adding the fund's cash to its government notes and bills (called cash equivalents) and then computing this as a percent of total assets.

While not as important as size or cash inflow, cash position data for individual funds can be a helpful analytical tool. Here is the general rule for the appropriate cash position for a maximum capital gains fund:

In a bull market, the fund should be fully invested, or even leveraged, in order to take full advantage of rising prices. Conversely, in a bear market, the fund should have a high portion of its assets in cash or cash equivalents in order to minimize losses as stock prices fall.

You will find that there is considerable variation among the various MCG funds in this regard. Therefore, you should select the fund whose investment policy most closely parallels your own outlook at that point in time.

The examination of the fund's cash position is also an easy way to recognize the exceptional risk-takers. For example, on August 31, 1971, two weeks after President Nixon announced his new economic plan, *Growth Fund Guide* reported that the speculative Berkley Dean Special Fund (now called New York Hedge Fund) had a negative cash position of 33%. This means they were not only fully invested but they had borrowed another third of their assets and invested it. This is analogous to an individual investor being on margin. By comparison, many other MCG funds had moderate cash positions. Nicholas Strong, the number-one fund in the country at that time, had an 8% cash position. Edie Special, another top fund, was 20% in cash.

At that time, Nicholas Strong had been receiving heavy inflows of new money because of its leadership position. This made it easy for the fund to accumulate cash. But in any event, it chose not to invest all of it.

Berkley Dean, which had not been experiencing these heavy cash inflows, obviously thought the potential for gain in the market at that time was very good. It was willing to take the risk of being one-third leveraged! If the market had risen for any sustained period of time, Berkley Dean would have had a large leg up on other funds competing for the top growth position.

In this case, Berkley Dean was wrong. The market did not take off. Instead, after a short spurt, it retreated to levels even lower than recorded just before the President's announcement of Phase One. Since leverage works in both directions, the Berkley Dean Fund suffered losses greater than its rivals in the following month.

There are many other examples of bad timing. In February and March of 1970, many investors, both individual and institutional, thought the long bear market was finally bottoming out. Here was an investment opportunity that comes along only once in several years. If a fund were fully invested at the bottom of a major bear market, it would make a fast getaway. Then, when the first bull market rankings came out, the fund would be riding high. The profit potential here was enormous. Astute no-load investors, discounting the fund's bear market performance in the previous fourteen or fifteen months, would swarm to the new leaders.

To take advantage of this "favorable" market, some fund managers did take extraordinary chances. As of the end of February 1970, Pennsylvania Mutual was 10.5% leveraged, Investment/Indicators was 18.2% leveraged, and the Doll Fund was 9.0% leveraged. By way of comparison, other funds at that time had cash positions as high as 33%.

As it happened, the market did not bottom out in February 1970. It deteriorated rapidly, with the small growth stocks hardest hit. The leveraged funds, which held many of these growth stocks, declined precipitously between February and May. Both Pennsylvania Mutual and Investment/Indicators were off 49% for that three-month period. The Doll Fund was off 38% in the same period. The New York Stock Exchange's Composite Index was off only 18%. The fact that these funds were margined at the wrong time accentuated their losses.

Of the dozen or so funds followed by the *Growth Fund Guide*, the Schuster Fund had the largest cash position at that time. In February 1970, it was 33% in cash. Even though the Schuster Fund was an MCG fund holding the same kind of stocks the other funds held, it held its losses between February and May to 19%, about the same as the NYSE Composite Index.

Funds appear to be developing a more flexible attitude toward cash positions. In the past, few funds would radically increase their cash positions during bear markets. In all of 1970 no fund followed by *Growth Fund Guide* had a cash position greater than 48%. With hindsight we know a 100% cash position would have been correct in the first half of the year.

The funds' reluctance to go further into cash stems from two traditional attitudes. One, they feel they are collecting their management fees primarily to invest monies, not to sit on cash. Two, they know they lack the ability to consistently forecast the direction of the market.

In contrast, in the down market of 1973, some funds shook these traditional attitudes and made far more radical shifts. Janus Fund was 88.6% cash on June 19, 1973. Another small fund, Cambridge Appreciation, was 73.5% cash on June 29, with much of its remaining assets invested on the short side. It actually showed a 6% gain in the first six months of 1973.

Let's now examine a good cash position for an emerging bull market. Data were available for four of the ten best-performing funds in the first four months of the new bull market starting in 1970. All four funds had cash positions substantially below that of the industry as a whole. As of June 30, 1970, the industry cash position was 11.4% while the cash positions of these four funds ranged from +8% to a margined −7%.

INITIAL 1970 BULL MARKET CASH POSITIONS
Top-Performing Funds

Performance Rank 5/26 to 9/30	Fund	CASH POSITION %	Date
2	Mates	+6%	6/30
3	Afuture	+8%	6/19
8	Investment/Indicators	−7%	6/30
9	Sherman Dean	−3%	6/30

On the other hand, the Schuster Fund never did lower its cash position. In fact, as late as July 23, it was 42% in cash. In the same four months ending September 30, its gain was only 20%, a smaller gain than the Dow Jones Industrial Average posted (22%). Clearly, Schuster did not have an appropriate cash position in an emerging bull market.

The cases cited are particularly definitive illustrations of the principle of cash position. There were other funds with both high and low cash positions in this period whose performance differed from these examples. Performance is determined more by the stocks a fund owns than by the smaller segment of the portfolio typically kept in cash.

It is, of course, as hard to anticipate the end of a bear market as the beginning, and many good funds do not rush back to equities at the first sign of an upturn. Furthermore, the fact that some funds do well in the initial stages of a new bull market is primarily a consequence of their previous mistakes. They had not had a sufficiently large cash position in the preceding bear market, so they were automatically positioned correctly when the turn came; the stocks they held were so depressed their percentage gains in the initial stages of the bull market were most impressive.

Still, all in all, most early rebounders did all right as the bull market continued. There were thirty MCG funds in the top 10% of all funds in this four-month period according to *FundScope*. Eight of these funds maintained their top 10% ranking in 1971 (January through December), and twenty-three of the thirty remained in the upper half in 1971. On the other hand, five funds dropped to the bottom 10%. These were funds whose early spurt was due to their bear market mistakes.

In summary, cash position is important to examine, both as a meaningful indication of how fund management sees the future and as a measure of risk and reward. In an evident bull market, funds that are fully invested offer the greatest potential for gain. If you are willing to take the risk, by all means buy funds that are completely invested or even leveraged at key market junctures. On the other hand, if the outlook is uncertain, then look for funds with a greater cash reserve.

DON'T ANALYZE THE PORTFOLIO

Most funds issue quarterly reports listing the fund's portfolio as of the end of the period. As a general rule, don't try to predict future performance by analyzing the portfolio; it just can't be done. The facts are out of date before the investor receives the report and it's just too complicated to analyze.

Typically, a month or more has elapsed before the quarterly report is received by the shareholder. It is generally early May by the time you receive the report for the three months ending March 31. In the interim, a significant number of changes are likely to have occurred in the portfolio. Many stocks may have been sold and replaced by others.

Incidentally, to avoid "tipping its hand" and thereby inviting early competition in acquiring new holdings, a mutual fund is permitted to conceal temporarily new additions to its portfolio under a category titled "Other." This is allowed while a fund is in the process of actively building up its position in a stock, as long as the total of all concealed securities does not exceed 5% of the portfolio's total market value. The fund can wait as long as twelve months following the initial purchase before the holding must be disclosed in the next report to shareholders.

Secondly, a tremendous amount of time and expertise is needed to evaluate the portfolio. If the investor has that kind of knowledge, he doesn't need mutual funds; he can invest directly in stocks. And even a professional financial analyst with ready access to research material would find it time-consuming to analyze the 50 to 100 stocks in the typical fund portfolio and to compare their over-all potential to other funds owning an equally large number of stocks.

One thing that can occasionally be done is to examine the prospectus where the cost basis of the fund's portfolio is given. By comparing the cost of the individual stocks to their market value, the fund's batting average can be determined. Is it a strong portfolio over-all or have one or two stocks done phenomenally well, pulling up the average and making a lot of poor selections look good? However, since the prospectus is also usually out of date and quarterly reports seldom show cost data, this type of analysis actually rates management's long-term ability more than the strength of the current portfolio.

As noted earlier, you can examine the portfolio to get an indication of the type of stocks the fund invests in and the inherent risk in these stocks, but that is far different from trying to predict each stock's potential.

MANAGEMENT ABILITY

There is one other significant factor in fund evaluation—management ability. The underlying strength of a mutual fund, whether speculative or conservative, is in the ability of its investment adviser. The greater his skill, the greater the likelihood the fund will excel.

Now, the word "professional" carries the connotation of excellence; but, alas, this is not universally the case. All we really know about a professional fund manager is that he is engaged full time in his occupation. Some are excellent, doing an outstanding job for their shareholders; some are mediocre; and a few are so poor their shareholders would be better off selecting their own stocks at random.

Investors are invariably urged to select well-managed funds; but unfortunately, for the layman, management ability is the hardest factor to evaluate. This section will discuss the problems of evaluating management and will suggest the most logical alternative for the layman.

The fund's prospectus does provide a partial basis for an evaluation. In the case of new funds, the SEC demands detailed background about the fund manager so the prospective investor can be advised of his experience—or his lack of it.

In 1966, the initial prospectus of the ultraspeculative Hubshman Fund had this to say about its three principal officers:

HUBSHMAN FUND MANAGEMENT

Louis Hubshman, Jr., Chairman of the Board, President and Director. Mr. Hubshman previously was associated with Burnham and Co., New York, N.Y., members of the New York Stock Exchange, from April 1958 to December 1962. During that period he was a director of National Equipment Rental, Ltd., New York, N.Y., May 1960 to December 1961; Presidential Realty Corp., White Plains, N.Y., April 1961 to December 1961; Fairfield Equity Corp., a Small Business Investment Company, New York, N.Y., May 1961 to December 1965; International Stretch Products, manufacturer of stretch fabrics, New York, N.Y., March 1962 to July 1963; and American Theatre Press, Inc., publisher, New York, N.Y., January 1963 to November 1965. From December 1962 through August 1966 he was President and Chairman of the Board of L. Hubshman & Co., Inc., New York, N.Y., members of the New York Stock Exchange. He is also President, Chairman of the Board and a Director of Hubshman Management Corp., New York, N.Y.

Terry C. Graves, Vice President, Treasurer and Director. Mr. Graves was a full-time student prior to graduating from the Harvard Business School, Boston, Massachusetts, in June 1966. From June through August 1966, he was a security analyst with L. Hubshman & Co. He is also Vice President, Treasurer and a Director of Hubshman Management Corporation. Mr. Graves is 24 years old and has had no experience in the securities business prior to June 1966.

Dale A. Ketcham, Secretary. Miss Ketcham was a full-time student prior to graduating from Manhattanville College, Purchase, N.Y., in June 1964. From October 1964 through August 1966, she was employed as a secretary at L. Hubshman & Co., Inc. She is also Secretary of Hubshman Management Corporation.

According to the prospectus, the Hubshman Fund appears to lack broad management know-how. The vice president had only a few months' experience and the fund's secretary was one of the few corporate secretaries who actually was a secretary.

If, in 1966, you had avoided this fund on the basis of inadequate management, you would have been proven wise. In the 1969–70 bear market, the Hubshman Fund ranked last among all funds; it was off 72%. In the rising market that followed (May 1970 to April 1971), the fund *declined* another 2%, a most incredibly poor performance. The fund has since been sold and is now operated by new management under a new name, the Sagittarius Fund.

The prospectus, then, can be of help in evaluating the management of a new fund. On the other hand, it is of little help in analyzing the ability of the management of established funds. With few exceptions, the names in a prospectus are unfamiliar. So John Smith is president of the fund. This means very little to the average investor. Secondly, the prospectuses for established funds often list only the officers' current positions. Nothing in the way of background is provided.

Another difficulty in evaluating the management of many funds is that the president may or may not be the fund's portfolio manager; that is, he may or may not be the key person responsible for selecting the stocks and timing purchases and sales. Only the names of the fund's officers are listed in the prospectus, and it may not be clear which officer, if any, is actually making the investment decisions. In fact, key decisions at some funds are made by an employee who is not even an officer, and is, therefore, not listed in the prospectus. Often, these key people come and go, and shareholders are never aware of it.

In November 1971, Richard C. McKenzie, Jr., resigned the presidency of the Afuture Fund and became the portfolio manager of the new Oppenheimer Time Fund. Afuture was the number-two fund that year, and McKenzie was widely regarded as an extremely able portfolio manager. When he left, the Afuture Fund issued a supplement to its prospectus noting his resignation.

However, when McKenzie joined the larger Oppenheimer organization, he did not become an officer or a director. Even though as portfolio manager he is responsible for the key investment decisions, his name was not in the original prospectus of the Time Fund.

Practices vary considerably in the industry. The various investment advisers may give portfolio managers complete authority, partial authority, or delegate decision making to a committee.

With some funds, the loss of a portfolio manager may hurt performance, while in others, a change may have little effect on results because the president of the fund has built a strong organization or can replace one good portfolio manager with another. The fact is that insiders are the only people who know the roles played by specific individuals in the everyday business of the fund and the extent to which they contribute to the fund's success or failure.

There is also a temptation to select a fund because the manager has received favorable publicity. But the facts are that write-ups in the financial press don't insure true expertise or continued outstanding performance, nor does a lack of publicity imply poor management.

The financial columns on occasion profile the managers of funds that perform well over even short spans of time, while neglecting other funds equally outstanding. An interesting case in point of a fund being overlooked is Nicholas Strong. While their fund was turning in outstanding performances month after month during 1971 and 1972, Albert Nicholas and Richard Strong—located in Milwaukee, far from the financial centers and the New York media—received little recognition in the press and were thus unknown to the average investor.

That some fund managers are profiled and others aren't is probably due primarily to the posture they take toward publicity. Some managers court it, hiring public relations experts, while others shun it. Be skeptical of publicity. Don't make it the basis for fund selection.

Just as in the theater, there are stars in the mutual fund industry, and these stars attract a following. The book *The Money Managers* profiled the biggest stars of the bull markets of the 1960s. They romanced Dave Meid of Winfield Growth, Fred Carr of Enterprise, Gerry Tsai and George Chestnutt. From the hindsight of a bear market, we find that this stardom was as transient as an actor's. Dave Meid, Fred Carr and Gerry Tsai are no longer with the funds they spearheaded to fame; George Chestnutt's American Investors Fund has fallen on hard times.

There are reasons for these dislocations. Many fund managers develop their expertise and make their mark with a particular type of stock in a particular kind of market. Gerry Tsai, for example, made his mark in the 1950's and early 1960's buying quality growth stocks like Xerox, Polaroid, and Burroughs. He originally made his reputation with Fidelity Capital Fund, and even his Manhattan Fund performed passably in 1966 and 1967. Then in 1968, without warning, the Manhattan Fund collapsed as the era of the big glamour stocks, upon which Tsai had based his entire market philosophy, abruptly ended. While the Dow Jones Industrial Average was up 5% and many other performance funds were up 30% and 40%, the Manhattan Fund was actually down 7%. It had the worst record among 310 funds in the Arthur Lipper survey of mutual fund performance.

What had happened? In 1968, the other performance funds had switched to the small, usually over-the-counter special situations, such as mobile-home makers and franchisers. Tsai, in a different market environment, was like a fish out of water. He couldn't abandon an entire category of stocks that had been his trademark.

A similar fate befell George Chestnutt of the American Investors Fund, who made his reputation on the strength of his ability as a master chartist. Chestnutt made his big killings between 1962 and 1966 through his precision timing in buying and selling airline stocks, and later Xerox. The one thing these stocks had in common was long enough histories and broad enough markets so they could be effectively charted. Then in 1969 and 1970, his fund suffered huge losses investing in letter stocks and over-the-counter issues that seldom had a market or a past worth charting.

There is no guaranteed way of determining good management. For instance, many no-load funds are run by leading brokerage houses. While some of these funds are very good, some are not. The One William Street Fund is owned by Lehman Bros., one of the best-known and most highly respected brokerage firms on Wall Street, yet for many years the fund was a mediocre performer.

WHAT TO DO

There is, of course, expertise in the mutual fund field. There is good management and poor management. A few professional investors have the resources to personally evaluate management. They interview fund managers, determine who is making the key decisions, check their backgrounds, the size and expertise of their staffs, and the adequacy of their research.

To do this right is an expensive procedure. Funds under consideration are seldom located in the investor's community. (There are outstanding funds located in Denver, Washington, D.C., Kansas City, Houston, Minneapolis, Portland, Oregon, and Media, Pennsylvania—as well as in the New York, Chicago, Los Angeles, and Boston money centers.)

Laymen simply lack the time and resources to professionally evaluate all these funds, even if they have the skill. As a practical matter, you're not going to have the opportunity to meet fund management and personally inspect their organizations.

There are further difficulties. There is usually no way of knowing if a good portfolio manager has left a fund. If the prospectus does show previous experience, the layman can seldom evaluate it properly. The press can be misleading, too.

So recognize the difficulty of accurately measuring management ability, and concentrate on fund results. Examine an easily available mutual fund performance record in your home, in your leisure time. Continual gains in the value of the fund's shares are the most eloquent testimony of management's ability.

SUMMARY: MCG FUND SELECTION

This discussion has emphasized procedures for selecting the most volatile and growth-oriented MCG funds; however, this is not to imply that all MCG funds have exactly the same goals. They do not. There are many less speculative MCG funds with objectives falling in between the most aggressive MCG funds and quality growth funds. Careful reading of the prospectus and an analysis of past volatility will enable you to identify them.

When you select an MCG fund, look for:

· · · Top-flight management as evidenced by *superior medium- and short-term performance.*

· · · *Small size,* preferably under $100 million.

· · · *Heavy new-money inflows.*

· · · An *appropriate cash position.*

No one factor is sufficient for success. A fund can be small and perform poorly if management is inferior. Good management can be hampered by large size and lack of cash inflow. And, of course, no fund is insulated from unexpected political events or economic catastrophes. But the task of the successful investor is to select tomorrow's top funds. When a fund qualifies in all categories, *its likelihood of achieving superior future performance is great.*

CHAPTER 10 HOW TO SELECT QUALITY GROWTH AND GROWTH-INCOME FUNDS

Quality growth and growth-income funds are inherently less risky, less volatile, and perform more consistently than maximum capital gains funds. In view of this, different criteria are used in their selection.

WHAT TO LOOK FOR IN A PERFORMANCE RECORD

Since quality growth and growth-income funds are bought for the long haul, it makes sense to examine their performance records over a greater span of time than for MCG funds. Furthermore, since they should perform well in both bull and bear markets, they should be analyzed accordingly. This involves more than just inspecting a ten-year record. As was noted earlier, the broad picture often conceals more than it reveals.

Following are the steps that should be taken in analyzing quality growth and growth-income funds. First, look at long-term performance; specifically, the last two or three bull or bear markets, if the fund is old enough. Then check the fund's record over the last bear market and the last bull market. Finally examine medium-term performance, the last six months to a year and possibly the last up-and-down jog in the market.

Comparisons should be made to other quality growth or growth-income funds, and to the New York Stock Exchange's Composite Index or to the Dow Jones Industrial Average. The method is the same as that outlined in the section on maximum capital gains funds.

The information needed to select these funds is readily available from advisory services. Here is how to use three well-known services.

WIESENBERGER'S *INVESTMENT COMPANIES*

Investment Companies, which is available in many libraries, also provides data that can be used in making these analyses. In the section of *Investment Companies* titled "Management Results," the funds are first segregated by objective and the results are shown for varying annual periods of up to ten years.

Unfortunately, this "Management Results" section does not show performance data in terms of up and down markets. However, the "Price Volatility of Mutual Fund Shares" section does, and it can be used to evaluate performance. This section indexes the funds' performance to the NYSE's Composite Index. An index of 1.20 means the fund performed 20% better than the Index in a rising market, or in the case of a falling market, 20% worse. Look for funds with indices over 1.00 in rising periods and indices of 1.00 or less in declining periods.

Note that in this section there is a caveat which says volatility is not a measure of management performance. It's not if you are comparing an MCG fund to an income fund, but it is a measure of performance for comparing funds with the same objective.

FUNDSCOPE

FundScope provides past performance data over a broad base. Following are rankings in its 1-dcs (diversified growth stocks) category for the May 26, 1970, to December 31, 1972, rising market period. This category is equivalent to my quality growth term.

Even among funds with more modest objectives, there is a wide range of performance between the top and bottom funds. The investor should select funds in the upper half of all funds.

	% A.V. Gain or Loss 5/26/70 to 12/31/72		% A.V. Gain or Loss 5/26/70 to 12/31/72

GROUP 1-dcs

Diversified Growth Stocks

Putnam Inv	+128.6★★	Mut Omaha Gr	+77.5★
Johnston	+108.2★★	**Beacon Hill**	+77.3★
Morgan Gr	+106.5★★	First Virginia	+77.1★
Sentry Fund	+105.8★★	Commerce	+76.5★
Nat Investors	+105.7★★	Com Stk-SBM	+74.7★
C G Fund	+104.7★★	**DJIA**	**+ 74.6%**
Mathers Fund	+104.4★★	Inv Research	+74.1★
MONY Fund	+103.3★★	MEDIAN 1	+74.1★
First Inv Gr	+103.1★★	Fidelity Trend	+72.4★
Eaton Growth	+102.7★	**Fund Mut Dep**	+71.6★
Mairs Growth	+102.3★	Super Inv Gr	+71.4★
Mass Inv Gr	+100.2★	NEA Mutual	+71.3★
E & E Mutual	+100.5★	Nat Sec Gr	+69.2★
Price, TR Gr	+99.8★	Amer Growth	+68.5★
Channing Gr	+98.3★	**Variable Stk**	+67.4★
Pioneer Ent	+98.1★	**Price New Era**	+66.0★
Investors Var	+97.1★	Egret Growth	+65.8★
Westfield Gr	+96.8★	Paul Revere	+65.5★
Travelers Eq	+95.2★	Syncro Growth	+64.8★
Stein Stock	+94.0★	Hancock Gr	+64.7★
Keystone S-3	+93.8★	Hedbg-Gordon	+64.7★
One William	+92.7★	Fidelity Cap	+64.5★
Franklin Gr	+92.1★	MIF Growth	+64.5★
Newton	+91.9★	Unifund	+64.0★
BLC Growth	+91.5★	**ALL FUNDS**	**+63.7%**
Growth Ind	+91.2★	Sentinel Gr	+62.8
NEL Growth	+90.8★	Planned Inv	+60.8
Allstate Ent	+90.5★	Anchor Growth	+60.3
Country Cap	+88.7★	Knowledge	+59.5
Colonial Gr	+87.7★	**Beacon Inv**	+59.4
Trustees' Eq	+87.7★	Group-Apex	+57.4
Amer Nat Gr	+86.8★	Windsor	+57.1
Pioneer II	+86.8★	**Continental**	+55.4
Ivest Fund	+86.6★	Brown-Hawaii	+55.0
Mann, Horace	+84.7★	Capital Shares	+53.2
State Street	+84.3★	Value L Fund	+53.1
AMCAP Fund	+84.1★	Eberstadt	+52.8
First Sierra	+82.9★	Wash National	+50.1
Age Fund	+82.4★	Found Growth	+49.5
Aetna Fund	+82.3★	**Inv Guidance**	+47.6
Nat Industries	+82.1★	Fund of Amer	+47.5
Philadelphia	+82.1★	**Drexel Equity**	+41.7
United Accum	+82.0★	Equity Prog	+41.1
Pligrowth	+81.4★	Equity Growth	+40.3
Lincoln Cap	+79.4★	**Prof Portf**	+39.6
Pro Fund	+79.2★	Allen, LB	+39.5
Elfun Trusts	+78.9★	Salem Fund	+37.3
Imperial Cap	+78.9★	Am Birthright	+35.1
Lexington Res	+78.7★	Compass Gr	+32.6
Putnam Growth	+78.1★	Manhattan	+31.4
Scudder Com	+78.1★	Rinfret Fund	+27.1
MEDIAN 1-dcs	+78.1★	**General Sec**	+21.3

FORBES

Forbes ratings, published in its August 15 issue each year and available in most libraries, provide a convenient way to select quality growth and growth-income funds. *Forbes* ratings measure long-term performance meaningfully by rating up and down periods separately. Their major limitations are that worthwhile funds which haven't been in existence through at least two bull and bear markets aren't rated, and the ratings are published only once a year.

Here is a technical explanation of the *Forbes* system.

Forbes rates mutual funds over the last three bull and bear markets if they have been in existence that long. For newer funds they will rate over the last two bull and bear markets. In the case of the 1972 ratings, three bull or bear markets went back to December 31, 1961, while two bull and bear markets started on February 9, 1966. Each fund's performance is compared to the S & P averages in each bull and bear market separately, averaged, and then ranked twice. In up markets, grades A+/A, B, C, or D correspond to the resulting quartile distribution. In down markets, a fund receives a B or better if its performance over the last three down markets bettered the S & P 500. Otherwise, it receives a C, D, or F depending on how poorly it fared. In both the up and down market ratings, the funds were penalized one rank if they failed to perform as well as their average in the latest up and down period respectively.

In order for a fund to be considered, it should score well in both the up-market and down-market ratings. For quality growth funds, I would consider the following ratings acceptable in this order. Each fund gets a pair of ratings.

ACCEPTABLE *FORBES* RATINGS FOR QUALITY GROWTH FUNDS

Up Markets	Down Markets
B	B
A	C
B	C

For growth-income funds, somewhat lower ratings are acceptable because they are less aggressive on the up side and also because *Forbes* excludes dividend yield in their computations. This puts the income funds at a disadvantage relative to the other categories.

**ACCEPTABLE *FORBES* RATINGS FOR
GROWTH-INCOME FUNDS**

Up Markets	Down Markets
C · · · · · · · · · · · B	
D · · · · · · · · · · · A	
D · · · · · · · · · · · B	

These funds all come under the general objective categories of quality growth or growth-income. However, some services— *FundScope* and Wiesenberger in particular—use several subcategories to more precisely define risk and volatility. These include:

> diversified growth
> growth-income
> income-growth
> growth-income-stability
> stability-income-growth
> income
> balanced

With these definitions, the first word denotes the fund's primary objective, or that element emphasized by management. Ideally, the investor should make comparisons among those funds whose goals are most similar.

MCG GUIDELINES DON'T APPLY TO CONSERVATIVE FUNDS

When selecting MCG funds, we paid particular attention to size and cash inflow. These criteria are relatively unimportant in selecting good quality growth or growth-income funds.

Size is unimportant because the quality growth and growth-income funds are, for the most part, buying stocks of larger companies which have millions of shares outstanding. These stocks are liquid, and in any case, these quality growth and growth-income funds do not have the rapid portfolio turnover of the MCG funds.

Cash inflow, while it would certainly aid performance, is not a criterion here. Since quality growth and growth-income funds don't achieve the performance levels that attract massive sums of "hot" money, they almost never receive cash inflows that amount to a significant percentage of existing assets. As a result, new money has an insignificant impact on their performance.

The third criterion, appropriate cash position, is in some cases significant. Quality growth and growth-income funds should not try to call the turns of the market as some MCG funds attempt to do. If there is any uncertainty, they should go to a higher cash position than an MCG fund under the same circumstances. However, this is not a universal rule. Many quality growth and growth-income funds remain relatively fully invested at all times, reasoning that their stocks are inherently less volatile. Others also remain fully invested but switch from stocks to bonds in adverse markets.

DON'T BUY BALANCED FUNDS

Balanced funds have restrictions placed upon them that limit their response to various market conditions. Some, for example, agree to hold a combination of bonds, preferred stocks, and common stocks at all times. Often there is a maximum limitation of 75% for any single type of security. These funds have performed poorly because they can't be 100% invested in common stocks when the market is rising, and they must hold bonds even if bond prices are declining.

Balanced funds arose out of the philosophy that when bonds fall, stocks should hold or rise, and vice versa. While this was historically true, it has not been the case in recent inflationary times. Bond prices declined during the bull markets of the sixties when stocks rose and continued to decline in the last bear market as stock prices fell. As a result, balanced funds have performed poorly in both up and down markets. Investor disenchantment with this poor performance was reflected in shrinking sales. In the early sixties, 30% of all mutual fund sales were in balanced funds; in recent times, only 3%.

If an investor's primary goal is prudent growth with some protection in adverse markets, he should invest in conservative common stock funds that can own any desired proportion of stocks, bonds, or cash. These funds will buy bonds if market conditions indicate. On the other hand, if the investor wants income only, there are bond funds available that will provide substantially higher income yields than balanced funds.

IT'S EASY TO ACHIEVE GOOD RESULTS

Quality growth and growth-income funds are ideal for investors who desire an investment vehicle that performs reasonably well in all kinds of markets and yet doesn't require constant watching; in short, a fund where you can really leave the worrying to the investment manager.

Using past performance as a basic tool, it's easy to select good quality growth or growth-income no-load funds meeting these criteria. With the memory of the 1969–70 bear market still fresh in many people's minds, I made an acid test. My objectives were (1) to determine if the better no-loads were respectable performers under the most adverse conditions and (2) to prove that the investor could readily select them himself.

Since *Forbes* ratings are perhaps the most readily available and their cost is minimal, I used them to illustrate that good performance in the past is likely to continue into the future. I went back to the 1968 *Forbes* ratings and found six no-load funds that rated B or better in both up and down markets. To obtain this rating they had performed well during preceding bull and bear markets. On average, these funds made $100 grow to $238 from 1962 to 1968, an average annual growth rate of 15.5%. Five of these funds were quality growth funds and one was a growth-income fund. They were de Vegh, Guardian, Johnston, Mairs & Power Growth, Penn Square, and T. Rowe Price Growth.

I then examined their subsequent performance into 1971. My ground rules were strict. I assumed that even though the *Forbes* ratings were published in August 1968, no money was invested until December 3, 1968. Then a lump-sum purchase was made in these six funds the day the market reached an all-time high—that is, the day before the bear market started. This money remained fully invested throughout the entire bear market, into better times and, finally, on April 30, 1971, was evaluated.

The results: These funds all performed well. Two of the six B-B funds ranked in the upper 10% of all funds (fourteenth and twenty-fifth); the remaining four were all in the upper half. If $100 had been invested equally in these six funds on December 3, 1968, the investment would have been worth $103 on April 30, 1971. Four of the funds would have shown a profit and two a slight loss. An investment in the best performer would have resulted in an 11.4% gain; the worst, a 2.8% loss. By way of comparison, $100 invested in the 352 funds tabulated by *FundScope* would, on average, have ended as $90.72, showing approximately a 9% loss.

In addition, if the investors in these six funds avoided investing a lump sum on that fateful day in 1968 when the market peaked, they did even better. In fact, investors who dollar-cost averaged showed a substantial profit under the most trying market conditions in years.

BULL MARKET ROUND-TRIP PERFORMANCE
December 3, 1968, to April 30, 1971

	Rank Among 352 Funds	*$100 Ended As*
Rowe Price Growth	14	$111.40
Johnston	25	107.70
Mairs & Power Growth	60	103.10
Guardian	74	101.90
de Vegh	139	97.70
Penn Square	148	97.20
Average Fund	176	90.72

In summary, quality growth and growth-income funds are much easier to select than are MCG funds, and the penalty for a poor selection is small as compared to buying the wrong MCG fund. Ironically, most salesmen sell quality growth or growth-income funds. Since the information needed to buy them intelligently is easy and inexpensive to obtain, it is particularly wasteful to pay a salesman to assist you in making this easy selection.

CHAPTER 11 THE DANGERS OF BUYING NEWLY ORGANIZED FUNDS

In the following discussion, a new fund is defined as an initial offering, the same as a new issue of stock. A fund with a performance record, even a short one, is not considered a new fund.

There are arguments for and against buying new funds. Careful consideration of these arguments indicates that the weight of evidence is against buying them. Of primary importance, new funds—like established funds—can be good, bad, or average; you have to differentiate the good from the bad. When you buy an established fund this is relatively easy. There is a performance record to evaluate. Equally important, it is relatively simple to get an accurate fix on the fund's objective since both its volatility and portfolio can be checked.

With new funds there is no performance record, and you have only the prospectus, which may have vague wording, to go by to determine the fund's objective. Since there are 600 funds whose quality is a matter of record, there is no reason to buy an unknown entity and deny yourself vital analytical advantages.

As you might suspect, there are great variations in the performance of new funds. As a rough indicator, I analyzed the 1971 performance of 31 growth funds started in 1970; they ranked as high as 6 and as low as 490 (out of a total of 526). Similarly, 16 new income funds ranked between 67 and 496 in this list.

The 27 funds started in 1971 had even poorer records in 1972; only three in ten performed above their group averages. Again, the performance range was wide—from a high of 11 to a low of 524.

1972 PERFORMANCE OF FUNDS
First Offered to Public in 1971

Growth Funds	Change	Rank All Funds
Scudder Development	+31.1%	11
Afortress*°	+29.3%	14
Capital Trinity	+16.6%	111
Interfund	+11.1%	233
Americare Growth	+8.5%	274
Average Growth Fund	+9.9%	269
Eagle Growth Shares	+8.4%	317
Heart of America Growth	+8.1%	327
Mutual Benefit Growth	+7.8%	338
Equity Western	+7.7%	341
Mutual Benefit Fund	+5.6%	398
Compustrend Fund	−0.3%	487
First Spectrum Fund	−5.3%	523
Growth-Income Funds		
Pacific Mutual	+16.8%	109
Sentinel Trustees	+16.2%	119
La Salle Fund	+14.5%	160
Average Growth-Income Fund	*+11.4%*	239
Sun Growth	+11.0%	240
Mass. Financial Development	+10.4%	259
Colonial Convertible	+3.5%	441
Shearson Investors	+2.1%	452
Convertible Securities	−5.5%	524
Income Funds		
Average Income Fund	+7.9%	318
Fidelity Bond Debenture	+7.1%	359
Shearson Income	+7.1%	359
Lord Abbot Bond Debenture	+6.1%	387
Neuwirth Income Development	+5.7%	395
First Investors Fund for Income	+4.9%	414
Dreyfus Special Income Fund	+4.8%	417
Pax World	+1.0%	470

° Afortress changed objective in middle of year; it is now an income fund.
NOTE: No-loads are in boldface type.
SOURCE: *Mutual Funds Scoreboard,* capital gains distributions and income dividends added back in.

Should you consider age at all when buying a fund? To see, I examined the age of the top fifty funds in 1971 (roughly the top 10%) and found that if there is any lesson to be learned from fund performance in this period, it is that two-year-old funds are most likely to excel. Twenty-two percent of all two-year-old funds made the top fifty.

Funds organized before 1965 were underrepresented in the top ranks in 1971. This is due partly to the conservative objectives of most funds organized prior to the "go-go" era.

1971 PERFORMANCE BY AGE OF FUND

Year Organized	Total Funds	FUNDS IN TOP FIFTY	
		Number	% Total
1970	60	7	12%
1969	89	20	22%
1968	66	8	12%
1965–67	52	5	10%
1964 or Earlier	284	10	4%
All Funds	551	50	9%

Funds started by experienced management teams probably do better on average; but here, too, there are no guarantees. T. Rowe Price, which has two top funds, initially delivered only average performance with its third endeavor, the New Era Fund.

Of course, the classic example of proven management falling on its face in a new operation was the Manhattan Fund. Investors who bought the Manhattan Fund disregarded one of the basic guidelines of MCG fund selection: buy a small fund. The Manhattan Fund, on the strength of Gerry Tsai's reputation, initially attracted $247 million. Perhaps if it had started smaller it would have performed better.

While some new funds are immediate winners, can you reasonably expect to select them beforehand? Without performance records to analyze, it's a most difficult task.

NEW FUNDS ARE DIFFERENT FROM NEW STOCKS

New funds are *not* like new stock issues. With new stocks, it is often profitable to be in on the ground floor because there is a fixed number of shares available for sale. If demand is great, the price increases since the supply is limited.

This is not true of open-end mutual funds, which can create an unlimited number of new shares as public demand increases. Since all shares are sold at the fund's net asset value, buying early provides no advantage whatsoever.

Some quick arithmetic illustrates this. Assume a fund has $100,000 of assets and 100,000 shares outstanding. Each share is, therefore, worth $1. Now, suppose a new investor wants to purchase 10,000 shares. In the case of an open-end no-load mutual fund, the new investor would also pay $1 per share—the net asset value. Ten thousand new shares would be created; the total asset value of the fund would increase to $110,000; the number of shares would increase by the same percentage; and the per share value for both *old* and new investors would remain the same.

XYZ FUND

	Total Assets	Number of Shares	Price per Share
Originally	$100,000	100,000	$1
New Sale	$ 10,000	10,000	$1
After Sale	$110,000	110,000	$1

Unlike stocks, there is no advantage in buying early. You will always pay net asset value for a share—no more, no less.

PROS AND CONS OF BUYING NEW FUNDS

Advocates of new funds make the following points in favor of buying them:

· · · *There may be a large net cash inflow.* In some cases this can be an advantage; however, there may also be too much of a cash inflow for an inexperienced management team to invest wisely.

· · · *A new fund, with all cash in its coffers, has no mistakes to liquidate.* It hasn't done anything wrong yet. This is an advantage, particularly if the fund is started in the middle of a bear market. On the other hand, it hasn't done anything right yet either. At some point it has to invest the money to produce results.

· · · *The new fund may offer a tax advantage.* If you buy existing successful funds with substantial appreciation, you are buying somebody else's tax liability. This can't happen with a new fund. (A full explanation of tax consequences comes next.)

These advantages do not outweigh the disadvantage of not seeing the performance record.

THE IMPACT OF NEW FUNDS IN THE INDUSTRY

New funds have had a major impact on the industry, as the following 1971 *Wall Street Journal* article attests.

Due partly to $231 million in new fund offerings, the nation's mutual funds moved back into a net sales position in October. The Investment Company Institute, a trade group representing more than 90% of U.S. mutual fund assets, said October (1971) sales were $595.9 million. . . . If the $231 million in sales of new funds are subtracted from October sales, funds would have remained in net redemptions. The Investment Company Institute maintains, however, that at least some investors who bought the new funds probably would have purchased other funds' shares if the new ones hadn't been available.

This article raises an interesting question. Why should almost 40% of all mutual fund sales that month come from new funds? Further checking uncovered the fact that there were three new funds that month—all income funds with a load charge. Yet, in October 1971, a new income fund would have been inferior to many existing income funds that could have been bought with built-in tax losses.

An existing income fund would have a tax loss if its portfolio stocks were either sold at a loss or declined in value below their cost basis. In 1971, this was likely. For example, AT&T common traded between 40¾ and 53⅜ that year. If a fund held Telephone at a cost basis of $60, there was an established tax loss if the stock had been recently sold; or if held, there was a potential tax loss.

New funds have no realized or unrealized appreciation, which may be a reason to buy them in good times. By the same token, they provide no purchasable tax loss either. In 1971, there was a definite tax advantage in buying an existing fund.

Secondly, there is no reason why a new fund should have a greater yield than an existing fund. Let's use Telephone as an example again. In October 1971, the Telephone dividend was yielding 6%. It makes no difference whether you buy an existing fund that already owns Telephone or a new fund that goes out and buys Telephone. In either case, you receive the same 6% dividend.

New funds appear to be unusually popular because investors think "getting in on the ground floor" is advantageous and salesmen, as a result, find them easy to sell. This became evident in 1971 when the Dreyfus Corporation brought out a new fund, the Dreyfus Special Income Fund. In the course of researching this book, I purposely put my name on many prospect lists in order to check fund salesmen's competence. Thus, within a short period of time, three salesmen tried to sell me this new income fund. This puzzled me as I had clearly indicated to each that I was looking for a growth fund. In addition, I noted that the fund had a management fee of ¾ of 1% per annum, which is above average. The fund did not appear desirable as a personal investment.

Why did salesmen push this particular fund? Perhaps because their firms had an underwriting commitment to meet; or possibly the commission was favorable; or they found the fund, with the respected Dreyfus sponsorship, exceptionally easy to sell.

As it turned out, the Dreyfus Special Income Fund was a below-average performer in its first full year. It was up only 4.8% compared to an 8% gain for the average income fund. It ranked 417 among all funds.

There is another reason why salesmen find new load funds easy to sell. The fund's sponsors usually set a limited period of time for the original underwriting. During this period there is no commission, only an underwriting fee. After this period is over, the fund is often closed for sales for forty-five days to two months. This sales tactic, albeit successful, is nothing more than a psychological gimmick to make the offering seem more desirable. The underwriting fee is the same as the load; closing the fund for a short period is done only to force the investor to make a decision before the underwriting period ends. You don't save anything and money can always be invested elsewhere during the closed period.

NEW CLOSED-ENDS

In 1972, closed-end fund sales were $1.2 billion. These funds are initially similar to load funds since their underwriters typically take an 8% sales commission off the top. Inasmuch as closed-end funds have been known to sell at discounts from net asset value, what is the advantage of buying a new closed-end fund? Again, I don't see any particularly cogent reason. Purchasers of these new funds may find they would have done better buying existing funds—either closed-end or open-end.

IN SUMMARY

There are no absolutes in selecting mutual funds, and a few new funds will become instant successes. However, you'll be ahead of the game in the long run if you restrict purchases to funds with at least a year's experience. Let somebody else go through the growing pains with new offerings. See if they go-go first. If they do, you can always buy later—at net asset value.

Furthermore, don't get taken in by new gimmick funds. If a fund wants to specialize in space ventures, peace stocks, low-cost housing stocks, etc., fine! But wait until it demonstrates that it can perform. Finally, don't get excited because a firm with four funds starts a fifth. That's no guarantee of success either. It may have started the new fund because, for one reason or another, the old funds became unsalable.

CHAPTER 12 WHEN TO SELL MUTUAL FUNDS

Most "experts" on mutual funds offer investors the following "conventional" advice: Buy, either in a lump sum or at regular intervals, and hold the fund long term—very long term . . . five years at a minimum and preferably ten or twenty. In other words, "marry" the fund. This is how the sales charge is rationalized and, of course, this advice is in the best interests of the mutual fund industry, whose profits are directly related to the total assets they manage.

These "experts" also offer simple advice as to the best time to buy. The standard injunction is: *now*. Any time is a good time to buy mutual funds. The rationale here is that in the long run you are almost certain to make money. To prove this, fund salesmen go back to the Civil War. They take every possible ten- or fifteen-year period and show that in an overwhelming number of cases, the stock market was higher at the end of each period than at the beginning. Since mutual funds go with the market, the fund industry is so certain of the market's long-term growth—and its own —a few funds will even sell you insurance on this basis. If a fund's value is smaller after ten years (in inflationary dollars, of course), it will pay the insured the difference.

You can, of course, buy a fund now. You can "marry" a fund, and in the long run you will very likely make money. But this is not the way to maximize your profits. It is all-important to realize that intelligent timing in buying and selling no-load mutual funds will enable you to make considerably more money than you could have made by holding even the top fund—load or no-load—over a period of years.

Despite the "conventional" advice, mutual funds (like most investments) should not be bought, locked in a safe-deposit box, and forgotten. Mutual funds should be periodically evaluated and, when necessary, sold for a variety of intelligent reasons.

SELL FOR PERSONAL REASONS

Mutual funds are generally thought of as a nest egg for retirement. And with a great many investors, retirement may be the only reason to sell them. But there are other compelling reasons why this nest egg should be cashed in: to buy a house, to pay unexpected medical bills, to put children through college, even to take an expensive vacation. While funds certainly may be held long term, accept the possibility that you may decide to sell them long before originally anticipated.

Logically, funds should be sold or switched when the investor's objectives change. A person owning an MCG fund may want to switch to a quality growth or a growth-income fund when he retires. On the other hand, an investor owning only quality growth funds and realizing that his financial situation is considerably improved due to a new job, an inheritance, or grown children, may even want to switch a portion of his capital to a more speculative MCG fund. Fortunately, no-loads are a flexible investment vehicle that readily accommodates personal selling decisions.

SELL WHEN PERFORMANCE LAGS

In this game, standing pat is no guarantee of a winning hand. Quality growth and growth-income funds should be sold when long-term performance begins to lag. In recent years, many balanced funds have been hard hit by inflation because the bonds they are committed to hold dropped in value.

An example of this is the Wellington Fund, a large balanced fund whose performance has declined steadily since the fifties. Wellington's ten best years were between 1949 and 1958; during this time, $10,000 invested in the fund grew to $29,666, or an annual compounded return of 11.5%. From that point, it has been downhill for Wellington. For the ten years ending in 1971, the average annual return was only 2.8%. Furthermore, this return came primarily from dividend payout, since the fund had few capital gains to speak of. In the ten years ending in 1972 the fund did somewhat better, primarily because 1972 was a very good year for conservative, cyclical stocks. Still, while its average annual return improved to 4.5%, this is less than the return available from a savings bank.

In a decade of inflation, the Wellington Fund did not achieve its stated objective of conserving principal. Despite this, Wellington still had 209,000 shareholders at the end of 1972. Why so many investors stood pat with Wellington is a mystery to me.

WELLINGTON FUND

Ten Years Ending	$10,000 Grew to	Average Annual Increase	Shareholders at Year End
1958	$29,666	11.5%	262,000
1960	25,871	10.0%	313,000
1962	23,378	8.9%	340,827
1964	21,729	8.1%	357,100
1965	19,822	7.1%	363,400
1966	17,739	5.9%	349,523
1967	20,058	7.2%	326,107
1968	16,844	5.4%	295,000
1969	14,266	3.6%	269,200
1970	14,429	3.8%	266,337
1971	13,208	2.8%	242,799
1972	15,462	4.5%	209,342

SOURCE: Wiesenberger Services, Inc., *Investment Companies, FundScope*. (All distributions reinvested in stock; sales charge deducted from initial investments.)

The Manhattan Fund's long-term performance can only be described as miserable. In the six years ending 1972, it declined 21% even after adding dividends back in. It was one of the seven worst funds in existence during this period. Similarly, in the five years ending 1972, it declined 43%, and in calendar 1972, it declined 3%. In all these three periods every market index showed gains. Despite considerable tax-loss selling, the Manhattan Fund still had 122,000 shareholders at the end of 1972. In my opinion, the remaining shareholders have been far too patient.

Similarly, in the fifties and early sixties, the Dreyfus Fund turned in an outstanding performance and attracted investors who wanted maximum growth. Then, as a result of its good performance, Dreyfus got too large to compete with other MCG funds. In recent years, the Dreyfus Fund, now classified as quality growth, has attained above-average results only in bear markets.

Now, if a Dreyfus shareholder is content with a quality growth fund that only excels defensively, that's one thing. But if he also wants above-average growth in bull markets, he should sell. Apparently most Dreyfus shareholders are content. While the fund's performance was below the average of all funds in 1970–72, there were 452,000 shareholders who continued to hold.

As a general rule, you should sell quality growth and growth-income funds when they rank in the lower half of all funds in their respective categories for an extended period of time—approximately two years. Since the managers of the quality growth and growth-income funds are selling on the basis of long-term performance, they are not promising to make money overnight. Logically, there should be a corresponding long-term commitment on the part of the investor. Poor performance over a short span of time should not be considered sufficient reason to sell.

However, don't make the mistake of "marrying" the fund. Do sell at some point after performance lags. Remember, there are always better-performing funds with the same objective to which the knowledgeable investor can switch.

MCG FUND STANDARDS ARE DIFFERENT

As you might expect, a different strategy applies to selling maximum capital gains funds. There is no great virtue in being patient with an MCG fund when performance has begun to decline. These funds take great risks seeking large profits and sometimes wind up with substantial losses. Long-term commitments here may be foolhardy.

There is another risk in holding MCG funds too long. When performance falters, other shareholders often decide to sell. When redemptions exceed sales by a sizable margin, the likelihood of the fund turning around in the near future is seriously reduced.

There are always alternative funds vying for your money. Even if the lag turned out to be a short-term fluctuation, the odds still favor selling and buying a more aggressive performer.

Here are some specific criteria for selling MCG funds.

Sell a volatile fund that is giving up all its up-market gains in periods of correction. The profits, if any, from this kind of fund will never outweigh the risks of holding it. A good example is provided by Pennsylvania Mutual's summer and fall 1971 performance which illustrates excessive downside volatility. In periods of correction, Pennsylvania Mutual's decline was more than twice that of the NYSE Industrial Index. Since it would take a very good market for this fund to recoup its losses, in this period its risk-reward ratio was decidedly inferior.

PENNSYLVANIA MUTUAL FUND
Percent Changes

	NYSE Ind. Index	Pennsylvania Mutual
Apr. 28–June 22, 1971	−7%	−15%
June 22–July 12	+3%	+5%
July 12–Aug. 9	−8%	−19%
Aug. 9–Sept. 8	+9%	+14%
Sept. 8–Nov. 24	−12%	−27%
Entire Period	−15%	−39%

In this same period of time Nicholas Strong lost only 4.5%.

Sell the erratic performers. A fund may be purchased because it qualifies under all the guidelines, yet it may unaccountably fail to maintain its expected performance. A case in point is the Sherman Dean Fund, which ranked twenty-fifth among all funds and eighth among all no-loads from May to December 1970. After this strong surge, it declined abruptly. By September 1971, Sherman Dean was in the bottom quarter of all funds. Nobody can invest with 100% accuracy. The only recourse with this type of fund is to sell.

Sell when cash position is inappropriate. If you believe the market may turn downward and the fund you own is highly leveraged or even fully invested, disagree with the fund's management and sell. Conversely, if you are bullish but your fund has a high cash position, switch to another fund whose cash position is more appropriate.

Sell to realize a tax loss. The money can easily be switched to another fund, and the government will share a portion of any loss. Note also that since the Tax Reform Act of 1969, it is more advantageous to take short-term losses (under six months) rather than long-term losses. A short-term capital loss is 100% deductible up to $1,000 each year, while a long-term loss is only 50% deductible. With funds (and stocks) it now pays to take losses short-term.

On the other hand, *size itself is not sufficient reason to sell MCG funds.* Some funds continue to turn in good performances even though they are past the $100 million level in total assets, so don't sell until the fund's performance falters.

IN SUMMARY

As a general rule, to substantially improve your investment results, sell funds ranking in the bottom 50% of all funds. In the up-market year of 1972, funds ranking in the top half appreciated from +10% to +68%, while funds ranking in the lower half ranged from +10% to a disheartening −34%. Don't be passive about poor holdings; switch from below-average funds into top-performing funds.

Furthermore, if you now own a below-average load fund, don't feel locked in by the commission. Consider this analogy. You paid a sales commission to buy a car, but that doesn't stop you from selling it when it no longer performs. Similarly, sell funds when they stop performing.

Incidentally, don't equate selling a fund with selling a stock. Many investors quite logically believe that if a stock achieves a certain goal—e.g., doubling or tripling in price—it should be sold. This is a good rule since individual companies seldom go through more than one period of rapid growth. Once this phase is completed, future growth seldom exceeds that of the economy. The stock then becomes a cyclical, and at this point, most investors interested in aggressive growth sell.

Funds are different. A fund is a managed portfolio of stocks and bonds that is constantly changing. A fund should continue to grow as long as the stock market gains. A fund can never become "fully priced" in the same sense as a stock. Therefore, a fund need never be sold because it has increased a given percentage. By the same token, an investor should never hesitate to buy a fund because its per share price has risen substantially. Assuming a long-term rising market, it can continue to grow indefinitely.

SELLING IS EASIER WITH FUNDS

The ability to sell stocks at the proper time is the single greatest factor that separates the professional from the amateur investor. Professionals understand that paper losses are real losses and accept the fact that it is better to take losses while they are small. They are also quick to sell if performance lags because they have preselected other stocks as candidates for purchase to cover this sure-to-happen eventuality. For example, T. Rowe Price Associates keeps a list of about 200 stocks from which to select investments for their funds and private clients. Since the key to successful investing is to be in the best possible stocks at all times, the pros have set up systems to achieve this goal. They work from a small list of alternatives. Psychologically they are attuned to taking action at the proper time, which makes them winners.

In contrast to the pros, most amateurs do not think or act this way. Instead, they nurture the often unrealistic hope that their losing stocks will come back so they can break even . . . they hope there will be better news in the future . . . they think perhaps suckers will bid the price of a stock back up . . . commission costs deter them from selling . . . most important of all, they either never consider the alternatives or they fail to evaluate them properly.

With funds, most of these reasons for inaction are eliminated. If you select no more than a half-dozen top-performing no-load MCG funds to follow, this brings your decision-making process down to manageable size. If a fund you own falters and another's performance is superior, you are presented with a simple, actionable decision. You don't have to worry about commission costs. You know that if an MCG fund drops out of the top rankings, it is unlikely to come back in the near future. And even if it did,

it should be dropped from your list because of its obvious inconsistent performance.

In addition, there is another interesting difference between
funds and stocks. Investing in a fund is usually a continuing
process over a period of time. Furthermore, funds sell fractional
shares and, from time to time, make distributions that are usually
reinvested in more shares. As a result, you are never quite as
aware of your cost basis as you would be with stocks. Your sell
decisions can be made more painlessly if the irrelevant cost is no
longer a factor.

With funds, you can act more professionally since you have
narrowed your alternatives and eliminated most of the psychological hang-ups that prevent investors from making money in
stocks.

If you take this professional attitude, you can invest in "hot"
funds with relative safety. Investment experts have always warned
against these hot funds because their performance lags after a
short time. This is logical advice if your thinking is confined to
load funds. However, with no-loads there is a strong argument
favoring the hot funds. The potential is far greater, while the risk
is not much more if you can discipline yourself to sell at the op-
portune time.

HOW DISTRIBUTIONS AFFECT BUY/SELL DECISIONS

Another important trick of mutual fund timing is to buy immediately after capital gains and dividend income are distributed.
There will be a definite tax advantage in doing so.

In the case of mutual funds, a distribution of either realized
capital gains or dividend income doesn't benefit the shareowner.
Here's why. Let's say a fund, over the year, has accumulated
dividends of 25¢ a share and realized capital gains of 75¢ a share,
a total of $1. Since funds enjoy a tax advantage if they act as
conduits by distributing at least 90% of these dividends, they will
generally do so. In this way, the distributions aren't taxed twice.
Only the shareholder pays. (In contrast, corporate profits are
taxed at two levels: once as corporate earnings and again when
dividends are paid to shareholders.)

Let's assume it's now time for the fund to distribute profits. The fund is selling at $10 a share. It goes ex-dividend and, since funds are always priced at net asset value, the per share price immediately drops to $9. The investor will then receive a check for $1 per share of distributions or, if he is reinvesting, a notice that his account has been credited with additional shares. In either case, the sum of the current value ($9) and the distributions is still $10. The distributions have not provided any real benefit to either new or existing shareholders; only a tax liability has been incurred.

The long-term shareholders should rightfully pay tax on these distributions because they shared in the growth that made them possible. But this is not true of a shareholder who bought shortly before the distribution was declared. He has only the tax liability.

The SEC and the NASD have declared it improper for a salesman to recommend that an investor purchase a fund just before the record date in order to receive the distribution. So heed their advice and don't buy just before the distribution. It doesn't make any financial sense.

How do you know when there will be a distribution? If you're buying a no-load you'll have to dig out the information yourself. *FundScope* and Wiesenberger's *Mutual Funds Panorama* provide approximate payout dates or you can ask the funds directly. Capital gains are usually paid once a year between November and February. Dividends may be paid annually, semiannually, or quarterly. The trend among MCG funds—where dividends are small—has been toward yearly payouts at the same time as the capital gains are distributed. Some funds, Weingarten for one, send a letter to their shareholders giving the payout date and suggest they wait until after that time before making any further purchases.

Tax consequences may also affect the timing of a sale of fund shares. If you're an investor who receives more than $100 a year in dividends, you might consider selling just before an income distribution. In this way the dividend income, instead of being taxed at ordinary rates, is converted into a capital gains distribution. Providing the fund has been held six months, it is then taxed at the lower long-term rates.

REINVEST DISTRIBUTIONS

Unless you need the current income, reinvest all dividend and capital gains distributions. If you don't, you lose the compounding effect, a major source of potential profits. The privilege of automatic reinvestment is one of the major advantages funds have over stocks. Take advantage of it.

One final tax tip. Don't forget that both dividends and capital gains distributions when automatically reinvested become part of your cost basis. For tax purposes, it's as if the fund had sent you checks for the amounts due and you cashed the checks and then returned the money to buy additional shares. And, of course, you paid taxes on each distribution the following April.

Here, for example, are the final tax consequences of a ten-year gain through December 1972 on an investment of $10,000 in the T. Rowe Price Growth Fund.

Value of shares initially purchased	$23,408
Value of shares acquired by reinvestment of dividends	4,080
Value of shares acquired by reinvestment of capital gains	5,622
Total Value of Investment After 10 Years	$33,110

While the only money the investor actually paid to the fund during the ten years was the initial $10,000, if he redeemed his shares on December 29, 1972, he should list as his cost:

Initial investment—Jan. 1, 1963	$10,000
Dividends used to purchase shares	2,680
Capital gains distributions used to purchase shares	3,903
Total Cost Basis	$16,583

Thus, although his original investment of $10,000 is now larger by $23,110, the capital gain he has to report for tax purposes is only $16,527 (the difference between $16,583 and $33,110). Taxes on the balance of the gains have already been paid.

CHAPTER 13 MAKING THE MOST OF MARKET CYCLES

There are two facets to successful investing in stocks: (1) selecting the right stocks and (2) achieving the proper timing. An investor buying individual stocks is confronted with both problems. And to achieve proper timing he must not only evaluate the over-all market cycles, he must also determine whether his stock will move with them.

Successful mutual fund investing is inherently simpler. The fund investor eliminates one of the major problems; he can leave the difficult chore of stock selection to fund managers while he watches the market trends.

BEAR MARKET STRATEGY: CONSERVATIVE VERSUS SPECULATIVE FUNDS

Mutual funds are basically designed as long-term investments, and the conventional advice always has been not to sell them in a bear market. If you are a conservative or middle-of-the-road investor holding quality growth or growth-income funds, it is acceptable advice for a number of reasons.

First of all, since nobody knows how long a bear market will run, or how deep it will fall, the best course of action for the investor holding quality stocks or funds is simply to ride out the down period. This is a viable course of action with quality growth and growth-income funds because while their performance is relatively unspectacular, it is usually consistent. Unlike MCG funds, quality growth or growth-income funds that performed well in the last bull market will generally perform well in the next bull market.

Secondly, the quality growth and growth-income funds will decline somewhat less than the MCG funds in a bear market, minimizing any losses from forced sales.

SELL MCG FUNDS IN BEAR MARKETS

In the sixties, MCG funds were sold as long-term investments. Investors were told that the advantages of diversification and the long-term record of growth were so overwhelming that temporary setbacks in a bear market could be ignored. With the experience of the 1969–70 bear market behind us, we know this advice was wrong.

MCG funds should be sold in a bear market. They lack defensive capability. The speculative stocks they hold can take terrible beatings. In 1969–70, the average performance fund rated by *FundScope* declined 49% as compared to a 36% drop in the market averages. This performance is particularly disastrous because when a fund declines 50%, it has to gain 100% in order to return to its original value.

Equally important, funds that led the lists in the last bull market are highly unlikely to do so again.

THE ENTERPRISE STORY

This is a classic example of how MCG fund investors failed to profit because of poor timing. While Enterprise was the number-one fund in the soaring sixties, few people investing in Enterprise in that period achieved the same results that the fund did. Most investors bought too late and sold too late, or just stood pat.

In three of the four years prior to 1967, Enterprise, under the name of Convertible Securities and Growth Fund, placed in the top 10% of all funds without attracting a great deal of attention. As late as December 1966, it had only 4,300 shareholders. It was in 1966 that Fred Carr joined the fund as portfolio manager.

Shortly thereafter, Enterprise became a household word when it gained 117% in 1967—number one among all funds available to the public. However, only the 4,300 shareholders from 1966 received the full benefit of this 1967 gain.

But in 1967, the fund added 30,000 new investors who shared in these huge profits, and it jumped from $28 million to $247 million in total assets.

ENTERPRISE FUND

| | Change in Per Share Value | AT YEAR END | |
		Number of Shareholders	Total Net Assets in Millions
1963	+28%	1,700	$ 3.3
1964	+25%	2,000	6.1
1965	+43%	3,000	17.2
1966	+4%	4,300	28.6
1967	+117%	34,574	247.0
1968	+44%	170,000	953.0
1969	−26%	237,000	769.7
1970	−26%	204,000	448.8
1963–70	+303%		

SOURCE: Wiesenberger Services, Inc., *Investment Companies*

Through 1968, more people bought Enterprise; at year end there were 170,000 shareholders. These people also profited, receiving some of the 44% increase recorded that year. The fund had not yet become completely unwieldy. Then in 1969, Enterprise, like most other MCG funds, registered a substantial decline of −26%.

However, a very strange thing happened that year. The number of Enterprise shareholders increased by 67,000. This means that substantially more than 67,000 investors bought Enterprise that year because some investors were redeeming their shares at the same time. Some sold in 1969 because of the market decline and because Enterprise was having administrative problems. There were also questions raised about the fund's holdings of letter stock; in fact, Enterprise was sued by Norman F. Dacey, the estate planner, on this score.

Why did so many people buy an MCG fund in the face of an apparent bear market and possible internal difficulties? Probably because they didn't realize the fund's 1967 and 1968 bull market performance was now meaningless and MCG funds should be sold in bear markets. Whatever the reason, a lot of people bought the wrong fund at the wrong time. And they all lost money. Some cut their losses, selling out during 1970. But the vast majority—probably 200,000—hung in for the full year, taking another 26% beating.

While Enterprise grew 303% between 1963 and 1970, no more than 1,400 investors actually held Enterprise long enough to realize that profit. All those investors who bought on January 1, 1968 (receiving the 44% gain that year), were still 21% behind at the end of 1970—three years later. Some investors bought too late, but most made the mistake of not selling in a bear market. It's incredible! Here's the greatest mutual fund success story of the decade, and yet the investors who actually made money in Enterprise are rare indeed.

Eventually, the losers should recoup, but perhaps not as fast as if they had switched to another fund. With Fred Carr gone, the fund now has a new orientation. Enterprise no longer looks for emerging growth situations. The fund, now managed by William Elliott, is run more like a typical large fund. There are only about 130 stocks in the portfolio, compared to as many as 430 in the late sixties, and, says Mr. Elliott, "the accent is on companies that are well financed and can get more financing if needed."

A CLICHÉ TO SUCCESS—"BUY LOW AND SELL HIGH"

The ultimate in successful fund investing would be simply to buy MCG funds in bull markets and switch to cash in bear markets. But to achieve this ultimate, the investor has to know whether he is in a bull or a bear market.

There are numerous guidelines for recognizing bear markets: the Dow Theory; volume indicators; the number of stocks posting highs and lows; contrary theories, e.g., the odd-lotter is always wrong; and numerous economic and monetary indicators. However, most investors fail to profit from these guidelines. The point is made most graphically when we analyze buy and sell activity in stocks.

The way to make money, the old cliché goes, is to buy stocks when they are low and sell when they are high. This cliché is now a joke, because few investors are sure when stocks are low or high. The strange thing, though, is that people do a disproportionately large share of their investing when the market is high.

When the market reaches new highs, brokers become ebullient. They're on the phone continuously, and the message is buy, buy, buy. Street-level brokerage board rooms are filled to capacity at lunchtime. Tip sheets take more and more advertising space in financial sections; the popular press talks about how strong the market is. Ironically, the higher the market, the greater the likelihood that the average investor will buy.

Conversely, when the market is at its lowest, brokers are discouraged and seldom phone, the papers are full of gloomy news and pessimistic forecasts. In this atmosphere, investors, despairing that prosperity will ever return, seldom buy.

Mutual fund buyers are no different. The all-time mutual fund sales record came at the end of 1968, just as the market reached a high. On the other hand, at market bottoms, mutual fund sales are at far lower levels.

These classic patterns may be changing. After good gains in 1971 and 1972, stock prices declined severely in 1973 without the usual signs of a bull market topping out. A probable reason is the market was dominated by the institutions throughout the entire period, with small investors notably absent.

The euphoria associated with market peaks was evident, though, among professional money managers. Indicative of their enthusiasm, *Barron's* had as its major feature on January 1, 1973, a roundtable discussion between its editors and ten experts from the world of finance. The headline for the series was: "Not a Bear Among Them—Our Panel Is Bullish on Wall Street, Business and the Market." The panel went on to predict 1,200–1,300 on the Dow for 1973. Instead, the market began to slide.

STRATEGIES FOR CYCLICAL MARKETS

Long-term investors in conservative funds can simply ignore market cycles. Investors in speculative MCG funds cannot. This book presents three strategies for the investor who wants above-average returns from his investments. All three strategies are designed to eliminate severe losses by replacing indecision and inertia with a self-disciplining system with built-in buy and sell points. Choose the system you will be most comfortable with, the one that best fits your temperament.

The first method is dollar-cost averaging, which is principally a conservative investing technique but one that can be used by MCG fund investors to good advantage, too. The second method is to set a stop-loss on funds, in the same manner stocks are stop-lossed. The third method involves switching between conservative and speculative funds depending on the market outlook.

DOLLAR-COST AVERAGING

There is one investing strategy that avoids the pitfalls just discussed by forcing the investor to buy when prices are low—dollar-cost averaging. It is an eminently satisfactory method of investing when followed over the long term, in this case, five years or longer. While dollar-cost averaging does not guarantee profits, it can make money for the long-term mutual fund investor when the long-term market trend is up, and, in many cases, even if the long-term trend of the market is level. It can also minimize losses if the long-term trend of the market is down.

Dollar-cost averaging is simply a system of buying equal *dollar* amounts of securities (not equal numbers of shares) at regular intervals, regardless of price levels. This reduces risks because shares are bound to be purchased at varied price levels and the investor obtains more shares for his money when the prices are low than when they are high.

Here are some hypothetical examples illustrating how this tactic can make money for the investor. First let's assume the market and the fund decline and then return to their original levels. Hypothetically, $100 is invested every month. In the first month, ten shares costing $10 each were acquired. In the next month, the per share price declined to $9, and 11.1 shares were purchased. In succeeding months, the price of the shares dipped to $7 and $100 bought a greater number of shares. Then, the market turned up and fewer shares were bought as the price gradually returned to $10. At this point, the investor who had dollar-cost averaged found that he owned 81.5 shares, which had cost him on average $8.59 per share. With the shares again worth $10, he had made a 16% profit (page 172).

Note that at any given time, the total value of the accumulated shares is determined by the per share price at the time. In the above example, there were months in which the investor had a loss.

In the previous illustration, the per share price declined $3 and came back. Now let's take a case of a rising market, in which the per share price started at $10 and rose gradually to $13 over six months (page 173).

As the months passed, fewer shares were acquired because the per share price increased. While the July value was $13, the total profit was still less than in the previous example, only 12%. The reason: there was less fluctuation in the period. Surprising as it may seem, fluctuations in price can produce greater profits than long-term growth alone.

For this reason, it is more profitable to dollar-cost average with MCG funds than it is with less volatile quality growth or growth-income funds—although the exposure to risk is far greater.

In our first example, the fund declined from $10 to $7 and then returned to $10, providing the investor with a 16% profit. If this same fund had exhibited greater volatility, declining to $5 before coming back to $10, and the investor had dollar-cost averaged at regular intervals, his profit would have been substantially greater, 34%. This is because the average price paid would have been $7.45, not $8.59 (page 174).

However, some MCG funds recoup very slowly after bear markets. Even with these funds, dollar-cost averaging makes sense. Hypothetically, if an investment program were started in an MCG fund when it was selling for $10 per share, and equal dollar com-

HOW DOLLAR-COST AVERAGING WORKS

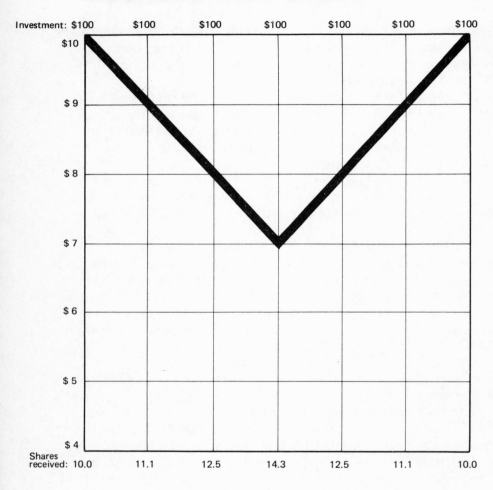

Investment: $100 $100 $100 $100 $100 $100 $100

Shares received: 10.0   11.1   12.5   14.3   12.5   11.1   10.0   Total 81.5

Summary		
	Per share	Total
Cost	$ 8.59	$700.00
End value	$10.00	$815.08
Profit	$ 1.41	$115.08 or +16%

HOW DOLLAR-COST AVERAGING WORKS IN
A RISING MARKET

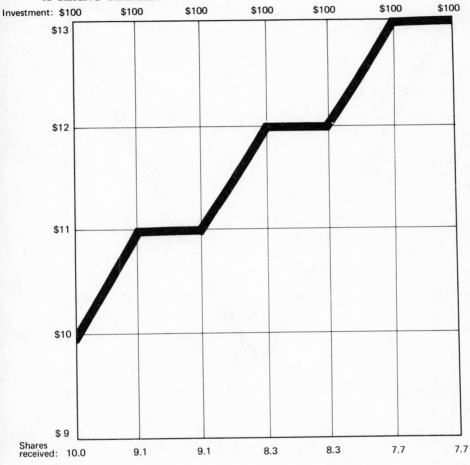

Investment: $100 $100 $100 $100 $100 $100 $100

							Total
Shares received: 10.0	9.1	9.1	8.3	8.3	7.7	7.7	60.2

Summary

	Per share	Total
Cost	$11.62	$700.00
End Value	$13.00	$783.04
Profit	$ 1.38	$ 83.04 or 12%

DOLLAR-COST AVERAGING WITH MORE VOLATILE FUNDS

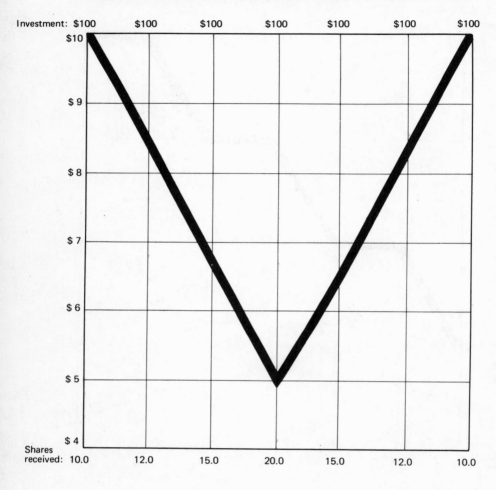

Investment: $100 $100 $100 $100 $100 $100 $100

Shares received: 10.0   12.0   15.0   20.0   15.0   12.0   10.0   Total 94.0

Summary

	Per share	Total
Cost	$ 7.45	$700.00
End value	$10.00	$939.96
Profit	$ 2.55	$239.96 or +34%

DOLLAR-COST AVERAGING WITH A FUND THAT
DOESN'T COMPLETELY RECOUP

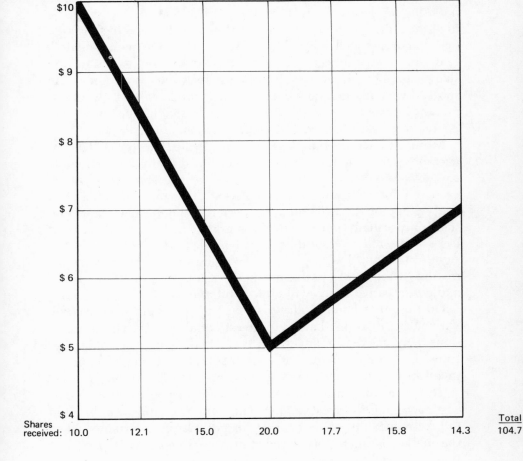

Investment:	$100	$100	$100	$100	$100	$100	$100	
Shares received:	10.0	12.1	15.0	20.0	17.7	15.8	14.3	Total 104.7

Summary		
	Per share	Total
Cost	$6.68	$700.00
End value	$7.00	$733.24
Profit	$0.32	$ 33.24 or +5%

mitments were continued as the fund declined to $5, and then went back to only $7, there would still be a 5% profit (page 175).

For dollar-cost averaging to work, the investor must make periodic purchases—even when the market is at its lowest. If the investor fails to carry a program of dollar-cost averaging through bad markets as well as good, its purpose will have been defeated.

If dollar-cost averaging is continued over a long period and shares are bought at various prices, dollar-cost averaging will succeed virtually independent of market trends. In fact, the greatest advantage of dollar-cost averaging is that it makes market fluctuations work for the investor, not against him.

Mutual funds are the ideal investment medium for dollar-cost averaging since equal sums of money in virtually any amount—e.g., $25, $50, $100 monthly—can easily be invested. In addition, each purchase represents a completely diversified investment at every stage of the accumulation period. Equally important, mutual funds usually move with the market. In the vast majority of cases, they will recoup after a bear market. However, don't lose sight of the fact that dollar-cost averaging's profitability is wholly related to the fund's performance. Investors in speculative funds and conservative funds will obtain different results.

On the other hand, dollar-cost averaging doesn't work as well with stocks. It is just harder to invest equal dollars. The commissions may make the investment of small sums uneconomical. Individual stocks might not come back after a long decline, as investors who have averaged down sometimes find to their sorrow.

This discussion has centered on the ways you can use dollar-cost averaging to invest money. The same principles can be used to take money out of the market. In periods of uncertainty when the market is high, partial redemptions spaced over a period of time may well be preferable to a lump-sum sale.

FEW INVESTORS DOLLAR-COST AVERAGE

When mutual fund sales statistics are examined, it becomes obvious that few investors dollar-cost average. Since the advantages of dollar-cost averaging are great, I find it difficult to understand why more investors do not adopt it as their basic investment strategy. I am sure that most investors are familiar with the method. Every investment book discusses it; every salesman explains its advantages. But people don't do it.

Perhaps one reason is that dollar-cost averaging has all the glamour and excitement of a payroll deduction plan. In short, despite its advantages, many investors find it a dull, unchallenging way to invest. And like payroll plans, dollar-cost averaging is a technique primarily used to invest relatively small sums saved from current income.

However, many people have large sums—from the sale of stock, bonus money, etc.—to be invested. If they don't want to buy lump sum, dollar-cost averaging can be used, particularly when the market outlook is uncertain. The sum ultimately to be invested can be divided into portions; one part—perhaps half—can be invested immediately, with the balance spread over the period of uncertainty. If prices rise, at least part of the cash was invested at lower levels; and if prices decline, money remains to be invested at the more advantageous levels.

Investors who are technically oriented (i.e., those who have studied charting principles) might consider dollar-cost averaging part of their capital by spacing buy decisions according to the market's technical action. For example, if the market is drifting with no apparent direction, no purchases would be made. Then if there was a breakout on the upside, a portion of the funds available could be invested. If there was a breakout downward, purchases might be made when the market had corrected a predetermined percentage (e.g., 50% of the previous rise) or had again reversed direction.

STOP-LOSS MCG FUNDS

The second option is to sell an MCG fund when it declines a certain percentage. This is analogous to putting in a stop-loss order on a stock. Here is how one "expert" has used the stop-loss technique. Fundpack is a multifund, investing solely in other funds; its managers are "professional" mutual fund investors.

Fundpack has publicly announced that it will sell any funds in its portfolio that decline more than 10% from any point—and buy back after a 10% rise or unusual positive newsbreak.

It did a hypothetical study proving that this method would produce far better results than leaving money in a fund continuously. In brief, the study imagined twenty-four investments of $10,000 each in twelve funds; each fund was allocated two investments for a total of $20,000 per fund. One $10,000 package was left in each fund. This investment was compared with the results that would have been recorded with the other $10,000 following the 10% guide—that is, buy on a 10% rise, sell on a 10% drop. The test period started with the stock market low of October 22, 1957, and ran to June 30, 1971, a 164-month period with many ups and downs.

THEORETICAL STUDY BY FUNDPACK
Using the Stop-Loss Technique

Funds	The Stay-in $10,000 Becomes	The In-out $10,000 Becomes
Keystone S-4	$ 43,559	$125,056
Dreyfus	42,854	67,586
T. Rowe Price Growth Stock	42,661	52,532
Putnam Growth*	38,305	92,590
Chemical Fund	37,966	57,415
Chase of Boston*	37,241	103,999
Investment Co. of America	37,101	48,953
Johnston Mutual	36,479	38,236
Massachusetts Growth	36,154	63,516
Affiliated	26,405	33,782
Colonial Growth	26,054	58,918
Scudder, Stevens & Clark Common	24,366	37,737
Total	$429,145	$780,320

* Started several months late.

Fundpack concluded that in-out investing wins each test: by 5% with the Johnston Mutual Fund, by 187% with Keystone S-4, and by an average margin of 82% in the twelve tests.

Fundpack has put its theories to practical test. The fund invoked its mechanical rule several times in 1971 and 1972, liquidating major portions of its portfolio. Interestingly though, it hasn't been rigid about its re-entry guidepost. Fundpack was 87% in cash on August 5, 1971, just prior to President Nixon's announcement of Phase One of his wage-price controls program. In view of the unusual nature of the news, Fundpack disregarded its 10%-rise-before-re-entry rule and reinvested immediately.

The great advantage of stop-lossing is that it eliminates the possibility of catastrophic loss (-50% or more) in a bear market or as a result of sharply eroding performance. The primary disadvantage is that on occasion the investor will be whipsawed—that is, the fund will be sold in an intermediate term decline only to have the market and the fund suddenly turn up.

Fundpack's guideposts have been the subject of a fair amount of controversy in the fund industry. One advisory service—*Fund Investment Engineering*—noted that the 10% stop-loss policy resulted in a number of whipsaws in 1972. It proposed that additional studies should be made on 8%, 10%, and 14% in and out, and also on 10% out and 6% back in, 12%/5% and 14%/10% to see if results would improve.

Fundpack replied to *Fund Investment Engineering*'s criticism, noting that 1971 and 1972 might be unusual because the Nixon Administration rescued the market from at least three intermediate declines: (1) Nixon's wage-price control speech, August 1971, (2) Kissinger's currency stabilization, Thanksgiving 1971, and (3) Federal Reserve supporting foreign exchange, July 1972. Fundpack termed such rescues unprecedented and felt whatever losses its shareholders suffered in liquidating and rebuying funds were "insurance premiums" and well worth it. However, after defending its policy, Fundpack shortly thereafter revised its guidelines to 14%/10%.

A different formula along the same lines is advocated by Melvin Roebuck. His research indicates using 12% out and 50% back in to minimize whipsaw. Roebuck's guidelines mean that if a fund declined 40% in a bear market it would have to rebound 20% (or half) before it would again be considered buyable. While waiting for a 50% rise certainly prevents being fooled by bear market rallies, it also means forgoing more bull market profits than under less stringent guidelines.

Despite its limitations, I believe stop-lossing MCG funds makes prudent investing sense. I would, however, recommend that a 12% to 14% figure be used on the downside, and on the upside, 10% or when an unusual positive newsbreak occurs.

BULL/BEAR MARKET SWITCHING

The stop-loss method will work for some investors, but the fact is that most investors—in stocks or in funds—do not sell in anticipation of a bear market; they remain fully invested at all times. For these investors, there is an alternative way of investing in MCG funds with relative safety. It is a plan that falls between unglamorous dollar-cost averaging and the difficult feat of going to cash in bear markets. While it does require some ability to recognize market cycles, it can work well in the face of considerable uncertainty since its goals need not be fully attained for it to be profitable.

The plan entails doing with no-load mutual funds what many sophisticated investors do with stocks: buy aggressive stocks in an apparent bull market, then switch to defensive stocks if the market's direction is uncertain.

The same thing can be done very easily with no-load mutual funds. Buy aggressive MCG funds if you are confident the market is rising; switch to conservative funds if you are worried that the market may turn down. This procedure can be much more profitable than being fully invested at all times in either type of fund.

An examination of mutual fund performance data from December 3, 1968, through April 30, 1971, explains the theory behind this strategy. FundScope, which calls this type of analysis a "bull market round trip," has figures available for this market cycle.

If you held the average mutual fund throughout this period, you would have lost 9% of your investment; if you held the average performance fund, your investment would have declined 25%. If you owned the average growth-income fund in this same period, you would have been better off, but still down 2%.

On the other hand, if you held the average growth-income fund in the bear market and the average performance fund in the bull market segment, *you would have made a 10% profit!*

BULL MARKET ROUND TRIP
% Gain and Loss

	12/3/68– 5/26/70	5/26/70– 4/30/71	$100 Ended As
Avg. Mutual Fund	−37%	+51%	$ 91
Avg. Performance Fund	−49%	+59%	$ 75
Avg. Growth-Income Fund (Flexibly Diversified)	−31%	+50%	$ 98
Growth-Income—Down	−31%		
Performance—Up		+59%	$110
NYSE Composite Index	−38%	+52%	$ 94

Let's take some specific examples using funds that were above-average performers. If you held the Babson Fund on the way down and New Horizons (the nineteenth-ranked fund) in the up period, you would have finished the period with a 32% gain. Similarly, owning de Vegh in the bear market and Afuture (#2) in the subsequent bull market would have resulted in a tremendous 68% profit. By way of comparison, the best single fund was up only 23% in this bull market round trip.

BULL MARKET ROUND TRIP
% Gain and Loss

	12/3/68– 5/26/70	5/26/70– 4/30/71	$100 Ended As
Babson—Down	−26%		
New Horizons—Up		+79%	$132
de Vegh—Down	−28%		
Afuture—Up		+133%	$168
Best Single Fund	−16%	+48%	$123

While the above examples (switching at the exact top and bottom) are, of course, strictly hypothetical, they demonstrate that a combination of two funds—one aggressive, one defensive—is likely to be superior to any single fund in negotiating the market cycle. This held true when both average and top funds were compared.

Needless to say, in practice, few investors, if any, would actually have timed their switches to coincide exactly with major turning points in the market. Actual results would depend on the exact point in the market cycle that funds were switched. Here are the de Vegh–Afuture results recomputed by introducing a time lag at both the top and bottom of the stock market cycle.

First assume the investor owned an "old favorite" MCG fund in 1968 which was sold in January 1969 after it declined 10%. Then, following the plan, the money was switched into de Vegh until October 7, 1970 (four months after the bear market had ended). At this point, Afuture was bought, held, and evaluated on April 30, 1971.

Under these more realistic conditions, $100 grew to $131 in less than two and a half years. Thus, under the most trying market conditions, the combination of a conservative and aggressive fund produced a better result than any single fund, and a substantially better result than the savings bank.

Specifically, the gain was achieved this way. The "old favorite" fund was sold on January 31, 1969, two months after the high point of the market. (In preparing this example I found great disparity in the rate of decline in the first stages of a bear market. Individual MCG funds declined from 2% to 13% in this two months. Enterprise, for example, was off 3.5%. Rather than pick a fund that might be atypical, an arbitrary 10% decline in the fund was assumed in this period.)

On January 31, 1969, it was decided to switch to de Vegh, which had declined only 2% up to that point. De Vegh lost another 26% in the down market and then gained 25% in the first four months of the subsequent up market. At that point, Afuture, up 50% in the same four months, had demonstrated superior growth potential. Therefore, on October 7, 1970, the money was switched to Afuture, which gained another 56% to end at $131.

ADVANTAGES OF THE BULL/BEAR MARKET PLAN

· · · The risk-reward ratio is very favorable, particularly if the plan is approached conservatively. Assume that you own MCG funds in the bull market, and fearing a downturn, you switch to a growth-income fund. If you are right, you have saved a significant amount of money. If you acted prematurely, you will lose only a portion of the potential profits realized by staying in the MCG fund. That is a small price to pay.

· · · The temptation to stay with the MCG fund too long is less than if the alternative is cash. The fact is that very few investors sell at the top of the market. However, you can switch to a quality growth or growth-income fund at any time, knowing you are still in the market and invested wisely.

· · · You eliminate the whipsaw problem.

· · · It is much easier to switch from aggressive to defensive funds than it is to do the same with stocks. With funds, you can simply concentrate your thinking on the market's direction since funds almost always follow the averages. With stocks, you have to evaluate the market and then consider the price trend of individual stocks. This is substantially more difficult.

· · · While this switching theoretically can be done with load funds, as a practical matter, the commission penalty for switching load funds would inhibit most investors from putting the plan into action. Thus, it is almost mandatory that you use no-loads if you wish to follow this switching strategy.

· · · This plan can be used with the package-of-funds concept, in conjunction with a varying cash position, and also with dollar-cost averaging.

INVESTING IN A PACKAGE OF FUNDS

Most sophisticated fund investors own a package of funds. For investors interested in growth, I recommend owning a minimum of two no-load funds, generally an MCG fund and a quality growth fund. Depending on your financial circumstances, somewhere between 25% and 75% of your money should be allocated to MCG funds, the balance to quality growth or possibly growth-income funds.

Owning two or more funds makes sense because it doesn't cost any more, and you have the benefits of additional diversification and more management expertise serving you. And, if you buy funds with different objectives, you also have a safer play in the market.

However, don't go overboard in the other direction. Buying funds is different from buying stocks. Individual investors with less than $100,000 in the market do not need more than four funds. No meaningful diversification is achieved after this point, and it becomes harder to achieve superior results.

Here is how bull/bear market timing can be used by an investor owning two funds.

A typical investor who could use this plan might be a 30- to 55-year-old businessman or professional with $10,000 to $100,000 in the market and with adequate current income. The plan would involve switching between two funds—a speculative MCG fund and a conservative fund—and cash.

First of all, our investor would keep at least 40% of his assets in a conservative fund—either quality growth or growth-income—at all times. In a healthy bull market, the other 60% would be invested in a MCG fund. As the bull market begins to mature, half (30%) would be switched from the MCG fund to the more conservative fund. Then, if there is any indication of the bull market's topping out, the MCG fund would be sold and all the money put in the conservative fund. When the market actually turns downward, some of the shares in the conservative fund would be liquidated and the money would be put in the bank.

The cycle reverses when the bull market ends. In the initial stages of the new bull market, cash would be gradually reinvested in the conservative fund. Then, as the bull market grows stronger, a portion of the money would be switched back into an MCG fund, in most cases a new one. At most points in the cycle, the investor is more or less fully committed to mutual funds. Psycho-

BULL MARKET ROUND TRIP

Point in Market Cycle	FUNDS		Cash
	MCG	Conservative	
A	60%	40%	
B	30%	70%	
C		100%	
D		70%	30%
E		100%	
F	30%	70%	
G	60%	40%	

logically, it is easier to switch to more conservative funds than to cash.

The full cycle, over major bull and bear markets, would take typically two to four years to complete. It would cover a variation of 200 to 300 points in the Dow Jones Industrial Average.

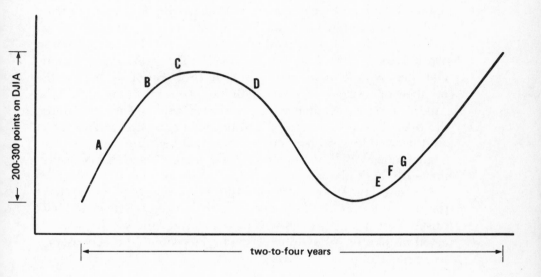

COMBINING THE SYSTEM WITH DOLLAR-COST AVERAGING

The bull/bear market strategy can easily be combined with dollar-cost averaging. Simply hold at least two funds—a speculative MCG fund and a conservative quality growth or growth-income fund. If you are bullish, make your regular payment into the MCG fund. If you are cautious, or bearish, invest in the more conservative fund.

INVESTING IN YOUR FUTURE

In this chapter I presented three methods of market timing because I find no single method works well for everyone. My own personal preference is for the third method, the bull/bear strategy combined with dollar-cost averaging. I prefer this method because while I have never found a consistently reliable way of predicting market cycles, I can assess the risks of holding various funds quite accurately. By paying close attention to volatility measures and cash position ratios—and by not trying for the last dollar—I find bull/bear timing a realistic method of optimizing profit while minimizing risk.

One day in the not-too-distant future, the Dow is going to break 1,100, 1,200, 1,300—you name it. The professional money managers will be unanimously bullish; brokers will be happy; the number of margin accounts will be at an all-time high. The American Stock Exchange daily volume will exceed 10 million; the over-the-counter market will be boiling. There will be 1,584 advisory services; 85 new go-go funds will be in registration. And Eliot Janeway will announce that the market has reached a permanently high plateau.

On that day, when everyone else's head is in the clouds, that's the day to follow the bull/bear market strategy. Sell your MCG funds, find a sluggish growth-income fund, and be happy you acted prudently. You will never go broke switching to a conservative fund too quickly.

CHAPTER 14 "TRADING" MUTUAL FUNDS

Trading is short-term in-and-out buying and selling. In the case of mutual funds, trading generally means buying and selling a fund to catch short-term swings of the market.

I am not in favor of trading mutual funds. Trading is not in the long-term interest of investors because it is detrimental to funds. Stockbrokers love traders; they make the bulk of their income from them. But with mutual funds, it's a different story. Mutual funds prefer not to open an account and then have to close it a few weeks later, since this short-term money can't be invested productively.

As a result, measures have been taken to curtail trading in funds. One major step was taken in 1968 when the SEC, with the support of the funds, eliminated the practice of backward pricing. Backward pricing meant that an investor could buy a fund at yesterday's price until noon of the following day. If the President made a favorable economic speech and the market reacted sharply upward, fund traders swarmed in. They bought huge blocks of fund shares, paying the previous day's price. If they sold the next day, they were virtually guaranteed an unearned profit—at the expense of the fund's existing shareholders. This practice has been stopped. Today, mutual funds operate on the principle of forward pricing. The price paid is established at the close of the day the order is received. (A mutual fund normally computes its price every day after the close of the New York Stock Exchange, 3:30 p.m. Eastern Standard Time.)

In another move to curb trading, some no-loads now demand redemption fees. Here's what W. S. Wurzberger, the astute president of the no-load Hyperion Fund, told his shareholders when he instituted a redemption charge of 1.5% on all shares redeemed within six months of purchase:

This [redemption fee] is aimed squarely at that small group of self-styled geniuses at market timing. The fact that buy and sell signals often come from calculations or sources no more reliable than their astrologer, or some flim-flam tip sheet, or the baby sitter, and their results show it, is immaterial. They are of no benefit to a fund from the standpoint of long-time fund investors. And we are managing this fund for the benefit of the long-time investor and not market players who think it's smart to use us because there are no in-or-out charges.

They affect the Fund in many ways. The market is going up and the timing genius comes in with a big purchase. It takes a week or longer these days for a check to clear and bank errors are so frequent that we hesitate to make purchases against a large check until we are sure it has cleared. Two weeks later, timer walks in and wants out. We have no compunction in liquidating shares of a portfolio fund if it isn't doing a job we think competent. But the last thing we want to do is to liquidate shares of a portfolio fund to satisfy a market timer. This is why the redemption charge.

A few funds simply refuse to sell to traders. If you call the Johnston Mutual Fund to place an order, you will be asked whether you have ever had an account there before. If you have had one, it better not have been recently. It doesn't matter how much money you have either, as the following story from *Forbes* indicates.

Last spring, Milton Mound, head of First Multifund of America, telephoned to find out why the Johnston Mutual Fund had returned Multifund's $500,000 check uncashed. Instead, he found out the difference between a go-go fund and an old-line mutual fund with long-run policies.

In November [1969], Multifund had invested $1 million in Johnston when the rest of the market had withered but Johnston's growth stocks had held up. Then, growth stocks began to slide, and about May [1970] Multifund took back its $1 million. Now, in June, Multifund wanted to reinvest half that amount.

"Multifund was shocked when we turned down their money, but we told them we only wanted long-term investors," says Johnston's president and chief executive, William I. LaTourette. "We don't permit anyone to trade our fund. For instance, a European fund from Liechtenstein sent us a check for $1 million. I was so happy I put it over the fireplace in my home. A few weeks later they took it back. I went home and threw the check into the fire. We don't want those kinds of investors. We'd have to keep higher cash reserves just for them."

Frequent trading has an additional drawback. If a mutual fund is sold at a profit without being held at least six months, the investor pays capital gains tax at ordinary income rates, not at long-term capital gains rates. As with any other investment, this is a good reason to hold for at least six months.

On the other hand, there are a sufficient number of top-performing funds available that aren't as rigid as Johnston, so that the astute investor would have no trouble following the bull/bear or stop-loss strategy suggested earlier.

You will recall Fundpack's policy of selling any fund after a 10% decline and buying back after a 10% rise. Portfolio fund managers are all aware of this policy and accept Fundpack's money under these conditions. It is interesting to note the amount of switching Fundpack has done to implement this policy.

The following chart, compiled from Fundpack quarterly and special reports, shows its portfolio fund holdings at various points of time in 1971 and 1972 before and after complete or partial liquidations.

There are a lot of good funds on this chart! And while a few didn't want to be in Fundpack's portfolio more than once (and some were saved because they didn't decline 10% every time), it is obvious that this multifund hasn't been prevented from implementing its stop-loss policy. Fundpack has more than $2 million invested and individual fund holdings can run as large as $300,000. If it can move in and out, so can the average investor whose holdings are far smaller.

In general, Fundpack buys and sells in accordance with its 10% rule. Its turnover rate for the fiscal year ending July 1971 was 95%. The more active First Multifund of America definitely appears to be trading. Despite its rebuff from Johnston, between

FUNDPACK PORTFOLIO FUNDS

Fund	July 31, 1971	Aug. 31, 1971	Jan. 31, 1972	July 31, 1972	Nov. 18, 1972
Acorn	●	●			
Afuture	●	●	●	●	
Burnham	●		●		
California Venture	●				
Columbia Growth	●	●	●	●	●
Edie Special	●	●	●	●	●
New Horizons	●	●		●	
Nicholas Strong	●	●		●	
Redmond Growth		●	●		
Berger-Kent			●		
Davidge			●		
44 Wall St.			●		
Hartwell & Campbell			●		
Hart. & Campbell Lev.			●		
Hawick			●		
Janus			●	●	
Oppenheimer Time			●	●	●
Weingarten			●	●	●
Channing Venture			●	●	●
Putnam Voyager				●	●
United Services				●	●

87% liquidation, August 1971

100% liquidation, November 1971 - January 1972

63% liquidation, July 1972

87% liquidation, September 1972

● Means in portfolio on date indicated

1969 and 1971 it held its portfolio funds, on average, about six months. Following are portfolio turnover rates for its fiscal years ending in November.

FIRST MULTIFUND TURNOVER RATES

1969	253.1%
1970	200.1%
1971	183.0%
(A 200% rate means that the average fund was held six months.)	

First Multifund, which typically holds fifteen to twenty funds at a time, states that even though it is buying and selling in $1 million lots, it has no particular problems since it gives its portfolio funds advance warning of its intention.

This high turnover rate may have hurt First Multifund's performance. It was in the bottom half of all funds in all three years. On the other hand, Fundpack, with a turnover rate of 95% in its fiscal year—and, according to its prospectus, a normally anticipated rate of under 50%—was in the top quarter of all funds in 1971.

Furthermore, Hyperion, with a notably low 12% turnover rate in 1971, ranked in the upper 10% of all funds and was the best-performing multifund.

In summary, if trading is your game, stick to stocks. Most no-load funds don't have redemption fees now, but if trading becomes a problem they will quickly slap them on. And nobody needs that.

CHAPTER 15 WITHDRAWAL PLANS

A mutual fund withdrawal program is a systematic means of obtaining regular monthly payments from dividends and invested principal. It is a logical outgrowth of the fund's capabilities and a highly convenient service.

These plans are flexible. The amount of the payout can be changed at any time, it can be terminated at will, or lump sums can be withdrawn when needed. The checks may be sent directly to you, your bank for deposit, or to any third person.

If you desire a fixed income on a monthly basis, the simplicity of a withdrawal plan gives it a tremendous advantage over stocks. Since most stock dividends are paid on a quarterly basis, you would have to own three stocks paying dividends in different months of each quarter in order to approximate the monthly payout principle of a fund withdrawal program.

Although mutual fund withdrawal plans are most commonly associated with payouts to the widowed and the retired, they can serve other objectives equally well. They can be used to:

· · · Care for dependents.

· · · Pay for school or college expenses. The program can be set up to cover a specific period, such as four years, in which the object is to deplete the principal.

· · · Make alimony payments.

· · · Make rent or mortgage payments, even if you're out of town.

ANTICIPATED INCOME

While any amount can be withdrawn, it is generally recommended that it not exceed 6% of invested capital annually. If the fund is well managed, its capital appreciation and dividends will be more than enough to cover these monthly payouts. To make the plan worthwhile, most funds require that a minimum of $10,000 be invested before withdrawals can be made. With $10,000 invested, a 6% payout would mean an income of $600 per year, or $50 per month. A few funds will set up a withdrawal plan for a $5,000 investment; but withdrawals of only $25 per month would, in many cases, make the plan hardly worthwhile.

DETERMINING THE KIND OF FUND TO BE USED

Since most people on withdrawal plans need the money for current expenses, the risk factor is the single most important consideration in selecting a fund for this program.

Therefore, if you need the greatest security in the immediate future, concentrate on growth-income funds. For greater long-term appreciation, with a consequent increase in risk, I recommend quality growth funds. It is also possible to use MCG funds for a withdrawal program, but I recommend the less volatile funds in this group, those that would in time mature into the quality growth category.

The major variables guiding your selection should be (1) other income and (2) life expectancy. If you retire at age 55 to 60, you have an average life expectancy of twenty-two more years and will be depending upon your fund to provide income for this period. In this particular case, it seems best to take a long-term view and invest in a quality growth fund where a greater opportunity exists for capital appreciation.

On the other hand, if you are approaching 70, select a fund that offers greater dividend income—and greater certainty that your capital won't depreciate rapidly in the immediate future.

Using an MCG fund for a withdrawal plan is far riskier; it should only be done if you have alternative sources of income. However, if you are financially able and willing to assume greater risk, the MCG funds offer the greatest growth potential.

ANALYSIS OF $10,000 INVESTMENT IN THREE DIFFERENT FUNDS

Let's see exactly what would have occurred if a withdrawal plan paying 6% annually had been started in 1961 with $10,000 in each of three different types of funds. As examples, we used Scudder, Stevens & Clark Balanced Fund, a growth-income fund; T. Rowe Price Growth Fund, which is representative of quality growth funds; and American Investors, an MCG fund.

In each case, the fund paid out regular monthly amounts totaling $600 per year for a period of ten years. However, there were significant differences in where the money came from. In the case of the growth-income fund, 53% of the payout came from dividends earned, the balance from the sale of shares. In the case of the growth fund, 35% came from dividends. For the MCG fund, only 11% of the payout came from dividends, with the bulk coming from the sale of shares.

On the other hand, after ten years of selling shares, the remaining shares of the MCG fund were worth $16,040; the quality growth fund was valued at $14,744; and the growth-income fund at only $9,084. Thus, in the decade of the sixties, an investor would have been better off buying an MCG fund for a withdrawal plan. Whether the payout came from dividends or from the sale of shares, in the final analysis, didn't really matter.

But what would have happened if the plan had been started in the bear market year 1970? By the end of the year, the value of all three funds would have declined because of the payouts made in a declining market. The remaining shares in the MCG fund would be worth only $6,319; the quality growth fund, $8,567; and the growth-income fund, $9,575.

Only time will tell whether the payout of the MCG fund was endangered on a long-term basis. But in any case, the value depreciated far more than with conservative funds. If a sudden emergency—such as major illness—forced you to reclaim your principal after only one particularly bad year (such as 1970), the more conservative funds would have proved to be the better choice.

EXAMPLES OF THREE WITHDRAWAL PLANS
Growth-Income

SCUDDER, STEVENS & CLARK BALANCED FUND, INC.

Group 5-gis

$50 Monthly Minimum Withdrawal—**$10,000** Assumed Investment—Based On Initial Net Asset Value of **$10,000**

	AMOUNTS WITHDRAWN (1)				VALUE OF REMAINING SHARES (1)		
Year Ended 12/31	From Investment Income Dividends	From Principal	Annual Total	Cumulative Total	Value Of Remaining Original Shares +	Value of Shares Acquired Through Capital Gain = Distributions (2)	Total Value Of Shares Held at Year-End
1961	$ 305	$ 295	$ 600	$ 600	$10,933	$ 453	$11,386
1962	304	296	600	1,200	9,317	880	10,197
1963	309	291	600	1,800	9,400	1,637	11,037
1964	317	283	600	2,400	10,027	2,150	12,177
1965	324	276	600	3,000	9,615	2,657	12,272
1966	337	263	600	3,600	8,203	2,338	10,541
1967	304	296	600	4,200	7,840	2,868	10,708
1968	295	305	600	4,800	7,313	3,473	10,786
1969	300	300	600	5,400	6,058	3,464	9,522
1970	357	243	600	6,000	5,608	3,476	9,084
	$3,152	$2,848	$6,000				

RESULTS IF PROGRAM HAD COMMENCED JANUARY 1, 1970

1970	$ 375	$ 225	$ 600	$ 600	$ 9,446	$ 129	$ 9,575

(2) Amounts of capital gains distributions accepted in shares were as follows: 1961 - $456; 1962 - $477; 1963 - $711; 1964 - $348; 1965 - $528; 1966 - $......; 1967 - $527; 1968 - $654; 1969 - $484; 1970 - $126; Total—$4,311. For the one-year period: 1970 - $133.

Quality Growth

T. ROWE PRICE GROWTH STOCK FUND, INC.

Group 1-dcs

$50 Monthly Minimum Withdrawal—**$10,000** Assumed Investment—Based On Initial Net Asset Value of **$10,000**

	AMOUNTS WITHDRAWN (1)				VALUE OF REMAINING SHARES (1)		
Year Ended 12/31	From Investment Income Dividends	From Principal	Annual Total	Cumulative Total	Value Of Remaining Original Shares +	Value of Shares Acquired Through Capital Gain = Distributions (2)	Total Value Of Shares Held at Year-End
1961	$ 171	$ 429	$ 600	$ 600	$11,487	$ 340	$11,827
1962	183	417	600	1,200	9,273	455	9,728
1963	185	415	600	1,800	10,185	706	10,891
1964	195	405	600	2,400	10,584	983	11,567
1965	218	382	600	3,000	12,310	1,566	13,876
1966	243	357	600	3,600	11,345	1,802	13,147
1967	250	350	600	4,200	13,496	2,544	16,040
1968	116	484	600	4,800	14,009	2,738	16,747
1969	249	351	600	5,400	13,484	3,216	16,700
1970	270	330	600	6,000	11,556	3,188	14,744
	$2,080	$3,920	$6,000				

RESULTS IF PROGRAM HAD COMMENCED JANUARY 1, 1970

1970	$ 160	$ 440	$ 600	$ 600	$ 8,359	$ 208	$ 8,567

(2) Amounts of capital gains distributions accepted in shares were as follows: 1961 - $340; 1962 - $168; 1963 - $184; 1964 - $219; 1965 - $382; 1966 - $319; 1967 - $338; 1968 - $......; 1969 - $488; 1970 - $364; Total—$2,802. For the one-year period: 1970 - $218.

Maximum Capital Gains

AMERICAN INVESTORS FUND, INC.

Group 1-pf

$50 Monthly Minimum Withdrawal—**$10,000** Assumed Investment—Based On Initial Net Asset Value of **$10,000**

	AMOUNTS WITHDRAWN (1)				VALUE OF REMAINING SHARES (1)		
Year Ended 12/31	From Investment Income Dividends	From Principal	Annual Total	Cumulative Total	Value Of Remaining Original Shares +	Value of Shares Acquired Through Capital Gain = Distributions (2)	Total Value Of Shares Held at Year-End
1961	$ 7	$ 593	$ 600	$ 600	$12,114	$ 689	$12,803
1962	78	522	600	1,200	8,675	1,739	10,414
1963	......	600	600	1,800	11,236	2,389	13,625
1964	21	579	600	2,400	11,686	3,378	15,064
1965	43	557	600	3,000	16,063	5,749	21,812
1966	102	498	600	3,600	15,438	6,512	21,950
1967	66	534	600	4,200	20,106	11,243	31,349
1968	216	384	600	4,800	29,906	4,150	34,056
1969	125	475	600	5,400	20,523	3,043	23,566
1970	......	600	600	6,000	13,889	2,151	16,040
	$ 658	$5,342	$6,000				

RESULTS IF PROGRAM HAD COMMENCED JANUARY 1, 1970

1970	$	$ 600	$ 600	$ 600	$ 6,319	$	$ 6,319

(2) Amounts of capital gains distributions accepted in shares were as follows: 1961 - $691; 1962 - $1,342; 1963 - $......; 1964 - $693; 1965 - $682; 1966 - $712; 1967 - $2,429; 1968 - $925; 1969 - $......; 1970 - $......; Total—$7,474. For the one-year period: 1970 - $......

WHAT IF YOU WITHDRAW MONEY FASTER
THAN THE FUND IS GROWING?

If your fund grows more rapidly than the 6% withdrawal rate typically recommended (and the average fund does), your capital will never be depleted. However, some elderly may find payments at 6% inadequate to meet current expenses and will need more even if it eats into capital. If you fall into this category, you must be careful that your capital won't be exhausted too soon.

In order to determine the maximum at which you can safely withdraw capital, here is a triangular table which gives the "financial life expectancy" of an investment where the rate of withdrawal from principal is higher than the rate of growth. The table is reproduced from "Brevits," a publication of Vance, Sanders & Co., mutual fund distributors.

Suppose you have $100,000 which is growing at 7% a year, and you withdraw at an 8% annual rate—$8,000 a year or $666.67 a month. Looking at the box where these two percentages intersect shows you that the principal will last thirty years. On the other hand, if the withdrawal rate is 9%, it will last only twenty-two

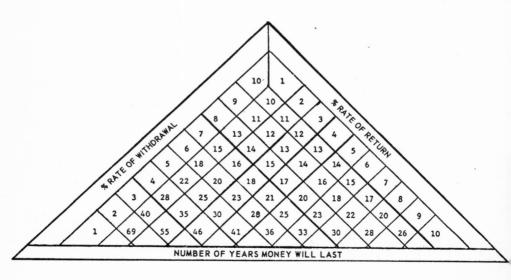

years, and at 10%, seventeen years. The chart should be used in conjunction with standard mortality tables to determine the number of years the payout is needed.

The table can also be read in the other direction. Assume you need withdrawals of 7% per year for twenty-five years. Then the right side of the chart shows that you need an investment that pays only 5% a year. Since a wise investor is "risk averse," the money should be placed conservatively.

CHAPTER 16 MUTUAL FUND ADVISORY SERVICES

Mutual fund advisory services are a valuable aid for the no-load investor. Their cost is reasonable for the services provided. The best advisory services cost no more than $60 per year, and satisfactory guidance may be obtained for less. As a matter of fact, for the one-time-only no-load investor, the advisory services' introductory offers, which cost as little as a dollar, may prove sufficient. The cost of these services is always tax deductible for people who itemize, and most investors will find the savings obtained from by-passing the loads will pay for the advisory service.

If you plan to invest in no-load MCG funds, it is vital to subscribe to an advisory service to keep abreast of fund performance and other news. On the other hand, if no-load quality growth and growth-income funds are for you, it is possible to make do with information obtained from periodicals or from big-city libraries. But even here the services can make the job of fund selection easier.

Most mutual fund advisory services are highly factual. Many simply provide data for the investor to interpret in the same way that *Moody's Investment Manuals*, the large 2,000-to-3,000-page books found in many libraries, detail "raw" facts on publicly held corporations. The heart of these advisory services are statistical sections where fund performance is computed, compared to stock market indices, and usually ranked so that investors are conveniently kept abreast of the top-performing funds. In addition, most services note fund size, objective, addresses, phone numbers, minimum investments, and summarize essential information from the prospectus. For these services alone they are worth their fees.

How the services summarize basic reference data from the prospectus is illustrated in the listing from the *Aggressive Growth Funds Report* on the following page. (Only the first third of the table is shown.)

Most important, the services provide data on funds too small to be listed in the daily newspapers. In fact, they have done a yeoman job alerting their subscribers to the many small, top-performing no-loads that would otherwise escape investor notice. Since these small funds will potentially remain good investments longer than larger funds listed in the papers, this is a most desirable feature.

Because it's a good rule to avoid investing in funds—or stocks—whose performance can't readily be followed, the advisory services provide a safe way of tracking these small funds. Consider these funds only if you subscribe to an advisory service. Otherwise, it's better to limit your investing to funds listed in the daily papers.

All mutual fund investors can benefit by using the advisory services as reliable sources of basic information. In addition to providing raw data, moreover, many of these services put it all together for the investor and make recommendations.

Mutual fund publications can thus be put into two general classifications—guides, known colloquially as "bibles," and advisory services. The guides are reference sources only. They do not make buy/hold/sell recommendations. The advisory services, in addition to providing reference data (usually in a less complete form), do recommend individual funds.

Following are services that provide reference data only.

FUNDSCOPE

The best "bible" for the serious mutual fund investor is *Fund-Scope*. It is published monthly, usually running about 150 pages. The annual *Mutual Fund Guide,* an exhaustive analysis of all funds, more than 500 pages long, appears each April.

FundScope shows performance results for more than 450 load and no-load funds on a medium- and long-term base. For exam-

BASIC REFERENCE DATA

FUND	% LOAD	PHONE	ACCEPT PHONE ORDERS	MINIMUM PURCHASE INITIAL/SUBS.	KEOGH PLAN	WITHDRAW PLAN (w)	LEVERAGE	PORTFOLIO TURNOVER	DATE STARTED
ACORN FUND, One First National Plaza #2580, Chicago, Ill. 60670	2.0v	(312) 641-3169	No	$1000/$250	No	No	Yes	'70/'71 NA 101%	6/70
AFUTURE FUND, 8 Pennell Road, Village of Lima, Pa. 19060	1.0v	(215) 565-3131	Yes (c)	$500/$30	Yes	$10,000	Yes	'70/'71 120% 123%	2/68
COLUMBIA GROWTH FUND, 621 S.W. Morrison, Portland, Ore. 97205	1.0v	(503) 226-7061	No	$500/$50	No	$10,000	No	'70/'71 69% 52%	6/67
DAVIDGE FUND, 1747 Pennsylvania Ave., Washington D. C. 20006	0	(202) 223-6090	No	$300/$50	Yes	No	Yes	'70/'71 194% 140%	3/69
EDIE SPECIAL GROWTH FUND, 530 5th Ave., New York, New York 10036	0	(212) 697-8900	No	$1000/--	No	No	No	'70/'71 72% 27%	8/69

Notes: (v) Fee charged on share redemption only. Afuture drops fee after one year invested.

SOURCE: *Aggressive Growth Funds Report*

ple, performance is usually shown for the duration of each bull and bear market cycle. Furthermore, data are shown several different ways for easy analysis—alphabetically, ranked for all funds, and ranked by objective. It also lists average performance for all funds and for funds grouped by objective.

In various issues it covers every conceivable subject of interest to the mutual fund investor. Basic reference data include addresses and phone numbers, size, management fees, dividends and distributions, classification of funds by objective, number of shareholders, shareholder services, investment restrictions, expense ratios, portfolio turnover, largest stock positions held, minimum purchase requirements, redemption fees, and more.

FundScope does many comprehensive special studies. It has analyzed no-loads versus loads, sales charges, contractual plans, withdrawal plans, dollar-cost averaging, unrealized appreciation, dual-purpose funds, multifunds, consistency of performance, cash inflow, and gifts to minors. It reports on mutual fund news and legislation and has an informative letters-to-the-editor department.

Since *FundScope* sells to investors, salesmen, and libraries, it maintains an impartial stance between load and no-load funds. However, in deference to no-load subscribers, it shows no-loads in heavy type face in all statistical tables.

FundScope's subscription rates are six months, $31; one year, $60. Its introductory offer, which includes the annual guide and three monthly issues, is $22. Its mailing address is Suite 700, 1900 Avenue of the Stars, Los Angeles, California 90067.

INVESTMENT COMPANIES

Usually referred to as "Wiesenberger's," this is the other "bible" in the industry. *Investment Companies* is a large hard-cover book, exceeding 400 pages, published annually. It costs $60 a year; this includes quarterly supplements, *Management Results*, which salesmen often carry.

Wiesenberger's is designed for the industry, not the layman; however, many libraries have it, and if available it is well worth your reading time. Its classification of funds by objective is, in my opinion, the most accurate of any guide or advisory service attempting to cover all funds. Its list of fund addresses, statistical histories, and facts on each fund are excellent and are arranged for ready reference.

Wiesenberger also issues another supplement annually (about May) called *Mutual Funds Panorama*. *Panorama* runs about thirty pages and provides a wealth of statistical data including objectives. It's $5 to investors and well worth it. Wiesenberger's address is One New York Plaza, New York City, New York 10004.

MUTUAL FUNDS SCOREBOARD

For the fund investor who requires complete performance data only, there is the *Mutual Funds Scoreboard*. This service, published quarterly, provides cumulative year-to-date rankings and previous-year data for more than 550 funds. The *Scoreboard* provides a most inexpensive way to keep you abreast of your fund's current performance. It tells you immediately if your fund is in the upper 10%, upper half, or below average. It costs only $6.50 per year (four issues) and can be ordered from the Hirsch Organization, 6 Deer Trail Road, Old Tappan, New Jersey 07675.

A companion publication is the *Mutual Funds Almanac*. The *Almanac* contains names, addresses, annual performance for the previous six years, assets, objectives, shareholder services, and minimum-investment information. The regular price of the *Almanac* is $5.95. Both reports can be purchased in combination for $10.

LIPPER ANALYTICAL SERVICES, INC.

Lipper Analytical Services has an outstanding mutual fund guide that provides performance data at frequent intervals. Since the data are presented in a manner that does not conform to the SEC's Statement of Policy, the service is specifically limited to professional money managers and is not available to salesmen or the public. However, you will on occasion see summaries of Lipper data in magazines and newspapers, produced in a slightly different form acceptable to the SEC. The data are excellent, so use this service when you come across it.

ADVISORY SERVICES COMPUTE PERFORMANCE DIFFERENT WAYS

When you examine published performance records, you will find that they have been computed in various ways. You will find such methodological descriptions as:

1. Results with all distributions taken in cash; or . . . as if taken in cash.

2. Results taking capital gains distributions in shares (or reinvested) and income dividends in cash.

3. Results reinvesting all dividends and capital gains distributions.

The essential difference between the three methods is whether the capital gains and dividends are reinvested or paid out to shareholders. The first method, which is probably the one most commonly used, takes into account these distributions without actually reinvesting them. It works like this: If a fund at the start of a two-year measured period had a per share value of $10, paid out $1 in distributions a year later, and ended the two-year period with a per share value of $12, the gain would be computed by adding $1 to the $12 and dividing by the beginning figure, $10. This would give the fund a 30% increase over two years.

A more proper method is to assume the reinvestment of the $1 at the end of the first year and have it compounding in year two. This is seldom done because it is difficult for a service to report on a large number of funds in this manner without a computer. In addition, it makes very little difference whether dividends are reinvested or added in at the end, except over a long period of time, ten years plus.

As far as the investor is concerned, the important thing is to make sure all comparisons are done the same way. Methods vary from service to service; some services use all the methods in different sections of their reports.

In a prospectus, where performance data must conform to the SEC Statement of Policy for sales literature, income dividends are shown separately from growth of capital. The SEC requires this since it puts funds on an equal footing with stocks. (In computing stock performance, dividends are not usually taken into account.)

Notwithstanding this, the best way to analyze mutual fund performance is with *both* capital gains and dividends either reinvested or added in at the end. Most fund shareholders reinvest all distributions; and this method also provides more accurate comparisons between growth funds, which pay little in the way of dividends, and income funds, which have substantial dividend payouts.

Advisory services that do not show income dividends separately do not conform to the SEC Statement of Policy and cannot be used by salesmen. They usually carry a warning to this effect. However, they can and should be used by the no-load investor.

ADVISORY SERVICES THAT RECOMMEND FUNDS

There are nearly a dozen mutual fund advisory services that in addition to providing basic data either make buy/hold/sell recommendations or provide judgmental ratings on funds. These services are very useful and in some respects even preferable to the guides since they provide analysis for the investor.

Unlike the "bibles," the advisory services usually have a "supervised" list. These are lists containing only a small number of funds that are examined in great detail. A typical "supervised" list might include approximately ten leading MCG funds and a few quality growth or growth-income funds. Supervised lists are very convenient. They usually include only the funds that are currently top performers and they cut down substantially on the investor's work load. No one wants to analyze 160 no-load funds!

The types of information often included in a supervised list are: size of fund, cash inflow and cash position, and estimates of volatility. These lists provide detailed information on the fund's portfolio, including largest stockholdings and the proportion of stocks listed on the NYSE, AMEX, or OTC market. They indicate whether a fund is permitted to leverage or to sell short. Most services provide periodic interviews with fund management directed toward management's appraisal of the current market—whether they are bullish, bearish, fully invested, or moving to a larger cash position. Personnel changes in a fund's management are sometimes reported.

Some services don't have a supervised list as such, but provide profiles of individual funds from time to time. This is not as useful as keeping tabs on the best funds month after month.

In addition to basic performance data and supervised lists, many advisory services provide general news about the fund industry. This includes industry sales and redemption figures, industry cash positions, and news about lawsuits, legislation, etc. Some services provide market forecasts, although seldom with any degree of sophistication. Most services publish monthly, which is the ideal frequency for serious investors.

HOW GOOD IS THEIR ADVICE?

While these advisory services are not infallible and vary in quality, they represent a far better source of advice than does the average salesman. They are experienced at evaluating the factors determining fund performance and they usually have a better idea of management potential than does the average investor since they interview management and communicate with them regularly in the course of obtaining data.

As an indication of how well advisory services are performing, here are the results of one independent study. It was conducted by *Medical Economics,* a conservative publication that often offers investment advice to that most affluent group who don't have their own businesses to put money into. For ease of comparison, this study was restricted to the most aggressive funds only. While many services also recommend more conservative funds, with one exception they weren't analyzed.

The study was based on two different up-market periods of relatively short duration—six months and a year. *Medical Economics* felt that one year was about all the advisory services could be checked without getting involved in "sells"—funds dropped from the recommended lists as they slowed up.

With some qualifications, the study concluded that the services "can indeed pick the big performers." Here is a summary of the results of the average June 1971 recommendation one year later.

FROM JUNE 30, 1971, THROUGH JUNE 30, 1972

Advisory Service	No. Funds Recommended	Average Change of Recommended Funds
Fundline	6	+35.0%
Converse Fund Reports	5	+29.9%
Aggressive Growth Funds Report	6	+27.6%
Fund Investment Engineering	10	+25.8%
No-Load Fund Digest	5	+23.3%
Fundicator	7	+21.5%
Growth Fund Guide	5	+21.3%
United Mutual Fund Selector	8	+12.2%
Average Advisory Service Selection		+24.6%
Average All Growth Funds		+13.3%
Average All Funds		+10.0%
NYSE Industrial Index		+10.4%

SOURCE: *Medical Economics,* October 23, 1972

In this period, the average recommendation grew 25%. The best service, with six recommended funds, grew 35% and the worst of the group averaged a 12% increase with eight recommendations. By way of comparison, the average growth fund added 13% and the NYSE Industrial Index increased by 10%.

Whereas all the services did well, it would appear that *United Mutual Fund Selector* doesn't stack up to the others. That's because they are the most conservative of the group. Their "aggressive fund" list doesn't include the most speculative funds the others recommend.

Let's put this study in some perspective. First of all, while most services beat the averages easily, they should have since they were recommending MCG funds in a rising market. While *Medical Economics* made no study in a down-market period, we would expect these MCG funds to do worse than the averages— and possibly the advisory services, too, if they stayed with their most aggressive recommendations.

As noted, the study did not adjust the performance figures for sell recommendations since funds commonly are held at least a year. However, the *Medical Economics* analysis did note that at least two services had recommended the Shamrock Fund, a hot little go-go that turned cold and fell apart late in 1971. In this case, both advisories dropped Shamrock in late November 1971 before they were too severely burned. Redemptions of Shamrock's shares officially ceased on March 1972. The fund is now in the hands of a receiver.

Here are the results based on the shorter, six-month period. Most services, again, beat the averages by a substantial margin.

FROM DECEMBER 31, 1971, THROUGH JUNE 30, 1972

Advisory Service	No. Funds Recommended	Average Change of Recommended Funds
Growth Fund Guide	1	+29.1%
Fund Investment Engineering	8	+22.9%
Aggressive Growth Funds Report	5	+22.5%
No-Load Fund Digest	4	+21.7%
Converse Fund Reports	5	+18.9%
Fundline	10	+17.1%
Fundicator	10	+16.0%
United Mutual Fund Selector	9	+11.6%
Average Advisory Service Selection		+20.0%
Average All Growth Funds		+10.5%
Average All Funds		+6.5%
NYSE Industrial Index		+7.8%

Source: *Medical Economics*, October 23, 1972

You, of course, want to know which fund *Growth Fund Guide* recommended. It was Nicholas Strong, which was eighteenth among all funds in this period. Moreover, Nicholas Strong was recommended by six of the eight services.

SOME CAVEATS

If you decide to accept a service's buy/sell advice, here are two caveats to consider.

(1) Services sometimes overemphasize short-term performance

at the expense of medium- or long-term performance. In some cases, a top-ten performance over a short period will result in recommendations for funds that have not demonstrated that they can perform at this level with any degree of consistency.

(2) Some services, lacking rigorous sell points, keep MCG funds on their recommended lists too long after performance starts to erode. In fact, there is a tendency not to recommend the outright sale of a fund at all. The service's reasons are much the same as the ones that inhibit brokerage firms from recommending sales of stocks: there is a continuing need to maintain close liaison with management. For this reason you may sometimes have to read between the lines when interpreting their ratings. For example, if an advisory service rates funds from A to F, with an F rating meaning sell, watch carefully to see if any fund is actually given an F rating. If not, sell when a fund's rating declines to D.

Some other advisory services evade this "problem" by merely delisting a fund. In other words, they simply delete it from their report. If a fund you own is delisted, sell quickly. It is no longer in the advisory service's golden circle of winners.

To sum up, you can always use the services to obtain basic data, but realize that buying the advisory's recommendations is not a guaranteed path to profit. *You* have to continually monitor the funds you've bought, weeding out the losers and adding new winners as the advisory services spot them.

Following are details on individual advisory services that "rate" funds. Since the information is subject to change, look for their ads in financial periodicals for the latest facts.

AGGRESSIVE GROWTH FUNDS REPORT

Aggressive Growth Funds Report specializes in rating the maximum capital gains no-load funds, publishing an eight-page letter-size report monthly. It maintains a supervised list of eight or more of the best-performing funds, rating each monthly on an A, B, C scale. Funds that are rated A are buys, B funds are holds, and funds rated C or delisted are given a sell recommendation. *AGFR* makes capsule comments on its A-rated funds on the "most attractive" list.

AGFR intends its ratings to "express their opinion of the fund's intermediate to long-term prospects. Evaluation is based upon a system of complex weighted factors involving market performance, fund size, and imponderables that must be assessed individually."

In addition, *AGFR* evaluates the general market outlook and recommends whether to buy or to hold funds or to go to cash.

AGFR's regular subscription is $39 for fourteen months. It also has a three-month trial subscription for $11 and frequently advertises its current report for $1. The address is P.O. Box 667, Los Altos, California 94022.

CONVERSE FUND REPORTS

Converse Fund Reports covers about forty aggressive funds which are grouped in several categories, including a speculative and growth fund select group. Subscribers are advised when to buy and sell, based on major market trends. *CFR* bases its ratings on performance, cash flow, ratio of portfolio gainers to losers, cash positions, fund portfolio turnover, and management. However, only the performance data are actually shown in the report. Performance is shown for the latest month, latest year by quarters, and for two preceding years.

CFR analyzes the economy and the market, advising readers of major market trends. Its discussion of these trends is by far the most complete of any of the mutual fund advisory services. In making its market forecasts, it utilizes odd-lot studies, Dow Theory, breadth of market, and monetary indicators, all charted in the report.

The report, published monthly, runs twelve letter-size pages. Annual subscribers also receive a directory and special reports. An annual subscription is $36; three-month trial, $10; and the current issue, $3. The address is P.O. Box 885, Livermore, California 94550.

FUNDLINE

This service puts the accent on timing, publishing a "Master Indicator Chart" to guide the investor in recognizing major bull and bear market trends. *Fundline* charts forty no-load funds, including twenty-six-week moving averages for each fund.

Fundline is published by David H. Menashe & Co., P.O. Box 663, Woodland Hills, California 91364. A complete handbook is published every fourth week; an update of ratings and prices is sent two weeks later. One year (twenty-six issues), $48; three-month trial (six issues), $14; introductory offer, $2.

GROWTH FUND GUIDE

Growth Fund Guide is an excellent advisory service for the investor who wants to build a portfolio of top-performing no-load MCG funds. *Growth Fund Guide* provides comprehensive reports on a supervised list of approximately ten "aggressive growth" funds, five "growth" funds, and five "quality growth" funds (its terms). These funds are charted, and performance is shown over medium- and short-term periods including market cycles. Cash position and inflow ratios, estimates of volatility, and current size are detailed. Management comments are elicited, and portfolio holdings are summarized.

Growth Fund Guide rates all funds on its supervised list. The ratings express its opinion of the fund's potential for intermediate to long-term growth.

The *Guide* has an introductory section on general economic news, industry fund sales, and redemptions. Basic reference information is provided.

Growth Fund Guide is published by Growth Fund Research, Inc., P.O. Box 2109, San Clemente, California 92672. It is issued monthly, typically running about twenty-four book-size pages. The annual subscription is $36; the special introductory offer for new subscribers can usually be obtained for $1.

MUTUAL FUND REPORTER

Each monthly issue of the *Mutual Fund Reporter* reports the comparative performance (alphabetically by investment objective) of more than 250 mutual funds, including 40 no-load funds. Performance is shown for the latest three-month and twelve-month period. A fund address directory is provided. Each issue also contains a short analysis of some aspect of mutual fund investing.

Mutual Fund Reporter is published by Investors Research Service, 1312 Carolyn Drive, N.E., P.O. Box 8415, Station F, Atlanta, Georgia 30306. An annual subscription is $15; single current issue, $2.

NO-LOAD FUND DIGEST

The *No-Load Fund Digest* follows more than 100 no-load funds, including funds of every shade of investment objective. All funds are charted for the current year, and performance is shown over the short, medium, and long terms. Addresses are provided for all funds.

No-Load Fund Digest has a supervised list of approximately ten to fifteen funds in growth-speculative, growth, growth-conservative and income categories. *No-Load Fund Digest* rates its supervised list, indicating its preferences for new fund commitments. In addition, growth, risk, and volatility indices are computed.

No-Load Fund Digest is approximately sixteen letter-size pages, including a monthly review and a commentary on the market. The annual subscription is $33; three months, $11. When advertised, its special introductory offer is $3. The address is Box 61, Wayland, Massachusetts 01778.

PERFORMANCE GUIDE PUBLICATIONS

For the investor who wants frequent evaluations, *Performance Guide Publications* reports the performance of 500 funds weekly, excluding some summer and holiday periods. In addition, it provides a monthly letter devoted to market timing and management interviews.

Its PGP Timing Index recommends a percent to be invested in the market at a given time. It is based on five market indicators: the level of speculation (AMEX volume as a percentage of NYSE volume), money supply, interest rates, federal budget deficits, and the number and trend of secondary issues offered. Based on its findings, *Performance Guide Publications* suggests that subscribers should be anywhere from 50% short to 180% long (margined) in the market.

A weekly subscription (forty-five issues) is $35 per year; a monthly subscription (twelve issues) is also available for $20. The address is P.O. Box 2604, Palos Verdes Peninsula, California 09274.

UNITED MUTUAL FUND SELECTOR

United Mutual Fund Selector is a division of United Business Service, an old-line market and economic advisory service. The *United Mutual Fund Selector* is a semimonthly eight-page letter-size publication.

The first issue of each month includes performance data for approximately 400 funds. The second monthly report includes from two to four full-page write-ups on various individual funds, and also includes *United's* supervised list. Filling out each issue are columns covering general financial and fund news, informative special studies, interviews with fund managements, and an interesting question-and-answer column from readers.

United's monthly performance tables show only year-to-date, previous two-year, and five-year comparisons. Approximately fifty no-loads are shown in a separate section.

United's supervised list consists of twenty quality growth, growth-income, and some of the less volatile speculative growth funds. About 60% of the funds on the supervised list are no-loads; the balance, loads. All funds on the list are recommended. At intervals, *United* publishes a ranking of the top twenty-five funds.

The annual subscription rate is $45; an introductory offer is advertised at $2. *United*'s address is 212 Newbury Street, Boston, Massachusetts 02116.

Following, for easy comparison, is a summary of the information offered by the various mutual fund advisory services.

SUMMARY OF ADVISORY SERVICES

	Aggressive Growth Funds Report	Converse	Fundline	FundScope	Growth Fund Guide	Mutual Fund Reporter	Mutual Funds Scoreboard and Almanac	No-Load Fund Digest	Performance Guide Publications	United Mutual Fund Selector	Wiesenberger's Investment Companies
No. of Funds Followed	17	60	40	450	40	250	600	100	500	400	550
Ranks Top Funds		●		●	●		●		●	●	
SUPERVISED LIST OF FUNDS											
MCG	●	●			●				●	●	
Quality Growth					●				●	●	
Growth-Income					●				●	●	
Rates Funds - Buy/Sell/Hold Advice	●	●	●		●				●	●	
STRATEGY INFORMATION											
Cash Inflow					●						
Cash Position				●	●						●
Size of Fund		●		●	●		●	●	●	●	●
Volatility				●	●			●			●
Portfolio Turnover	●			●						●	
Largest Holdings				●	●						●
Dividend Yield				●			●			●	●
Management Interviews		●		●	●				●	●	
Economic and Market Commentary	●	●	●		●	●		●	●	●	
Addresses	●	●	●	●	●	●	●	●	●		●
Minimum Investments	●		●	●	●		●	●	●		●
Investment Restrictions	●			●	●			●			●
Shareholder Services	●			●	●		●	●			●
Expenses				●							●
Annual Cost	$39	$36	$48	$60	$36	$15	$10	$33	$35	$45	$60

FORBES

In addition to an advisory service, the mutual fund investor might find it helpful to subscribe to *Forbes* magazine, a semi-monthly business periodical.

Each issue of *Forbes* has a newsworthy column on mutual funds which highlights trends in the industry and profiles individual funds and their managements. Always interesting, these columns keep the investor abreast of what is happening in funds.

Secondly, *Forbes* has five distinguished analysts who regularly comment on the stock market, giving particular emphasis to market trends. These columns are particularly helpful to an investor wishing to use the cyclical investment strategy discussed earlier.

Finally, *Forbes* rates funds in its August 15 issue ($1). This issue also features a comprehensive article commenting on the most significant developments in the field that year. The *Forbes* ratings are helpful in selecting quality growth and growth-income funds since they show performance over the last three bull and bear markets with two separate ratings.

Forbes offers its mutual fund ratings issue as a bonus to new subscribers. An annual subscription to the magazine, including the most recent fund ratings, is $12. Unless you have a copy of the introductory offer, specifically request the fund supplement when subscribing. The address is 60 Fifth Avenue, New York City, New York 10011.

DON'T RELY SOLELY ON MANAGEMENT

Most investors rely on their fund for progress reports. Yet the quarterly and annual reports that the management disseminates are often self-serving, particularly if the fund has had a bad year. Here is what some of 1972's losers told shareholders in their annual reports.

Anchor Capital Fund (rank: 458)
"Fellow shareholders:

"Performance over any short period can be an elusive element. However, we remain firmly convinced that the future potential for meaningful appreciation of your shares is encouraging. . . . We believe . . . investor's patience will soon be rewarded."

First Investors Discovery Fund (rank: 511)
"Dear shareholders:

"Although, as always, there seems to be some areas of concern remaining, we too are optimistic as to the potential of 1973 generally, and for the Fund particularly."

Value Line Special Situations Fund (rank: 542)
"To our shareholders:

"1972 was the year of the 'blue chip' stock. . . . In this market climate, special situations do not flourish. Second grade stocks are not of interest to institutional investors. . . . Prices of new, emerging, and still risky companies are at meaningless levels and the special situation investor's patience is sorely tried. The net asset value per share of the Value Line Special Situations Fund declined by 10.97% in 1972. Considering the character of the equity markets during the past 12 months, one should not be unduly alarmed."

Manhattan Fund (rank: 507)
"My fellow shareholders:

"By now, you probably are aware that, on January 29, I have resigned as president and board member of Manhattan Fund. . . . Your directors have elected as my successor Irwin Lainoff, an officer of the fund for the past six years. Mr. Lainoff has amply demonstrated his credentials in all areas of your fund's operation. Mr. Lainoff will have the assistance of a restructured and restaffed investment group. . . . The fund's new management team is dedicated to seeking satisfactory long-term growth of your investment capital. . . . Respectfully yours, (signed) Gerald Tsai, Jr."

Whatever their assurances, in the first nine months of 1973 these funds ranked 542, 519, 514 and 424 respectively.

As you can see, management often measures its own performance through rose-tinted glasses. So be on guard and don't rely solely on management's opinion. Consult an unbiased source of information; subscribe to an advisory service or at least obtain comparative fund statistics from newspapers or magazines.

CHAPTER 17 THE MUTUAL FUND PROSPECTUS

What, me read a prospectus! Why, I'd rather read the fine print in my insurance policy.

That's the kind of reader interest prospectuses generally enjoy. And let's face it, they are hard to read. That's because under SEC regulations, prospectuses are replete with highly technical jargon which is mostly incomprehensible to investors. The fund industry knows this and while it wants to make prospectuses more informative and easier to read, it's pretty hard to get the legal profession and Washington to change their ways.

Despite the drawbacks, it's worth learning about the prospectus. By federal law, you must be provided one when you buy a fund. Always save the prospectus; it is valuable.

Before getting into specifics, let's find out what the prospectus does in general terms. Its primary purpose is to provide "full and fair disclosure" of all relevant investment information. The document is valuable for this reason alone; it provides facts some funds would just as soon leave unsaid. It tells you when a fund is being sued, whether the management is inexperienced, or if the management fee is abnormally high. These are facts you won't get if you buy already issued stock, or if you select an investment counselor or broker. Most important, the prospectus gives you a clear, detailed explanation of the fund's objectives, not the one- or two-word descriptions the advisory services use.

What the prospectus does *not* tell you is how the fund compares to other funds. The SEC prohibits comparisons to other funds in a prospectus or in sales literature, and as a practical matter, you will find comparing a dozen prospectuses extremely difficult, if not impossible.

HOW TO GET PROSPECTUSES

You can obtain a prospectus by either writing or telephoning the specific fund. In addition, you can now obtain an up-to-date list of approximately 85 no-load funds by writing the No-Load Fund Association at 475 Park Avenue South, New York City 10016 (telephone 212-532-8811). The list will also include the fund's objective, age and size. The Association will also place your name on a list which is available to member funds. Some of these funds may send you prospectuses directly.

WHAT'S IN THE PROSPECTUS?

All prospectuses adhere to a basic form, which will be discussed briefly in the ensuing section.

The first page of the prospectus contains caveats, notes, unusual policies of the fund, or important facts the SEC feels should be highlighted. Typically, no-load funds emphasize their lack of a sales charge.

As an example of a caveat, here is a direct quote from the introductory section of the Ithaca Growth Fund prospectus:

During the fiscal years ended February 28, 1970, and 1971 the Fund had net losses of $8,105.58 and $11,917.50 respectively. The ratio of operating expenses to average annual net assets for said periods were 8.79% and 17.12% respectively. The foregoing ratios are considerably higher than the expense ratios of most other investment companies with similar objectives. This is because the Fund had a relatively low net asset value during those periods.

The Fund has no sales organization and employs no salesmen in connection with the marketing of its shares. To date virtually all of the sales have been concentrated in Ithaca, New York area. Although Management has attempted to increase the size of the Fund's net assets through the sale of Fund shares, the results to date have been largely unsuccessful.

As of February 28, 1971, the Fund had a net asset value of $76,026.05. Out of this sum $14,585.00, constituting approximately 18%, represents unamortized organization expenses. It should, therefore, be realized that only $64,441.05, constituting approximately 82% of the Fund's net assets, are actually available for investment purposes.

Prospective investors have been properly forewarned.

THE OBJECTIVE

The section on the fund's objectives, already discussed in previous chapters, is one of the most valuable in the prospectus. While the advisory services condense it into a few hyphenated words, the prospectus spells out the objective in detail, sometimes taking as much as a page. This often includes a discussion of how the fund intends to achieve its objective. For example, while American Investors, Fleming Berger, New Horizons, and 44 Wall Street are all no-load MCG funds, they hope to attain their growth objective in quite different ways.

American Investors notes that "stocks are selected almost entirely on the basis of market action. Heavy reliance is placed upon computer analysis in its decision-making."

Fleming Berger states that the Fund is "designed primarily for investors who desire to participate in a carefully supervised program of capital appreciation utilizing the speculative investment techniques of leveraging, short selling, hedging and purchasing option contracts and warrants. The Fund expects to trade to a substantial degree in securities for the short term. However, the Fund will emphasize research in attempting to identify undervalued situations which it is hoped will appreciate over the ensuing six to nine months in order to be able to distribute primarily long-term capital gains to its shareholders."

On the other hand, the New Horizons Fund's investment objective is to "find and purchase a diversified group of growth stocks of the future before they attain sufficient stature to become attractive to institutional investors generally."

Finally, the 44 Wall Street Fund "seeks growth of capital through investment in a limited number of securities. Investments will be selected for relatively long-term performance."

Similarly, you can find how the fund intends to meet varying market conditions. You will learn whether the fund will stay fully invested most of the time or will revert to cash in adverse markets.

The objective cannot be changed without the approval of the shareholders.

INVESTMENT POLICIES

This section (sometimes combined with the objective section) spells out how the fund intends to manage your money. Here it lists the investment techniques it is permitted to use in achieving the objective. These may include hedging, short sales, leveraging, buying warrants, foreign securities, puts and calls, restricted securities (letter stock), real estate, commodities, and investing for control. This doesn't mean the fund is using these techniques at any given time, only that it is permitted to do so if it chooses.

INVESTMENT RESTRICTIONS

This is a listing of techniques that the fund has agreed not to use. Most funds agree not to buy commodities and real estate, for example. Just as with the statements of objective and policies, these restrictions cannot be changed without shareholder approval.

After reading the fund's objective, investment policies, and restrictions, you should have an excellent understanding of the investment vehicle you contemplate purchasing.

OFFICERS AND DIRECTORS

As noted earlier, the listing of officers in the prospectus is primarily of value in pointing out inexperience. While the fund is required to list all officers and directors along with their principal occupations and affiliations in the last five years, it means little to the average investor, except in the case of new funds.

Directors can either be officers of the fund or outsiders independent of the fund. The better-known mutual funds have prestigious independent directors on their boards. However, there is no reason to suspect that these "names"—congressmen, presidents of other large corporations, etc.—contribute any more of their valuable time to mutual fund boards than to corporate boards of directors.

PORTFOLIO TURNOVER RATE

Portfolio turnover is the rate at which the fund buys and sells its holdings. For example, a turnover factor of 100% would mean all the fund's stocks were sold and replaced within a year's span. A 200% turnover rate indicates that stocks were held on average only six months.

Portfolio turnover is sometimes covered in the prospectus under investments or policies, and sometimes as a separate paragraph. The fund is required to disclose portfolio turnover for three years, if applicable.

My research indicates that there is no consistent relationship between turnover and performance.

BROKERAGE

Brokerage fees, which are paid when funds buy and sell stocks, are big money. While the prospectus states that "the fund will always seek the best price and execution available," it usually goes further and says that brokerage may also be allocated to brokers and dealers who furnish research and services. If the fund is managed by a brokerage firm or an affiliate, the prospectus will often state that a significant portion of the transactions will be cleared through the parent firm.

There should be an arm's length relationship between the fund and the broker. Funds have the size and muscle to negotiate lower commissions on the Big Board if the transaction is more than

$300,000 or deal in the third and four markets. When this is done, it is a saving to the shareholders. Judging from turnover ratios, some funds don't give top priority to minimizing brokerage fees. However, if these funds achieve *superior* performance by holding stocks short term, any extra commission expense becomes incidental.

While the dollar value of brokerage commissions is given in the prospectus, this figure is difficult to analyze. The turnover rate may be used as a rough means of comparing one fund's brokerage expense to another. Note, though, that if a fund deals extensively in over-the-counter issues, which are traded net without commissions, the commission expense will be less than the turnover rate might indicate.

THE INVESTMENT ADVISER

Mutual funds are owned by their shareholders. However, they are seldom managed along conventional corporate lines by their own officers and directors. The typical fund is said to be "externally managed." This means that most or even all of its work is done for it, not by its own officers or employees, but by a separate company usually called the *investment adviser*. The adviser presides over the fund's birth and generally remains in control of it throughout its life since fund shareholders almost always vote to renew the adviser's management contract.

This section of the prospectus should spell out the background of the adviser, noting whether he manages other funds and whether he is also an investment counselor; or the adviser may be a brokerage firm.

The principal item of interest in this section is the management fee. How big is it? Is it scaled down as the fund increases in size? Are there any incentive features? What portion of the fund's expenses are paid by the adviser out of the management fee? What portion is borne directly by the fund?

The management fee is usually .5%, and it should be scaled down as the fund grows larger. There are exceptions though. Recently, many of the smaller MCG funds have increased their fees to .75% up to 1% to compensate for their lack of size.

In recent years, incentive, or performance, fees have come into vogue. About 10% of all funds now have these bonuses paid for superior performance. Performance fees used to be on a heads-I-win, tails-you-lose basis. The Investment Company Amendments Act of 1970 now mandates penalties for inferior performance where incentives are in effect. These bonus and penalty fees are generally determined by the fund's performance relative to one of the market averages.

Here's the incentive fee schedule for the O'Neil Fund:

Its adviser receives a basic fee of ⅜ of 1% per annum of average net assets of the fund. In addition to this basic fee, management receives an incentive fee of ⅛ of 1% per annum if the performance of the fund during the fiscal year exceeds that of the Dow Jones Industrial Average by six percentage points or more. Similarly, a penalty fee of ⅛ of 1% per annum is charged the adviser if the performance of the fund during the fiscal year is less than that of the DJIA by six percentage points or more. Management receives its basic fee if the fund's performance differs by less than six percentage points from the Dow.

Performance analyses have failed to show that funds with incentive fees outperform other funds. Therefore, this should not be a consideration in choosing a fund.

Another matter of interest is the expenses paid out of the adviser's fee. The adviser is generally required to pay for the cost of providing investment advice, office space, bookkeeping, statistical and clerical expenses, executive salaries and expenses, and promotional expenses incurred in connection with the distribution of fund shares.

On the other hand, the fund itself pays for printing and mailing costs of shareholder material and prospectuses, legal and auditing fees, brokerage commissions, taxes, registration fees, expenses of independent directors (sometimes reimbursed by the adviser), and custodian and transfer agent fees.

If there is any significant variation from the above—such as the fund, rather than the adviser, paying the rent—it should be highlighted in the prospectus.

As far as the investor is concerned, the most important thing is that all these expenses are included in the fund's performance results. As a general rule, don't worry about minor differences in expenses among funds. They are insignificant compared to the wide performance variations possible among funds.

THE CUSTODIAN

Mutual funds have custodial banks that safeguard the fund's securities and cash. In many cases the bank also handles the administrative details of the shareholders' accounts.

SHAREHOLDER SERVICES

Special services such as Keogh (a tax-sheltered retirement program for self-employed persons), withdrawal, insurance plans, automatic reinvestment of capital gains and dividends, systematic investment plans, etc., are discussed in detail under this heading.

HOW SHARES ARE PURCHASED

This section lists the minimum investment the fund will accept. Minimum initial investments, with a few exceptions, range from $25 to $1,000. There is a good selection of quality no-loads requiring minimum initial investments in the $200 to $500 range. Minimum subsequent investments are often less than $100.

No-loads are generally bought directly from the fund, not from salesmen or broker-dealers. An application blank is usually included with the prospectus. It requests such information as your social security or tax number, the name and address under which you want the shares registered, if share certificates should be mailed or held by the fund, and if dividends and/or capital gains should be reinvested or sent to you. It tells where to send the application and to whom to make the check payable.

Funds are far ahead of corporations in doing away with stock certificates. In fact, funds issue certificates only upon request. Unless you need the certificates as collateral, have the fund hold them. It facilitates both buying and selling and is safer.

If you want to buy a fund but don't have a prospectus, first call the fund and place an order. Call collect. If the fund won't accept charges, it will say so. It doesn't cost anything to try.

If the fund doesn't accept phone orders at all and you don't want to wait for the prospectus to arrive, send the following letter:

DEAR SIRS:

Please purchase as many shares as the enclosed check for $_____ will buy. Register the shares under (*name and address*). My social security number is _____. Please reinvest all distributions. Do not send me the certificates.

Sincerely,

Normally, you should enclose a check with the purchase letter; however, some funds will accept your order at the closing price on the day they receive your order and will then bill you. In all cases make sure that your order meets the fund's minimum initial or subsequent investment requirements.

FUNDS AREN'T ALWAYS AVAILABLE FOR SALE IN EVERY STATE

Mutual funds are organized and operated under federal laws; but, in addition, they must be registered in accordance with local and state laws where they carry on their business. Since it is expensive and time-consuming to obtain registrations in all states, many funds don't register everywhere. Then, too, funds using the most speculative investing methods may not be able to satisfy all the blue-sky laws and may be banned in some states.

Salesmen usually avoid selling load funds in states where they are not registered. Since no-loads don't have salesmen, it is sometimes assumed that purchases are unsolicited if the investor learns of the fund through national advertising, publicity, or an advisory service. No-loads making this assumption will accept unsolicited orders from states where they are not registered, contending that the purchase is actually consummated at the fund's home office, not at the investor's residence.

Sales practices in this area are, to say the least, murky. The reason why some funds exercise caution is the possibility of *rescissions;* that is, investors holding fund shares sold improperly can, under some circumstances, demand that the sale be rescinded. In this case, the investor gets back the same amount he paid for the shares, plus interest. That's pretty tempting if the value of the fund's shares has dropped below what the investor paid for them. The laws and practices governing rescissions are complex, varying from state to state, so fund policies differ.

Most advisory services list the states in which funds are qualified for sale. If you want a particular fund and it isn't qualified in your state, try anyway. The fund may accept unsolicited orders. The worst that can happen is that it will say no or will not answer your request.

In addition to dealing with the fund directly, you can buy approximately twenty-five no-load funds through stockbrokers. Typically, these brokers work for firms that sponsor no-load funds as an investment counseling subsidiary. Since the funds are no-load, there is no cost to the investor; however, you should realize that in some cases these salesmen are rewarded for their services with "reciprocal" commissions. The money to pay these reciprocal commissions comes from the brokerage fees generated when the fund buys and sells its portfolio stocks.

This arrangement can result in a loss of objectivity. Keep in mind that the broker selling a no-load fund will receive commissions only from the sale of his house fund or—in a few rare cases—from as many as a dozen no-load funds. When possible, it is convenient to order no-load funds from a broker, but be sure to evaluate his advice as carefully as you would if he were a load fund salesman.

REDEMPTION OF SHARES

You should always retain the prospectus for ready reference to this section. It is to your advantage to follow the fund's procedures for redeeming shares. If you do not, it will take longer to get your money.

Shares must be redeemed by mail, although a few funds will

accept a sell order over the phone, giving you that day's price. In these cases, written confirmation is still required.

Recently, many banks have instituted a new red-tape procedure: you must have your signature guaranteed by a stockbroker or the bank where you have your checking account. This policy was instituted after a case of fraudulent redemption of shares held by a custodial bank. Banks are now cautious. The prospectus will tell whether a signature guarantee is needed.

Here is a sample redemption letter:

Please redeem _____ shares of (or completely liquidate my position in) XYZ Fund. My account number is _____. Enclosed is certificate number [if you have certificates] for _____ shares. Please send proceeds to (*give name and address*) as soon as possible.

Sincerely,

The account number isn't required but it is handy in case there is any confusion over name or address. Send the redemption letter to either the fund or its transfer agent, as described in the prospectus. If you aren't certain where to send it, send it to the fund. It will see that it goes to the right place.

If you are concerned about the market and want to sell fast, send the letter airmail special delivery. Also, for large sums you might register the letter with return receipt requested. It costs more, but you will have a record of the date the fund actually received your request. Your shares should be sold at the closing price on that date.

According to SEC regulations, payment for shares redeemed must be made within seven days after the letter of redemption has been received or after issued shares have been deposited with the fund. While checks are usually sent out promptly, it is not unknown for the custodial banks to hold up payment for the full seven days and sometimes even longer. Considering weekends and slow mail, it may take as much as two weeks for your check to arrive. So, if you are planning to redeem to meet a specific financial deadline, I would allow two weeks between letter of redemption and receipt of check in order to be sure to have the money available when it is needed.

THE "MOUNTAIN"

The "mountain" is the fund's performance chart shown on an annual basis. One is illustrated on page 228.

While it's not required to show a "mountain" in the prospectus, if the fund has performed well (or even moderately well), it will generally elect to show one. To avoid misrepresentation, the SEC requires that performance data be shown for the life of the fund, for ten years, or for periods longer than ten years in multiples of five.

What you should realize is that the longer the period used, the more impressive the "mountain" becomes, since money has been growing longer. Because of the 1969–70 recession, long-established funds that used to show only a ten-year performance record suddenly started showing fifteen-to-twenty-five-year records.

Since the periods shown are seldom the same from prospectus to prospectus, they cannot be compared directly. In the preceding example, $10,000 invested in the Stein Roe & Farnham Balanced Fund grew to $47,742 in slightly less than twenty-two years (excluding dividends). Now consider the "mountain" of Stein Roe & Farnham's more aggressive Stock Fund on page 229. In this case, $10,000 invested grew to $29,206 (also excluding dividends). There was less growth, but the money was invested for a shorter period of time—only thirteen years.

However, if both growth charts are reduced to average annual increases, we find the Stock Fund outperformed the Balanced Fund. The Stock Fund grew at the average rate of 8.6% per year, compounded annually, while the average growth rate for the Balanced Fund was less—only 7.4% annually. "Mountains" can be deceptive. Note that even this method does not provide completely comparable data since different periods of time are being compared.

To compare "mountains" you can use the tables on the following pages to determine annual percentage increases. These tables show what $10,000 will increase to at various growth rates, com-

ILLUSTRATION OF AN ASSUMED INVESTMENT OF $10,000

With Capital Gains Distributions Reinvested in Additional Shares

The chart below covers the period from August 25, 1949 to June 30, 1971. This was a period during which common stock prices fluctuated but were generally higher at the end of the period than at the beginning. The results shown should not be considered as a representation of the dividend income or capital gain or loss which may be realized from an investment made in the Fund today.

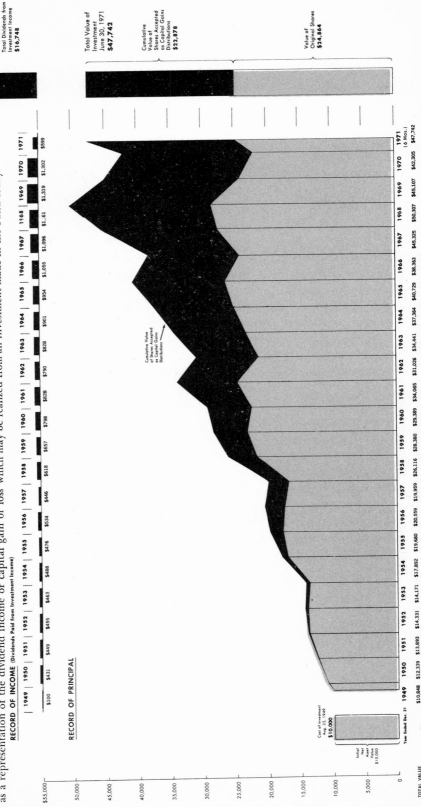

ILLUSTRATION OF AN ASSUMED INVESTMENT OF $10,000

With Capital Gains Distributions Reinvested In Additional Shares

The chart below covers the period from July 1, 1958 to June 30, 1971. This was a period during which common stock prices fluctuated, but were generally higher at the end of the period than at the beginning. The results shown should not be considered as a representation of the dividend income or capital gain or loss which may be realized from an investment made in the Fund today.

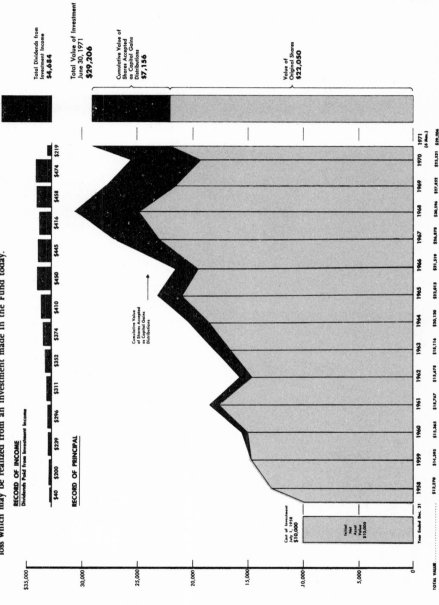

RECORD OF INCOME
Dividends Paid from Investment Income

RECORD OF PRINCIPAL

Cumulative Value of Shares Accepted as Capital Gains Distributions

Total Dividends from Investment Income
$4,684

Total Value of Investment June 30, 1971
$29,206

Cumulative Value of Shares Accepted as Capital Gains Distributions
$7,156

Value of Original Shares
$22,050

pounded annually. The data are also useful to show the range of investment results over a period of time.

For example, you wish to find the average annual compounded growth rate of a fund whose "mountain" shows $10,000 increasing to $33,800 in eighteen years. Using the table, first run your finger down the first column of the table to the line showing growth at eighteen years. Then look across till you find the number closest to $33,800—in this case, $33,799. Then note the percentage at the top of the column. In this example it is approximately 7%. This is the average annual growth rate with annual compounding.

LITIGATION

If there is litigation against the fund or the adviser, it is noted in the prospectus. Even if the adviser and not the fund is being sued, it can pose a problem; judges have, on occasion, ordered the fund (i.e., the shareholders) to pay certain litigation costs.

ACCOUNTING STATEMENTS

Prospectuses contain several accounting statements from which it is possible to glean investment information. Here is how these statements can be effectively used as an investment tool.

(1) *Per Share Income and Capital Changes.* This is usually the first table in the prospectus. The last three lines of the table are of primary interest to the investor. One is called the "Ratio of Operating Expenses to Average Net Assets." This is the expense ratio. Following this is the "Ratio of Net Income to Average Net Assets." This is the fund's dividend yield, an important figure to check if you are buying an income fund. The final line shows the number of shares outstanding. This figure and the per share value determine the fund's total asset size.

In the center of the table is a section called "Capital Changes." By comparing net asset value at year end plus distributions paid out (the preceding line), it is possible to compute the fund's growth. But this is the hard way to do it. If the fund has a "moun-

WHAT $10,000 WILL BE WORTH IN A GIVEN NUMBER OF YEARS

% INCREASE COMPOUNDED ANNUALLY

Year	5%	6%	7%	8%	9%	10%	11%	12%
1	$ 10,500	$ 10,600	$ 10,700	$ 10,800	$ 10,900	$ 11,000	$ 11,100	$ 11,200
2	11,025	11,236	11,449	11,664	11,881	12,100	12,321	12,544
3	11,576	11,910	12,250	12,597	12,950	13,310	13,676	14,049
4	12,155	12,625	13,108	13,605	14,116	14,641	15,181	15,735
5	12,763	13,382	14,026	14,693	15,386	16,105	16,851	17,623
6	13,401	14,185	15,007	15,869	16,771	17,716	18,704	19,738
7	14,071	15,036	16,058	17,138	18,280	19,487	20,762	22,107
8	14,775	15,938	17,182	18,509	19,926	21,436	23,046	24,760
9	15,513	16,895	18,385	19,990	21,719	23,579	25,580	27,731
10	16,289	17,908	19,672	21,589	23,674	25,937	28,394	31,058
11	17,103	18,983	21,049	23,316	25,804	28,531	31,518	34,785
12	17,959	20,122	22,522	25,182	28,127	31,384	34,984	38,960
13	18,856	21,329	24,098	27,196	30,658	34,523	38,833	43,635
14	19,799	22,609	25,785	29,372	33,417	37,974	43,104	48,871
15	20,789	23,966	27,590	31,722	36,425	41,772	47,846	54,736
16	21,829	25,404	29,522	34,259	39,703	45,950	53,109	61,304
17	22,920	26,928	31,589	37,000	43,276	50,545	58,951	68,660
18	24,066	28,543	33,799	39,960	47,171	55,599	65,436	76,900
19	25,270	30,256	36,165	43,157	51,416	61,159	72,633	86,128
20	26,533	32,071	38,697	46,609	56,044	67,274	80,623	96,463
21	27,860	33,996	41,406	50,338	61,088	74,002	89,492	108,038
22	29,253	36,035	44,304	54,365	66,586	81,403	99,336	121,003
23	30,715	38,197	47,405	58,714	72,579	89,543	110,263	135,523
24	32,251	40,489	50,724	63,412	79,111	98,497	122,392	151,786
25	33,864	42,919	54,274	68,484	86,231	108,347	135,855	170,001

WHAT $10,000 WILL BE WORTH IN A GIVEN NUMBER OF YEARS

% INCREASE COMPOUNDED ANNUALLY

Year	13%	14%	15%	16%	17%	18%	19%	20%
1	$ 11,300	$ 11,400	$ 11,500	$ 11,600	$ 11,700	$ 11,800	$ 11,900	$ 12,000
2	12,769	12,996	13,255	13,456	13,689	13,924	14,161	14,400
3	14,429	14,815	15,209	15,609	16,016	16,430	16,852	17,280
4	16,305	16,890	17,490	18,106	18,739	19,388	20,053	20,736
5	18,424	19,254	20,114	21,003	21,924	22,878	23,864	24,883
6	20,820	21,950	23,131	24,364	25,652	26,996	28,398	29,860
7	23,530	25,023	26,600	28,262	30,012	31,855	33,793	35,832
8	26,584	28,526	30,590	32,784	35,115	37,589	40,214	42,998
9	30,040	32,519	35,179	38,030	41,084	44,355	47,854	51,598
10	33,946	37,072	40,456	44,114	48,068	52,238	56,947	61,917
11	38,359	42,262	46,524	51,173	56,240	61,759	67,767	74,301
12	43,345	48,179	53,503	59,360	65,801	72,876	80,642	89,161
13	48,980	54,924	61,528	68,858	76,987	85,994	95,964	106,993
14	55,348	62,613	70,757	79,875	90,075	101,472	114,198	128,392
15	62,543	71,379	81,371	92,655	105,387	119,737	135,895	154,070
16	70,673	81,372	93,576	107,480	123,303	141,290	161,715	184,884
17	79,861	92,765	107,613	124,677	144,265	166,722	192,441	221,861
18	90,243	105,752	123,755	144,625	168,790	196,735	229,005	266,233
19	101,974	120,557	142,318	167,765	197,484	232,144	272,516	319,480
20	115,231	137,435	163,665	194,608	231,056	272,930	324,294	383,376
21	130,211	156,676	188,215	225,745	270,336	323,238	385,910	460,051
22	147,138	178,610	216,447	261,864	316,293	381,421	459,233	552,061
23	166,266	203,616	248,915	303,762	370,062	450,076	546,487	662,474
24	187,881	232,122	286,252	352,364	432,973	531,090	650,320	794,968
25	212,305	264,619	329,190	408,742	506,578	626,686	773,881	953,962

tain," use it instead. Compare growth (the total value line at the bottom of the chart) plus accumulated dividends (the very top line) for the period you are interested in.

(2) *Statement of Assets and Liabilities.* This is the balance sheet. There are two figures of importance here. One is "Net Assets," which tells you the size of the fund. It is also possible to compute the amount of unrealized appreciation or depreciation from this statement. At the top of the table under "Assets" there is a line called "Investments, at Market Quotations." This shows the market value of the portfolio and, in parentheses, the identified cost. Subtract the cost from the market value and you can see whether you are buying someone else's unrealized gain or a tax loss.

(3) *Statement of Income and Expense.* This table shows the income derived from dividends and interest, and various expenses such as the adviser's fee, the custodian fee, etc., charged against it. This is usually shown as a percentage on the line titled "Ratio of Operating and Management Expense As a Percentage of Investment Income." In the case of MCG funds, the ratio is high, since dividend income is low or nonexistent. The average MCG fund pays out more than one-third of dividend income for expenses, and the ratio can go over 100%.

Since fund expenses are always laid off against income before any dividends are paid, this figure is basically of concern to buyers of income funds. For an income fund, the expense-to-income ratio should be 10% or less with dividend payout undissipated by high fund expenses.

(4) *Statement of Realized and Unrealized Gain or Loss on Investments.* The amount of unrealized gain or loss can be picked up directly from this table. Most prospectuses omit this table, in which case you will have to compute it from the balance sheet (see 2). Some funds, though, have another table called *Statement of Sources of Net Assets* in which the unrealized figure is given.

(5) *Statement of Changes in Net Assets.* This statement is a condensation of what has happened to the fund's assets during the year after taking into account investment income, plus realized and unrealized gains and losses. This figure shows the *change* in realized and unrealized gains or losses from the previous year. This figure is not as important as the *total* figure given in the other tables.

INVESTMENTS

This shows the portfolio holdings as of a certain date. Funds are required to break down holdings by industry and show the acquisition cost.

By scrutinizing the portfolio you can also see whether the fund is *diversified* or not. Not all funds are. Technically, a diversified fund is one in which 75% of the cash and stocks must be spread around so that not more than 5% of this money is placed with any one issue. A *nondiversified* fund need apply this 5% limitation to only half (50%) of its portfolio. Of the other half, as much as 25% can be invested in one company. There is generally more risk in buying nondiversified funds.

Similarly, it pays to check to see whether there is an undue concentration of assets in a particular industry. If so, it is a good idea to investigate independently the investment potential of this industry.

Finally, by adding the cash to short-term notes, the fund's cash position can be calculated.

Note: A fund can use the same prospectus for sixteen months before it must be updated. Therefore, the fund's latest quarterly or annual report may furnish more up-to-date financial and port-folio data than the prospectus does.

A PAT ON THE BACK

A philosopher once remarked that a pat on the back is a great incentive to success—if delivered early enough, hard enough, and low enough. So, dear dedicated investor, because you have taken the time and effort to complete this intricate journey with me, please consider this book a pat on the back.

You've gotten it early enough (because it's never too late to make money with no-load funds); you've gotten it hard enough (because I've attempted to state the principles of successful no-load investing, and to document their validity in as clear and concise a manner as is possible); and you will have gotten it low enough if this book will make you get your seat out of your chair and get to work on an intelligently conceived and carefully monitored no-load investment program of your own.

Remember, the potential rewards and personal satisfactions are both great. Good luck—and good fortune.

APPENDIX I ALPHAS AND BETAS: THE NEWEST INVESTING TOOL

In Chapter 7, I described a rough method of measuring volatility by comparing a fund's price action to the market averages. This rule-of-thumb method is sufficiently reliable for most purposes. However, it is possible to measure volatility and consequent risk much more precisely and therein lies the latest trend in investment technology.

Some have called this new tool the "beta revolution" and believe it will bring far-reaching benefits to investors. Others contend it is nothing but sophistry and that Wall Street is becoming enamored of just another gimmick made impressive by statistical formulas and computer print-outs. In any case, beta theory is now widely covered in the financial press and is one of the most popular subjects at professional investment seminars. Since the beta will almost inevitably filter down to the lay investor, here is a short overview of what the pros are talking about.

BETA = MARKET RISK; ALPHA = ALL OTHER FACTORS

Beta theory is based on two simple ideas: (1) That there is a fairly close relationship between the movement of most stocks and portfolios and the movement of the market as a whole, and (2) that to get higher rewards, you must take greater risks. The beta coefficient is essentially a measure of market risk. It measures a fund's sensitivity to, or volatility relative to, the stock market in general. It differs from our rule-of-thumb measurement in Chapter 11 by isolating market risk (beta) from all nonmarket (residual) factors influencing the price of a stock or portfolio. These other nonmarket risks are then defined as alpha.

For example, if a stock declines because of a bear market, that's beta. If a company goes bankrupt and the stock becomes worthless, that's alpha. Conversely, if a cyclical stock goes up with the market, that's beta; but if a company develops a unique product (like the Polaroid camera) and its stock shoots straight up regardless of what the market does, that's alpha.

The performance of portfolios such as mutual funds can be similarly determined. The market (as determined by a convenient index) by definition has a beta of 1.0. If a fund has a beta of 1.0, its portfolio stocks can be expected to gain or lose at the same rate as the market. For example, if the market goes up 10%, a fund owning stocks that previously have been about as volatile as the market would expect to rise 10%. If the fund actually goes up 15%, the additional 5% gives the fund a positive alpha. Alphas, the nonmarket influences, are also thought of as a measure of "reward adjusted for risk." Alpha represents the difference between the actual net asset performance of a fund and the performance that should have been achieved because of the movement of the market, that is, on the basis of the fund's observed beta.

Investors can use betas to confirm precisely the objectives (MCG, etc.) of their funds. They can use alphas to measure management performance adjusted for risk-taking.

BETA'S ORIGINS

Portfolio managers have always spoken of downside risk, but it is only in the last twenty years that efforts have been made to quantify this risk. Furthermore, while beta theory was first propounded in 1952, widespread practical applications had to wait until computers made the necessarily voluminous calculations economically feasible.

Beta theory actually received its biggest impetus from the SEC in its *Institutional Investor Study* of 1971. The SEC noted that competition between bank trust departments, insurance companies, and investment companies had become intense and that "performance consciousness" by the money managers and their beneficiaries (i.e., mutual fund shareholders, among others) was a predictable consequence. The disquieting result of these pressures was to provide an incentive for investment managers to assume higher and higher levels of investment risk to achieve greater performance. In the past, most people have equated "performance" with "price action" without adjusting for the risk borne by the portfolio. In many cases increased risk taken by management was not apparent to the beneficiaries (i.e., you and me).

The SEC concluded that:

· · · Performance measures should be adjusted for volatility and rankings made in terms of achieved alphas.

· · · Serious and prompt attention should be given to disclosing risk policies in mutual fund prospectuses and basing incentive fees only on volatility-adjusted investment returns.

The Commission stated that "such disclosures would not only better inform portfolio beneficiaries of the risks to which they may be subjected, but also can moderate existing pressures on portfolio managers to assume more aggressive investment postures than otherwise would be warranted by the investment objectives of the accounts under management."

HOW ALPHAS AND BETAS ARE CALCULATED

Technically, these measures are determined by what statisticians call least squares regression analysis. Graphically, a fund's performance is plotted against that of a market index such as the S & P 500. For example, for a one-year beta, weekly data (52 points) might be used. These points when plotted on graph paper produce a large number of dots that approximate a straight line. The formula for the line, found in every high-school math book, is: $y = a + bx$. β (beta) is the slope of the line; a (alpha) is the point at which the line intersects the vertical axis. Here, visually, are two typical equations, reproduced from the *Institutional Investor* magazine. In the interests of comprehensibility, certain statistical refinements are omitted from the graph.

The portfolio with the steeper line has a beta of 2.0; it is twice as volatile as the market. The portfolio with a beta of .5 is half as volatile as the market. This latter fund also has a positive alpha of about 2%, which means that the stocks this portfolio manager selected did well for nonmarket reasons. On the other hand, the higher volatility portfolio had a negative alpha of about 5%, which means this manager was a less successful stock picker after taking market risk into consideration.

It can thus be seen that there are two ways for a portfolio manager to achieve superior performance. The first method is to forecast the market accurately and own a portfolio of high-beta stocks in up markets and low-beta stocks in adverse markets. The beta permits the manager to get a better fix on the stocks that will do well in each type of market. The second method is to achieve a positive alpha. If the fund manager is able to select stocks that benefit from technological breakthroughs, management shifts or mergers, he can achieve good performance even in mediocre markets.

As might perhaps be expected, there is an intense debate among beta theorists as to whether the statistical quantification of these prin-

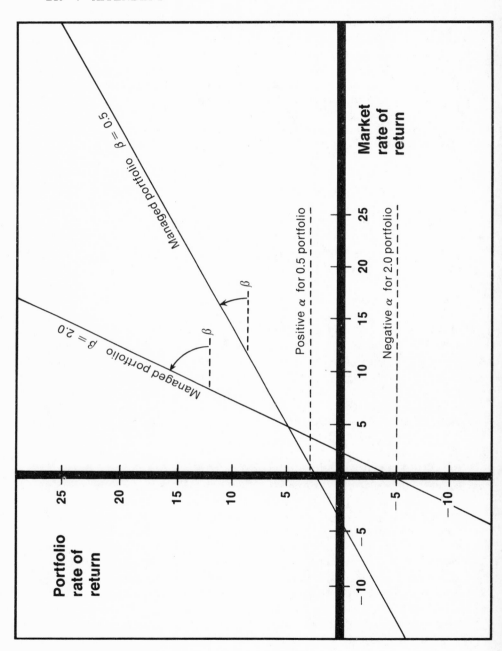

SOURCE: *Institutional Investor*, from an article by Chris Welles

ciples will actually enable the manager to achieve successful results over long periods of time.

The Wiesenberger advisory service, whose pioneering beta report is described next, believes the predictive value of the alphas is highly questionable but that the beta coefficients tend to be stable and may be used to estimate expected betas for future periods.

HOW ALPHAS AND BETAS ARE BEING USED

The first syndicated service providing mutual fund alphas and betas was the *Mutual Fund Performance Monthly,* started in October 1972 by Wiesenberger ($360 per year for those who can afford it; however, the year-end data are in *Investment Companies*).

Wiesenberger provides the following examples for the nontechnically oriented users of its report.

	1	2	3	4 Anticipated Fund Return on Basis of Measured BETA Col. 1 × Col. 3	5
	Fund's Measured BETA Coefficient	*Percent Change in Net Asset Value*	*Percent Change in S&P 500*		*ALPHA Coefficient Col. 2 − Col. 4*
Fund A	1.50	+15.55%	+8.44%	+12.66%	+2.89%
Fund B	2.00	+15.55%	+8.44%	+16.88%	−1.33%

SOURCE: Wiesenberger Services, Inc., *Mutual Fund Performance Monthly*

In the case of Fund A, the measured beta is 1.50. This fund has, for a particular period, registered a return (percentage change in adjusted net asset value) of +15.55%, while the stock market, as measured by the S & P 500, had a return of +8.44%. On the basis of the measured beta, this fund's return should have been +12.66%, or 50% higher than that of the S & P 500. Since in this period it recorded a performance of +15.55%, this fund's alpha would be shown as +2.89%, or the difference between actual performance and anticipated performance based on its measured beta. Put another way, by more familiar scorekeeping methods, the fund has done about 84% better than the S & P 500, but when the risk was taken into account, the fund had actually done only about 23% better (15.55% ÷ 12.66%).

In the other example, Fund B had a negative alpha because its growth in net asset value was less than was anticipated in view of the degree of risk it was taking. While both funds outperformed the S & P 500 by the same percentage (column 2), if the more familiar score-keeping method were used, there was a significant difference in the real "efficiency" of the funds' managers (column 5) when risk was taken into account.

Since both funds performed equally in a rising market, some may argue that the risk (beta) justified the means. However, Fund B could be expected to decline more in a poor market, and considering the risk to which the investors' money was exposed, Fund B failed to live up to expectations.

Obviously alphas and betas are going to take some time to get used to, and the prime initial users will be the fund managers themselves, or those institutions that hire them.

Here is what these fund managers are now looking at. Following are Wiesenberger's top fifteen funds ranked by alphas for January–October 1972. (Don't try to check the math; it won't come back exactly because of a complex error factor called rho.)

Rank by Alpha

| | | | | Year To Date Jan 1,1972 to Oct 31,1972 S&P 500 +12.28 | | | | |
| | | Total Net | | Alpha | | | Adjusted Change Net Asset Value | |
Objective	Pol-icy	Assets	NAME OF FUND	Value	Rank	Beta	%	Rank
MCG	CS	45.2	Omega Fund	+ 19.2	1	.87	+ 33.76	1
G	Spec	16.1	Scudder International Investments	+ 19.1	2	.29	+ 24.97	5
MCG	CS	44.6	Putnam Voyager Fund	+ 17.8	3	.93	+ 31.46	2
G	Spec	90.3	Life Insurance Investors	+ 13.7	4	.69	+ 23.94	6
G	CS	834.6	Chemical Fund	+ 10.9	5	.86	+ 23.39	8
G	CS	7.2	Over-The-Counter Securities	+ 10.9	6	.03	+ 11.89	53
G	CS	483.7	Putnam Investors Fund	+ 10.6	7	.92	+ 23.79	7
MCG	CS	102.4	Putnam Vista Fund	+ 10.6	8	1.29	+ 28.45	4
MCG	CS	15.4	Twentieth Century-Growth	+ 9.6	9	1.43	+ 28.49	3
G	Spec	32.2	Canadian Fund	+ 9.2	10	.42	+ 14.80	34
G	CS	56.7	Boston Common Stock	+ 7.5	11	.65	+ 16.29	24
G-CI	CS	314.3	Financial Industrial Fund	+ 7.2	12	.99	+ 14.04	41
LG-I	CS	85.4	Babson Investment Fund	+ 6.9	13	.76	+ 17.22	18
MCG	CS	29.7	Explorer Fund	+ 6.8	14	1.01	+ 20.18	9
G	CS	298.0	Johnston Mutual Fund	+ 6.2	15	.90	+ 18.16	13

SOURCE: Wiesenberger Services, Inc., *Mutual Funds Performance Monthly*

The Omega Fund had the highest alpha and the best performance of any fund in the first ten months of 1972. Furthermore, the top five funds by alphas were all in the top ten in performance (change in net asset values). It is also interesting to note that all five top-ranked funds had betas less than 1.00. In this period, owning a portfolio of conservative stocks was the way to achieve maximum performance.

An exception, though, was the Over-the-Counter fund. Here, the exceptionally low beta of .03 means that the unlisted securities that this fund invests in weren't influenced at all by the movement of the listed stocks included in the S & P Index. As a result, while it ranked sixth by alpha, it ranked fifty-third in growth.

The previous year was completely different. In 1971, the top five funds by alpha all had betas over 1.00. In 1971, it paid to own an aggressive, volatile portfolio.

Rank by Alpha

Objective	Pol-icy	Total Net Assets	NAME OF FUND	1971 Jan 1,1971 to Dec 31,1971 S&P 500 +14.12				
				Alpha		Beta	Adjusted Change Net Asset Value	
				Value	Rank		%	Rank
MCG	CS	85.6	Nicholas Strong Fund	+ 40.1	1	1.75	+ 85.51	1
MCG	CS	52.6	Afuture Fund	+ 33.1	2	1.46	+ 67.46	2
MCG	CS	470.9	Rowe Price New Horizons	+ 26.6	3	1.30	+ 53.92	3
MCG	CS	272.5	IDS New Dimensions Fund	+ 22.3	4	1.37	+ 48.62	4
MCG	CS	24.3	Security Ultra Fund	+ 20.8	5	1.45	+ 47.62	5
MCG	CS	27.5	Pace Fund	+ 20.4	6	1.24	+ 43.59	7
MCG	CS	27.8	Union Capital Fund	+ 19.8	7	1.14	+ 39.17	11
MCG	CS	247.5	IDS Progressive Fund	+ 17.9	8	1.48	+ 44.06	6
MCG	CS	68.5	Vance Sanders Special Fund	+ 17.4	9	1.26	+ 40.11	10
I	FL	8.3	Admiralty Fund-Income Series	+ 16.2	10	.61	+ 27.30	57
G	CS	483.7	Putnam Investors Fund	+ 16.1	11	.92	+ 32.13	26
MCG	CS	23.9	Keystone Apollo Fund	+ 16.1	12	1.58	+ 43.22	9
MCG	CS	56.4	Edie Special Growth Fund	+ 15.8	13	1.05	+ 34.26	19
MCG	CS	74.4	Polaris Fund	+ 15.2	14	1.65	+ 43.29	8
G	Spec	117.0	Century Shares Trust	+ 15.1	15	.93	+ 30.96	31

SOURCE: Wiesenberger Services, Inc., *Mutual Funds Performance Monthly*

Following is a partial listing of no-load funds available for the investor's consideration. Names, addresses, and phone numbers are shown.

The listings are for informational purposes only; buy decisions should be made only after studying the prospectus and up-to-date performance data. The omission of a fund doesn't mean it is undesirable. Some funds have been excluded because they are not generally available—they may be offered in only one or two states or to only certain categories of investors.

One in five people move each year. Mutual funds move, too. Consult an advisory service or the No-Load Fund Association (475 Park Avenue South, New York, N.Y. 10016) for up-to-the-minute data.

NO-LOAD MAXIMUM CAPITAL GAINS FUNDS

ABLE ASSOCIATES FUND
174 Birch Drive
Manhasset Hills, N.Y. 11040
212–563–2441

ACORN FUND
One First National Plaza
Chicago, Ill. 60670
312–641–3169

AFUTURE FUND
8 Pennell Road
Lima, Pa. 19060
215–565–3131

AMERICAN INVESTORS FUND
88 Field Point Road
Greenwich, Conn. 06830
203–661–5010

ARGONAUT FUND
1020 Prospect Street
La Jolla, Calif. 92037
714–459–4251

BURNHAM FUND
60 Broad Street
New York, N.Y. 10004
212–344–1400

CAMBRIDGE APPRECIATION FUND
747 Third Avenue
New York, N.Y. 10017
212–753–7710

COLUMBIA GROWTH FUND
621 S.W. Morrison Street
Portland, Ore. 97205
503–222–3601

NO-LOAD MAXIMUM CAPITAL GAINS FUNDS

COLUMBINE FUND
1600 Broadway
Denver, Colo. 80202
303–292–9680
800–525–6494

COMPUSTREND FUND
424 Falls Building
Memphis, Tenn. 38103
901–527–3493

COMSEC FUND
88 E. Broad Street
Columbus, Ohio 43215
614–228–7000

CONCORD FUND
15 State Street
Boston, Mass. 02101
617–742–7077

DAVIDGE EARLY BIRD FUND
1747 Pennsylvania Avenue, N.W.
Washington, D.C. 20006
202–223–6090

DOLL FUND
Thackery Lane
Mendham, N.J. 07945
201–543–2388

EDIE SPECIAL GROWTH FUND
530 Fifth Avenue
New York, N.Y. 10036
212–697–9538

ELDORADO FUND
18158 Westover Street
Southfield, Mich. 48075
313–354–3529

FINANCIAL DYNAMICS FUND
FINANCIAL VENTURE FUND
900 Grant Street
Denver, Colo. 80203
303–292–5880
800–525–6148

FINOMIC INVESTMENT FUND
600 Jefferson, Cullen Center
Houston, Texas 77002
713–224–2611

FIRST MULTIFUND OF AMERICA
32 East 57th Street
New York, N.Y. 10022
212–759–2311

FLEMING BERGER SPECIAL FUND
899 Logan Street
Denver, Colo. 80203
303–744–6081

44 WALL STREET FUND
150 Broadway
New York, N.Y. 10038
212–374–1146

GREENFIELD (SAMUEL) FUND
25 Broad Street
New York, N.Y. 10004
212–344–2760

HARTWELL AND CAMPBELL FUND
HARTWELL AND CAMPBELL
LEVERAGE FUND
345 Park Avenue
New York, N.Y. 10038
212–421–3530

HYPERION FUND
126 Barker Street
Mount Kisco, N.Y. 10549
914–241–1830

INTERFUND
P.O. Box 550
Bellevue, Wash. 98009
206–455–2425

INVESTMENT GUIDANCE FUND
Investment Plaza
Cleveland, Ohio 44114
216–696–3070

JANUS FUND
444 Sherman Street
Denver, Colo. 80203
303–744–6081

LENOX FUND
666 Fifth Avenue
New York, N.Y. 10019
212–582–5900

MATES INVESTMENT FUND
237 Madison Avenue
New York, N.Y. 10016
212–686–0300

MEDICI FUND
120 Broadway
New York, N.Y. 10005
212–233–3370

MUTUAL SHARES CORPORATION
200 E. 42nd Street
New York, N.Y. 10017
212–687–2277

NEUWIRTH CENTURY FUND
NEUWIRTH FUND
Middletown Bank Building
Middletown, N.J. 07748
201–671–9511

NICHOLAS STRONG FUND
312 E. Wisconsin Avenue
Milwaukee, Wis. 53202
414–272–6133

OCEANOGRAPHIC FUND
15 Exchange Place
Jersey City, N.J. 07302
201–434–8281

ONE HUNDRED FUND
1600 Broadway
Denver, Colo. 80202
303–292–9680
800–525–6494

O'NEIL FUND
10960 Wilshire Boulevard
Los Angeles, Calif. 90024
213–473–2911

PENNSYLVANIA MUTUAL FUND
80 Broad Street
New York, N.Y. 10004
212–269–8533

REDMOND GROWTH FUND
1750 Pennsylvania Avenue, N.W.
Washington, D.C. 20006
202–298–9150

ROWE PRICE NEW HORIZONS FUND
One Charles Center
Baltimore, Md. 21201
301–547–2000

SCUDDER DEVELOPMENT FUND
SCUDDER SPECIAL FUND
10 Post Office Square
Boston, Mass. 02109
617–482–3990

SEQUOIA FUND
One New York Plaza
New York, N.Y. 10004
212–344–6700

SHERMAN DEAN FUND
140 Broadway
New York, N.Y. 10005
212–425–2121

SMITH, BARNEY EQUITY FUND
1345 Avenue of the Americas
New York, N.Y. 10019
212–333–7200

S&P/INTERCAPITAL DYNAMICS FUND
S&P/INTERCAPITAL SPECIAL FUND
1775 Broadway
New York, N.Y. 10019
212–581–3360

STEADMAN AMERICAN INDUSTRY
919 18th Street, N.W.
Washington, D.C. 20006
202–223–1000

TUDOR HEDGE FUND
120 Broadway
New York, N.Y. 10005
212–349–6660

TWENTY FIVE FUND
1600 Broadway
Denver, Colo. 80202
303–292–9680
800–525–6494

WESTERN/AMERICA FUND
212 College Club Building
Seattle, Wash. 98101
206–623–3170

NO-LOAD QUALITY GROWTH FUNDS

AID INVESTMENT FUND
P.O. Box BA
Des Moines, Iowa 50304
515-280-4244

ALLIANCE GROWTH FUND
Box 1032, Wall Street Station
New York, N.Y. 10005
212-269-6363

AMERICAN ENTERPRISE FUND
50 Broad Street
New York, N.Y. 10004
212-425-0400

AMERICARE GROWTH FUND
601 Sixth Avenue
Des Moines, Iowa 50304
515-284-1414

ARMSTRONG ASSOCIATES
3200 First National Bank Building
Dallas, Texas 75202
214-744-5558

BANK STOCK FUND
P.O. Box 367
Colorado Springs, Colo. 80901
303-473-8100

BEACON HILL MUTUAL FUND
75 Federal Street
Boston, Mass. 02110
617-482-0795

CONSULTANT'S MUTUAL INVESTMENTS
1500 Walnut Street
Philadelphia, Pa. 19102
215-545-4100

CONTINENTAL MUTUAL INVESTMENT
FUND
2285 S. Main Street
Salt Lake City, Utah 84115
801-485-2471

DE VEGH MUTUAL FUND
20 Exchange Place
New York, N.Y. 10005
212-269-3313

DREXEL EQUITY FUND
1500 Walnut Street
Philadelphia, Pa. 19101
215-545-4100

EAST/WEST ADVANCED TECHNOLOGY
FUND
9100 Wilshire Boulevard
Beverly Hills, Calif. 90212
213-278-0890

E&E MUTUAL FUND
4400 N. High Street
Columbus, Ohio 43214
614-267-7492

ENERGY FUND
120 Broadway
New York, N.Y. 10005
212-344-5300

F. G. MUTUAL FUND
4680 Wilshire Boulevard
Los Angeles, Calif. 90010
213-931-1961

FIRST SPECTRUM FUND
230 Park Avenue
New York, N.Y. 10017
212-684-3664

GROWTH INDUSTRY SHARES
135 S. LaSalle Street
Chicago, Ill. 60603
312-346-4830

HARVEST FUND
1809 Walnut Street
Philadelphia, Pa. 19903
215-568-5935

IVY FUND
441 Stuart Street
Boston, Mass. 02116
617-261-1900

JOHNSTON MUTUAL FUND
460 Park Avenue
New York, N.Y. 10022
212-679-2700

MAIRS & POWER GROWTH FUND
2062 W. First National Bank
Building
St. Paul, Minn. 55101
612–222–8478

MATHERS FUND
One First National Plaza
Chicago, Ill. 60670
312–236–8215

NELSON FUND
345 Park Avenue
New York, N.Y. 10022
212–486–0610

NO-LOAD SELECTED FUNDS
3300 Whitehaven Street, N.W.
Washington, D.C. 20007
202–333–7140

PENN SQUARE MUTUAL FUND
451 Penn Square
Reading, Pa. 19603
215–376–6771

PRO FUND
Valley Forge Colony Building
Valley Forge, Pa. 19481
215–783–7604

ROCHESTER FUND
31 E. Main Street
Rochester, N.Y. 14614
716–232–2540

ROWE PRICE NEW ERA FUND

T. ROWE PRICE GROWTH STOCK FUND
One Charles Center
Baltimore, Md. 21201
301–547–2000

SCUDDER INTERNATIONAL
INVESTMENTS
44 King Street, W.
Toronto, Ontario, Canada
416–362–2531

SCUDDER, STEVENS & CLARK—
COMMON
10 Post Office Square
Boston, Mass. 02109
617–482–3990

STEIN ROE & FARNHAM CAPITAL
OPPORTUNITIES

STEIN ROE & FARNHAM STOCK FUND
150 S. Wacker Drive
Chicago, Ill. 60606
312–368–7820 (Cap. Op.)
312–368–7800 (Stock)

UNITED SERVICES FUND
110 East Byrd Boulevard
Universal City, Texas 78148
512–658–3562

USAA CAPITAL GROWTH FUND
4119 Broadway Street
San Antonio, Texas 78215
512–824–9011

VIKING GROWTH FUND
6006 N. Mesa Street
El Paso, Texas 79912
915–584–4481

WADE FUND
63 S. Main Street
Memphis, Tenn. 38103
901–527–8693

WEINGARTEN EQUITY FUND
331 Madison Avenue
New York, N.Y. 10017
212–697–9600

WILLOW FUND
One Chase Manhattan Plaza
New York, N.Y. 10005
212–558–3300

NO-LOAD GROWTH-INCOME FUNDS AND INCOME FUNDS

AFORTRESS INCOME FUND
8 Pennell Road
Lima, Pa. 19060
215–565–3131

BABSON (DAVID L.) INVESTMENT
FUND
301 W. 11th Street
Kansas City, Mo. 64105
816–842–2611

NO-LOAD GROWTH-INCOME FUNDS AND INCOME FUNDS

BRIDGES INVESTMENT FUND
8401 W. Dodge Road
Omaha, Neb. 68114
402–397–4700

CAPITAL PRESERVATION FUND
459 Hamilton Avenue
Palo Alto, Calif. 94301
415–328–1550

CHESAPEAKE FUND
527 St. Paul Street
Baltimore, Md. 21202
301–727–6400

DAVIDGE CAPITAL FUND
1747 Pennsylvania Avenue, N.W.
Washington, D.C. 20006
202–223–6091

DODGE & COX BALANCED FUND
DODGE & COX STOCK FUND
3500 Crocker Plaza
San Francisco, Calif. 94104
415–981–1710

DREXEL INVESTMENT FUND
1500 Walnut Street
Philadelphia, Pa. 19101
215–545–4100

FINANCIAL INDUSTRIAL FUND
FINANCIAL INDUSTRIAL INCOME FUND
900 Grant Street
Denver, Colo. 80203
303–292–5880
800–525–6148

GENERAL SECURITIES
133 S. Seventh Street
Minneapolis, Minn. 55402
612–332–1212

GUARDIAN MUTUAL FUND
120 Broadway
New York, N.Y. 10005
212–233–5900

LA SALLE FUND
One IBM Plaza
Chicago, Ill. 60611
312–828–1111

LOOMIS-SAYLES MUTUAL FUND
225 Franklin Street
Boston, Mass. 02110
617–482–2450

MAIRS & POWER INCOME FUND
2062 W. First National Bank
Building
St. Paul, Minn. 55101
612–222–8478

MUTUAL TRUST
301 W. 11th Street
Kansas City, Mo. 64105
816–842–2611

NASSAU FUND
P.O. Box 629
Princeton, N.J. 08540
609–924–0314

NATIONAL INDUSTRIES FUND
1880 Century Park East
Los Angeles, Calif. 90067
213–277–1450

NEUWIRTH INCOME DEVELOPMENT
Middletown Bank Building
Middletown, N.J. 07748
201–671–9511

NORTHEAST INVESTORS TRUST
50 Congress Street
Boston, Mass. 02109
617–523–3588

NORTH STAR FUND
600 Dain Tower
Minneapolis, Minn. 55402
612–371–7780

ONE HUNDRED AND ONE FUND
1600 Broadway
Denver, Colo. 80202
303–292–9680
800–525–6494

ONE WILLIAM STREET FUND
One William Street
New York, N.Y. 10005
212–269–3313

PAX WORLD FUND
224 State Street
Portsmouth, N.H. 03801
603–431–8022

PINE STREET FUND
20 Exchange Place
New York, N.Y. 10005
212–269–3313

SCUDDER, STEVENS & CLARK—
BALANCED
10 Post Office Square
Boston, Mass. 02109
617–482–3990

SMITH, BARNEY INCOME & GROWTH
FUND
1345 Avenue of the Americas
New York, N.Y. 10019
212–333–7200

STEADMAN ASSOCIATED FUND
STEADMAN INVESTMENT FUND
919 18th Street, N.W.
Washington, D.C. 20006
202–223–1000

STEIN ROE & FARNHAM BALANCED
FUND
150 S. Wacker Drive
Chicago, Ill. 60606
312–368–7810

VIKING INVESTORS FUND
6006 N. Mesa Street
El Paso, Texas 79912
915–584–4481